BEST OF BRITAIN'S
Birds

As the sun sinks slowly towards the horizon on the island of Unst, in the Shetland Isles, thousands upon thousands of puffins return from a day's fishing far out to sea to feed their young on the seabird cliffs of Hermaness. A visit to this, or any of Britain's outstanding birdwatching sites, is enough to inspire an interest in ornithology in even the toughest sceptic – and the excitement of such a spectacular natural event will live with you forever.

While special expeditions or days out can provide wonderful opportunities to view Britain's birds, the delight of a hobby like birdwatching is that you can pursue it almost anywhere. Rambles through the countryside may have much to offer, but careful observation from the comfort of your own home can yield a wealth of observations as well.

Edited by
Paul Sterry

Produced by AA Publishing © Automobile Association Developments Limited 2004

Published by AA Publishing (a trading name of Automobile Association Developments Limited, whose registered office is Millstream, Maidenhead, Windsor SL4 5GD; registered office 1878835)

A01911A

ISBN 0 7495 4045 1

A CIP catalogue record for this book is available from the British Library.

Produced for AA Publishing by The Bridgewater Book Company

Printed and bound by Leo Paper, China

Visit AA Publishing at www.theAA.com

Acknowledgments *Abbreviations for terms appearing below: (t) top; (b) bottom; (l) left; (r) right; (c) centre*
All images and illustrations belong to the Automobile Association's own library (AA WORLD TRAVEL LIBRARY)
R ALLEN 20c, 20bl, 20bc, 21tc, 21ct, 21cb, 21bl; N ARLOTT 3b, 10t, 10br, 28t, 29t, 30t, 30c, 31t, 35b, 42t, 42b, 43t, 43b, 44t, 44b, 45t, 45b, 55t, 55b, 56, 57t, 57b, 58t, 58b, 59, 60t, 60c, 60b, 61t, 61b, 62t, 62b, 63t, 63c, 63r, 64t, 64b, 65t, 65c, 65br, 66c, 67, 69bc, 82, 86, 89c, 89b, 90t, 90b, 91t, 91bc, 91br, 94t, 94c, 94b, 95t, 95b, 96t, 96b, 97t, 97b, 98t, 98b, 100c, 104t, 104c, 105, 106, 130c, 131t, 141t, 142t, 142bc; A BAKER 50ltl; J BEAZLEY 25ltl, 40tl; J BLANDFORD 40c; T BOYER 1, 4l, 5b, 23ct, 23b, 24cl, 26cl, 26b, 27t, 27b, 28cr, 28b, 29cl, 29b, 30b, 31c, 31b, 76, 77b, 78t, 78b, 83c, 83b, 84ct, 84b, 85ct, 85b, 98c, 99t, 99b, 100t, 100b, 101, 102, 103t, 103b, 116, 117t, 117b, 118t, 118b, 120t, 120b, 121t, 121b, 122t, 122b, 123t, 123b; I BURGUM 40tr; H BURN 18t, 18b, 19, 20t, 21clt, 21bc, 22, 24t, 24c, 27c, 29c, 30tc, 30cr, 48, 49l, 49r, 51t, 51b, 52t, 52b, 53t, 53b, 54c, 54b; J COX 7l, 23tc, 23tr, 23cbl, 23cbr, 26tc, 26tr, 26c, 26cr, 28cl, 28c, 89l, 97c, 130t, 130b, 131c, 131b; D DALY 57c, 58c, 64c, 66l; R GILLMOR 12, 13b, 14t, 14b, 15tl, 15tc, 15bc, 16, 17ct, 17bc; J GALE 15br, 46t, 47t; P HAYMAN 7crt, 17bl, 126t, 126b, 127, 128, 129t, 129b, 132, 133, 134t, 134c, 134b, 135t, 135b, 136, 137t, 137b, 138, 139t, 139c, 139b, 140t, 140b, 142cr, 142br; I LEWINGTON 7cr, 119l, 123c, 142cl; S & O MATHEWS 25tl, 124/125c, 125; E MEACHER 25tr; R MOORE 25trt; D QUINN 7crb, 13l, 38b, 69cl, 69cr, 69rcr, 69bl, 69br, 70t, 70cl, 70cr, 70rcr, 70bl, 70br, 72c, 72b, 77t, 141b, 142c; D REES 99c; C ROSE 2, 3t, 4t, 4r, 5t, 6t, 6b, 7t, 8t, 8b, 9t, 9cl, 10cl, 10cr, 10bc, 11t, 11b, 17t, 25t, 32t, 32ctl, 32ct, 32ctr, 32cbl, 32cbr, 32b, 33t, 33c, 33b, 34t, 34b, 35t, 35c, 36, 37t, 37c, 37cb, 37b, 38c, 39t, 39b, 40t, 41t, 41c, 41b, 46c, 46b, 47c, 47b, 50t, 68t, 68b, 69t, 69lcl, 70lcl, 71t, 71b, 72t, 73t, 73b, 74t, 74c, 74b, 75t, 75b, 79, 80t, 80b, 81t, 81b, 83t, 84t, 84cb, 85t, 85cb, 87, 88, 92, 93t, 93b, 107t, 107bl, 107br, 108t, 108b, 109t, 109b, 110t, 110b, 111t, 111b, 112t, 112b, 113t, 113b, 114, 115, 119r, 124/125t, 131cl; M SHORT 50tl, 50tr; P TRENCHARD 50rtr; H WILLIAMS 25bl, 50b; P WILSON 40rt

Front Cover l (Nuthatch) AA/Norman Arlott; r (Greenfinch) AA/Peter Hayman;
Inside flap (Welney Marshes) AA/S & O Mathews
Back Cover bl (Shag) AA/Robert Gillmor; bc (Kestrel) AA/D Quinn; br (Barn Owl) AA/T Boyer; background (Kingfisher) AA/Chris Rose

Contents

Dipper

Using this Book

Puffin chick under three weeks

Four weeks

Five or six weeks

Six months

Adult puffin in winter

Adult puffin in summer

Many people are first attracted to birdwatching by the visual variety of birds in this country, from colourful species such as the kingfisher to the subtly camouflaged, such as the stone curlew. The marvellous, detailed paintings of birds in this book may be browsed through simply for pleasure, of course, but they also serve as a practical and accurate guide to bird identification, with many species shown in flight, or engaging in some characteristic behaviour, such as courtship or feeding. Some species are illustrated at different stages of growth, and any differences between summer and winter plumages are highlighted.

The notes that accompany each bird portrait are a quick guide to key points for identification, and are designed to enable the observer to distinguish a particular species from a similar one, and to tell the sexes and ages apart. Accurate identification, of course, enables the enthusiast to learn more, and the main text provides practical and interesting background information about each species. Curious aspects of behaviour may be discussed – why, for example, is the nuthatch known as the plasterer? – along with details such as breeding habits, numbers and status in the British Isles, the size of the breeding population and overwintering numbers. Each species has a panel packed with essential information relating to the bird's size, weight, preferred habitat, and breeding and feeding patterns.

Sometimes an illustration to show characteristic behaviour is included, like these Manx shearwaters, gliding close to the water's surface, tilting from side to side.

Birds in the Garden

Birdwatching need take you no further than your own window, especially if you look out onto a garden. Even without extra encouragement, there are sure to be common species such as blackbirds, starlings, robins and blue tits around in fair numbers.

   If you are able to put out nesting boxes and food in the winter, you will attract larger numbers of birds and almost certainly increase the variety of species seen. Different foods attract different birds, and sometimes presentation can be important – for example, siskins are known to favour the red plastic bags of peanuts. A small pond or birdbath is another popular attraction for garden birds, both during the summer months and in winter if you keep it ice-free. Remember to locate birdbaths and feeders in open places, where prowling cats cannot hide.

Flocks of fieldfares may be attracted to fruit and berries in a winter garden.

Going Birdwatching

Certain fieldcraft skills can be learned, and these will improve with time and experience. For example, your ability to identify species at a glance will develop with repeated observations of common species – as will your ability to find the best spot for watching. You can soon learn to move quietly through woodlands, using your ears as much as your eyes to detect the presence of birds around you. Wherever you are, remember to use natural cover whenever possible to break up your outline. Be patient, and try remaining motionless in one spot: once birds are used to your presence, you have a better chance of observing their general activity at close range.

If you are going birdwatching in search of a particular species, then it is well worth undertaking some research before you set off. By focusing on the correct habitat you will greatly improve your chances of successful observation.

Visual clues may be the most obvious way to distinguish species, but do not forget that the calls and songs of birds are also invaluable aids to their identification. With practice, most birdwatchers can learn to recognise the songs of common garden and woodland birds. Flight and alarm calls may take longer to master – not least because you cannot always track down or see the bird in question, to relate the sound to the species. Having a more experienced birdwatcher as a companion and mentor can greatly speed up the learning process, so why not tag along with an expert? Many nature reserves have wardens who can give you general advice, and a guided walk with an expert ornithologist can be a real revelation. Membership of an organisation such as the Royal Society for the Protection of Birds (RSPB) will also offer more opportunities to broaden your knowledge.

When watching birds in unfamiliar locations or habitats, many people find it useful to carry a field guide with them, to help identify a species on the spot. Without this aid – and sometimes even with a field guide – there will always be birds which defy ready identification. Making some simple notes on the spot can help you here, where relying on memory alone can be extremely misleading. Try and note down the bird's size in relation to others of known species around it. Look for distinctive marks or patterns, both at rest and in flight; beak shape and white rumps or wing bars are examples of less obvious but essential diagnostic aids. Try to describe any call or song heard, and note down any interesting or unusual behaviour. Your notes will make it much easier to recall details when you get back to your reference books, or want to ask for somebody's help.

The song of familiar garden birds such as the robin may be easily learned.

Male snow bunting in winter

SOME BASIC EQUIPMENT

Although good eyesight and keen hearing are the best tools to help you enjoy birdwatching, a good pair of binoculars enables closer observation, and along with a good identification guide they can make all the difference. Their powers of magnification allow you to see distant and often shy species without actually disturbing the birds; and they can also add to the enjoyment of watching common and familiar birds by bringing them into close range, allowing you to pick out the detail of every feather.

When selecting a pair of binoculars, the best advice is to try out as many different makes as possible and to buy the best you can afford. Binoculars are described by a set of numbers – 8x30, for example. The first number denotes the magnification, and the second the light-gathering capacity of the lenses. Do not be misled into thinking that larger magnification binoculars are automatically better than their low magnification counterparts. With greater magnification comes greater bulk, and cumbersome equipment is much more tedious to carry around with you or hold steady. Although some people prefer 10x magnification, 8x will be fine for most birdwatchers.

For the dedicated birdwatcher, and especially one with a serious interest in coastal birds, a telescope is essential equipment. Again, try out as many as possible before you choose – and remember, having bought a telescope, you will also need a tripod to hold it steady.

The green woodpecker is the largest of Britain's woodpeckers. It is more often heard than seen.

Male snow bunting in summer

Female snow bunting

Red-throated Diver
GAVIA STELLATA

LENGTH: 53–69CM **WEIGHT:** 1,200–1,600G **WHERE TO LOOK:**
BREEDING BIRDS ARE CONFINED TO LOCHS AND SMALL FRESH
WATER POOLS ON MOORS. IN WINTER WIDESPREAD AROUND
UK COASTS, OFF BOTH ROCKY AND SANDY SHORES **NEST:** A
FLAT PAD CLOSE TO WATER **EGGS:** 1 OR 2, DARK, SPECKLED
BROWN **FOOD:** NEARLY ALWAYS FISH, BUT SOME CRABS,
SHRIMPS **VOICE:** ONLY IN BREEDING SEASON, WAILING AND
RHYTHMIC GOOSE-LIKE CALLS; LOUD DEEP QUACKING IN FLIGHT,
RAPIDLY REPEATED *KWUK-UK-UK*

Adult male

Adult female

R ed-throats take off more easily than other divers and can take advantage of
smaller pools, but are restricted to areas with very little human disturbance. The
range has expanded recently to southwest Scotland. The nest is a mere cushion of
aquatic vegetation, often very close to water.

Young birds and adults from the far north start moving south in late August,
usually appearing in the south in September. They stay until April, even May, often in
large, loose groups but more usually in ones and twos. By May many birds will have
acquired their smart summer plumage, a sight not often seen outside Scotland. They
are then distinguished from other divers by their unpatterned backs, but a close view
shows delicate striping on the nape and side of the neck; the white breast is more
obvious. In summer they are seen in flight more often than black-throated divers, as
they move from their breeding loch to and from their feeding places on the coast,
usually calling loudly as they go.

■ *On water the general appearance is of a slim, long-necked bird, low in the water with
head and bill uptilted. It swims long distances under water.*
■ *A longer body and thicker neck distinguish it from grebes. The feet look smaller than
those of other divers.*
■ *In winter, adults have paler face and neck than juveniles, with the dark eye obvious
against the white background. Upper parts have fine white speckling, not seen on
other divers.*

Black-throated Diver
GAVIA ARCTICA

L ike all divers, the black-throated faces many potential dangers all
year round. Because it feeds in the larger lochs where it breeds,
instead of flying to the sea, disturbance by boats or noisy groups of
people can cause the sensitive divers to desert their nests. Even on
ideal lochs, breeding density is low because each pair needs a
territory of up to 142 hectares. And whereas red-throated divers can
breed on acidic, peaty pools and feed out at sea, there is some
evidence that black-throats have been affected by acid rain reducing
fish stocks in the large lochs they use. In autumn and winter all divers
can fall victim to fishing nets in inshore waters, or to oil. Despite these
problems, the British population, though small, seems stable after a
decline prior to the 1940s.

Breeding birds may be helped by the provision of artificial floating
islands to remove the problem of flooded nests, but this idea, which
seems a very good one, has yet to be proved successful.

■ *The summer plumage is distinctive and, in winter, the dark upper parts,
greyer nape and white flank patch are useful identification features.*
■ *On water, black-throats look relatively bulky.*

LENGTH: 58–73CM **WEIGHT:** 2,000–3,000G
WHERE TO LOOK: BREEDING BIRDS ON
LARGE SCOTTISH LOCHS. IN WINTER MOVE
SOUTH, TO BOTH SANDY AND ROCKY COASTS
NEST: BESIDE WATER, OFTEN ON ISLAND
EGGS: 1 OR 2, OLIVE-BROWN WITH BLACK
SPOTS **FOOD:** ALMOST ENTIRELY FISH **VOICE:**
RAVEN-LIKE CROAKING, OFTEN REPEATED, AND
WAILING CALLS BUILDING UP TO LOUD, FAR-
CARRYING CLIMAX

Divers dive smoothly without the forward
leap of the shag. Young cormorants have pale
undersides but longer tails. In flight, divers look
hump-backed, legs trailing. Black-throats form
small groups, have pale, horizontal, dagger-like
bills and white flank flash; red-throats have
uptilted bills.

Adult male

Adult female

Great Crested Grebe
PODICEPS CRISTATUS

LENGTH: 46–51CM **WEIGHT:** 800–1,400G **WHERE TO LOOK:**
INLAND LAKES, ESPECIALLY GRAVEL PITS, OCCASIONALLY ON
SLOW-FLOWING RIVERS AND OFTEN OFF SANDY STRETCHES OF
COAST IN THE WINTER **NEST:** OFTEN A FLOATING HEAP OF
AQUATIC PLANTS ANCHORED BY SURROUNDING VEGETATION
EGGS: 3-4, WHITE BUT FREQUENTLY STAINED BY WATER PLANTS
ON NEST **FOOD:** SMALL FISH, INSECTS, MOLLUSCS AND
SOMETIMES VEGETABLE MATTER **VOICE:** BARKING *RAH-RAH-RAH*
AND A CLICKING *KEK*; LOUD WHISTLES FROM CHICKS

A male and female great crested glebe perform an elaborate courtship display, shaking out their ornate head plumes.

Adult in winter.

Very young grebes often ride on their parents' back.

Red-necked Grebe
PODICEPS GRISEGENA

Red-necks are similar to great crested
grebes, but can be told by their smaller
size, stocky build and, in summer, by their
red neck and white cheeks. They are seen mainly
as winter visitors to reservoirs and sheltered coastal waters.

The display of the great crested grebe is as incredible as its history. In the mid 19th century these beautiful grebes were the height of fashion, when skinned and converted into ladies' hats – so much so that by 1860 the UK population had been reduced to just 42 pairs. Today, after a steady increase, the population is standing at around 4,700 pairs. This remarkable recovery has been aided by the flooding of many old gravel pits, which, after a few years, provide an ideal habitat with overhanging bank vegetation in which grebes can nest.

The extraordinary springtime display was first recognised and documented in the early 20th century. 'Cat display', 'penguin dance', 'habit preening' and 'head shaking' are all parts of the ritual in early spring. The fluffy, striped young are regularly carried aboard the parents' backs from soon after hatching. It is thought the young do not recognise their parents by sight during the first six weeks, as they have been known to follow anything that moves – including boats! The first two weeks of a great crested grebe's life are especially hazardous as they often fall prey to large fish.

People on the shore do not particularly worry grebes, but if they are disturbed and leave their nests their eggs might be taken by predators. Escaped mink present a new menace to these elegant birds, and the wash from power boats is also a threat, sometimes swamping nests and chicks.

■ *Large young remain striped until they moult into winter plumage. The stripes help the young conceal themselves in vegetation around the edge of the water. They make long whistling calls.*
■ *The head ruffs are lost during the winter.*
■ *The pink bill is specific to the great crested grebe.*
■ *This bird is best identified in flight by its vivid wing pattern; the long neck and trailing feet reduce possible confusion with mergansers, which have similar white patches.*
■ *Grebes move long distances under water and this can be frustrating for the birdwatcher: after a long dive they come up far from where you expect them.*

Little Grebe
TACHYBAPTUS RUFICOLLIS

LENGTH: 25–29CM **WEIGHT:** 140–230G **WHERE TO LOOK:** SHALLOW-EDGED LAKES, SMALL PONDS AND SLOW-MOVING RIVERS **NEST:** FLOATING TANGLE OF AQUATIC VEGETATION ATTACHED TO LARGER PLANTS **EGGS:** 4-6, WHITE, BUT OFTEN STAINED **FOOD:** SMALL FISH, SHRIMPS AND MANY TYPES OF AQUATIC INSECTS **VOICE:** DISTINCTIVE, HIGH-PITCHED, TITTERING GIGGLE

Nest

Adult

Juvenile

From a dumpy little puffball on the water's surface the little grebe transforms to a sleek, highly developed hunter beneath the water. All of its features are geared to fast movement when submerged. Its legs are set well back on the body to allow as much movement as possible. Its tail is reduced to mere bristles so as not to collide with its thrusting feet. The toes, with wide lobes, can be folded over each other on the forward stroke, and even the bones in the leg are flattened to give extra propulsion on the backward stroke but less resistance on the forward stroke.

Beneath water the little grebe appears silver because air bubbles are trapped under its feathers. This helps to keep the grebe warm and also enables it to float to the surface while concentrating on holding on to its prey – often diving beetles and sticklebacks.

Little grebes, or dabchicks, are found on tiny ponds and narrow rivers, but also on the bigger, more open waters that larger species inhabit, especially in winter. Then they appear smaller than ever.

■ *The rich burgundy sides to the face and neck show up well.*
■ *Young birds have unusually striped heads.*
■ *In flight its very small size and upper wing with no white make the little grebe easy to distinguish from other grebes.*

Slavonian Grebe
PODICEPS AURITUS

The spectacular golden-yellow eye stripe and tufts are only present during the summer when they are used in great crested grebe-like displays. It is during these displays that the North American name, horned grebe, seems more appropriate. A penguin-like dance varies from the great crested grebe's in several ways. Aquatic plants are gathered from the bottom of the pond and the birds surface to face each other as though to start the dance. When raised out of the water the two grebes immediately turn parallel to each other and race across the surface together. This ceremony is termed the 'weed rush'.

The first records of Slavonian grebes nesting in Britain were in the early 1900s. Today there are still about 60 breeding pairs. During the winter they move from the coast or estuaries only when the weather is too bad for them to fish easily. The stocking of lakes with large numbers of trout, which alters lake ecology, causes some concern for the wellbeing of these rare grebes.

LENGTH: 31–38CM **WEIGHT:** 350–450G **WHERE TO LOOK:** RARE BREEDER IN THE HIGHLANDS OF SCOTLAND. IN WINTER ALMOST EXCLUSIVELY FOUND AROUND THE COAST, PARTICULARLY IN SHELTERED BAYS AND ESTUARIES **NEST:** MADE OF FLOATING WEED ANCHORED BY SURROUNDING VEGETATION **EGGS:** WHITE, BUT SOON STAINED BY VEGETATION USED TO COVER THE NEST AS THE ADULT BIRD LEAVES **FOOD:** FISH

Winter plumage

Summer plumage

Winter flight

■ *In winter the birds have well-defined black and white plumage.*
■ *Summer plumage is unmistakable.*

Black-necked grebe
PODICEPS NIGRICOLLIS

The summer plumaged bird is easy to identify; in winter the appearance is similar to the Slavonian grebe, but note the peaked forehead and uptilted bill.

Manx Shearwater
PUFFINUS PUFFINUS

The Manx shearwater has remarkable navigational abilities: a bird released in Boston, USA, took just over 12 days to return the 5,150km to its nesting burrow on a Welsh island. Even to feed they may travel more than 300km. Perhaps the most remarkable colony in Britain is to be found 600 metres up on a mountain on the Hebridean island of Rhum. The birds are vulnerable to predators on land, and so gather at dusk in rafts offshore before coming into their burrows in darkness.

Like other members of the shearwater family, the adult abandons its young in the nest burrow, where it lives off its fat reserves for two weeks, and then finds its own way to the sea, and winter quarters, 8,000km away off the South American coast.

Manx shearwaters are perhaps most easy to find, though after dark, on some of the Welsh seabird islands, including Skomer. During on-shore gales, however, they often pass close to shore and can then be seen during the daytime from headlands off the west coast of Britain.

LENGTH: 30-38CM
WINGSPAN: 76-89CM **WHERE TO LOOK:** MAINLY OFF WEST COAST, SPRING TO AUTUMN. ASHORE ONLY AT COLONIES AT NIGHT **NEST:** IN BURROWS ON ISLANDS **EGGS:** I, WHITE **FOOD:** SMALL FISH, SQUID **VOICE:** EXCITED CACKLES

Storm Petrel
HYDROBATES PELAGICUS

LENGTH: 14–18CM **WINGSPAN:** 36–39CM **WHERE TO LOOK:** AT SEA, OFF WEST COAST DURING GALES. FOLLOWING BOATS **NEST:** IN HOLES, BURROWS ON ISLANDS **EGG:** I, WHITE **FOOD:** PLANKTON **VOICE:** CHURRING FROM BURROW

It is a memorable sight to see Britain's smallest seabirds, only sparrow-sized, battling against a fierce autumn gale, apparently at the mercy of the elements. However, the weak-looking, bat-like flight with rapid wing-beats and very short glides is deceptive, for much of their life is spent far out of sight of land, and birds 20 years old have been recorded. They only come to land, after dark, to breed in colonies. Inland records are quite exceptional.

Their habit of following ships, fluttering back and forth across the wake, has made them familiar to sailors. Large numbers can be attracted by 'chum' – a mixture of fish oil and offal; within minutes, an apparently empty sea is dotted with tiny black birds heading purpose-fully low over the surface towards the slick, attracted by the smell.

Petrels are named after St Peter, from their habit of apparently walking on water. In fact they simply flutter and patter with their feet, or merely lower their legs to stabilise themselves above the waves.

The pale underwing bar can show well. At a distance it resembles a sea-hugging house martin.

It feeds by dipping to the water's surface, wings raised, legs dangling.

Boat trips in late summer, or sea watching in autumn gales, can be very exciting. Huge numbers of kittiwakes and gannets may pass; petrels and the rarer shearwaters are keenly sought. Identification of distant 'tubenoses' rests largely on their flight action – a few stiff-winged flaps and long glides of shearwaters and the weak fluttering of storm petrels.

Fulmar
FULMARUS GLACIALIS

LENGTH: 45–50CM WINGSPAN: 102–112CM WHERE TO LOOK:
PRESENT ROUND ENTIRE COASTLINE WHERE CLIFFS SUITABLE,
ALL YEAR EXCEPT LATE AUTUMN. NON-BREEDERS AT SEA. VERY
RARE INLAND NEST: IN COLONIES ON CLIFF LEDGES, LESS
OFTEN UNUSED BUILDINGS, SAND DUNES; GRASS OR SOIL
PREFERRED TO BARE ROCK EGG: 1, WHITE FOOD: OFFAL,
CRUSTACEANS, CARRION, REFUSE, SMALL FISH, USUALLY TAKEN
FROM SURFACE. ATTENDS TRAWLERS IN LARGE NUMBERS VOICE:
LOUD, EXCITED CACKLING AND CROONING AT NEST, GRUNTS
AND CACKLES IN FEEDING FLOCKS, OTHERWISE SILENT

Nostril tubes

Adult

Chick

Fulmars are perhaps Britain's longest-living birds, many probably reaching 40 years of age; and at least one has celebrated its 50th birthday. Immature birds remain at sea for several years, not breeding until nine or ten. Young birds looking for future nest sites are sometimes trapped in old roofless buildings: in three years 274 were found in this way on North Ronaldsay, Orkney.

In the last 200 years there has been a spectacular spread from Icelandic stock, with birds first recorded breeding in Britain, away from the ancient colony of St Kilda, on Foula in 1878. In 1969/70 the British and Irish breeding population was 305,000 pairs, with 40,000 on St Kilda. Today more than 550,000 pairs nest around the British and Irish coasts. This increase is thought to have resulted from the availability of whaling and trawling offal as food. The St Kilda population has remained stable and still has a plankton-based diet; it also behaves differently, avoiding ruined buildings, so it is possible that a new adaptable type of fulmar arose on Iceland, capable of exploiting man's fishing waste – just as the collared dove has extended its range more recently by filling a vacant niche.

Fulmar-oil is a foul smelling liquid, ejected by both adults and young as a form of defence, although also used, mixed with regurgitated food, for feeding the young. It is rich in vitamins A and D. The smell of fulmars is said to stay on oil-stained clothing for many years. Predators including peregrines have been found dead, completely coated in the oil.

■ *A heavy body, straight wings and lack of neck distinguish the fulmar from superficially similar gulls such as the herring gull.*

■ *The stout, hooked bill is made up of several plates, topped with a prominent pair of nostril tubes. The dark patch of modified bristly feathers in front of the eye may help to reduce glare.*

■ *Fulmars swim buoyantly, and may spend much of the day resting on the water. They feed from the surface, and also occasionally by shallow plunge diving.*

■ *Fulmars are faithful to their mate and nest site. They wave their heads and bow and cackle at their mates and rivals. The inside of the bill, shown in display, is a striking mauve or purple colour.*

■ *The nest site is vigorously defended, though once incubation has started the adults are rarely together.*

■ *The downy white chick is attended constantly for the first two weeks. Later, the parents visit only briefly to feed the chick.*

■ *At fledging, the young bird resembles its parents. Despite the long period of immaturity, there are no plumage differences with age, sex or season.*

Gannet
SULA BASSANA

LENGTH: 87–100CM **WINGSPAN:** 165–180CM **WHERE TO LOOK:** BREEDS MAINLY ON ROCKY ISLANDS IN NORTH AND WEST, BUT SEEN OFF ALL COASTS, LESS NUMEROUS IN WINTER. VAGRANT INLAND **NEST:** PILE OF SEAWEED, VEGETATION, AND EARTH, IN LARGE, DENSE, NOISY COLONIES **EGG:** 1, PALE BLUE, CHALKY, TURNING WHITE, THEN STAINING **FOOD:** FISH, ESPECIALLY MACKEREL AND HERRING, CAUGHT IN SPECTACULAR PLUNGE-DIVE; ALSO OFFAL **VOICE:** *ARRR, URRAH*

Britain and Ireland now hold 201,000 pairs of this largest and most spectacular seabird of the North Atlantic, a large proportion of the world population. It was formerly taken for food by sea-fowling communities, the fat, unfledged young or 'guga' providing considerable quantities of protein and fat. The inflated dried stomachs were used on St Kilda as containers. Cessation of most persecution has enabled numbers to increase to a new peak, doubling between 1949 and 1969, and still rising, with several new colonies.

Gannets have no brood patch, so the egg is incubated under the large webbed feet, and the newly hatched chick brooded on top of the webs. Another special adaptation is the lack of external nostrils, enabling the birds to dive headfirst into the sea from up to 30m, reaching 100kph as they hit the water.

Each young gannet eats about 30kg of fish before leaving the colony. After 13 weeks, they jump off the cliffs and flop-glide to the sea below, unable to take off again for a week or more, until their excess fat reserves have been used up. They move south to waters off the West African coast and may remain there for two years, before returning north.

■ *The central long, thin, angled wings, long, pointed bill and tail give the gannet a characteristic silhouette.*

■ *In flight the body is often angled above the horizontal, and the bird has steady, powerful wingbeats.*

■ *Distant birds of all ages are identifiable by their shape.*

■ *One or other parent is always in attendance at the nest to defend it and to tend the downy, white chick.*

■ *Gannets take about four years to attain full adult plumage, each stage being recognisable. When fledged, juveniles are black to avoid being taken for trespassing adults. First-years have white under parts, head and neck, but otherwise are dark above; second-years have largely white forewings but still have dark flight feathers. Third-years resemble adults, but retain some black feathers on the inner wing and tail. They hang around the edge of the colony in 'clubs'.*

■ *The magnificent adult is gleaming white with black outer wings, and a rich buff head and nape.*

■ *Fishermen may use the spectacular sight of fishing gannets to locate fish shoals. Many hundreds of birds may gather if the fishing is good, feasting, for example, on mackerel or other shoal fish. To watch a diving mass of gannets it is a wonder that they do not impale one another.*

Juvenile

2nd year

1st year

3rd year

Juvenile

Adult and chick

Adult

Cormorant
PHALACROCORAX CARBO

LENGTH: 80–100CM **WINGSPAN:** 130–160CM
WHERE TO LOOK: BREEDS ROUND ALL
COASTS, BUT LARGE GAPS IN THE EAST;
OTHERWISE WIDESPREAD ON ESTUARINE AND
INLAND WATERS, ESPECIALLY WINTER. **NEST:**
PILE OF TWIGS, SEAWEED, LINED WITH FINER
MATERIAL, IN LOOSE COLONIES ON CLIFF
LEDGES. ABROAD, ALSO IN TREES, REED BEDS
INLAND. **EGGS:** 3-4, CHALKY WHITE **FOOD:**
FISH, ESPECIALLY BOTTOM-DWELLING
SPECIES, EELS **VOICE:** GUTTURAL
CROAKING AT NEST AND ROOST

Feeding on eels

Adult, summer

Cormorants are widely distributed over five continents. They eat a variety of fish, many of no commercial value, but fishermen, who see them as competitors, have long persecuted them. When not feeding, cormorants sit like bottles, upright in rows on a sand bank, buoy or other man-made structure; shags prefer rocks.

The cormorant uses its large webbed feet to incubate its eggs, carefully placing them under the eggs so they are warmed between the feet and body. The young are born blind and naked, and look distinctly reptilian at this stage. They were formerly eaten in the Netherlands, where some tree colonies are very large – at one time the famous Nardermeer colony had 3,800 nests.

Cormorant feathers have modified barbs, which allow air to escape and water to penetrate the plumage. This makes for more efficient underwater swimming. However, it also means that the bird becomes waterlogged and must dry out in the familiar heraldic posture. Vultures have been observed in similar pose, and it is thought this may also aid digestion in some way.

■ *In full breeding dress they are very handsome; black, glossed blue and bronze, with a white throat and thigh patch, flashed in courtship display. A few white plumes adorn the loosely crested nape formed of elongated feathers. Outside the nesting season adults are much duller, and lose most of their white.*
■ *Immatures are brown with varying amounts of white underneath.*

Shag
PHALACROCORAX ARISTOTELIS

Chicks

Adult, spring

LENGTH: 65–80CM **WINGSPAN:** 90–105CM **WHERE TO LOOK:**
ROCKY COASTS, ABSENT FROM MUCH OF EAST AND SOUTH
ENGLAND. IMMATURE BIRDS DISPERSE MORE WIDELY IN WINTER.
NOT INLAND EXCEPT AFTER GALES **NEST:** HEAP OF WEED,
VEGETATION, ON SHELTERED LEDGE, SEA CAVE, AMONG
BOULDERS **EGGS:** 3, PALE BLUE, WITH CHALKY DEPOSIT
FOOD: FISH, MAINLY SAND EELS AND HERRINGS
VOICE: GRUNTS AND CLICKS

The shag, or green cormorant, like most British seabirds, has been steadily increasing this century, despite periodic disasters. It is highly susceptible to paralytic shellfish poisoning, contracted from a natural toxin produced by a small marine organism, and concentrated in the fish upon which the shags feed. In 1968, 82 per cent of Farne Island breeding birds died within a few days. However, in the following year, numbers were rapidly replaced by incoming young birds, which had dispersed from the colony. Shags take four years to mature, and, once adult, have a high life expectancy. Young birds are prone to disorientation in adverse weather and may end up inland in considerable numbers. Such influxes are called 'wrecks'.

It is an early breeder; nesting usually timed so that the young are in the nest when most sand eels are available in May and June, but occasional nests have been found in winter. The long fledgling period of 53 days is followed by a further four weeks, during which the adults still feed and tend the young. The female chick loses her voice after five weeks, able only to hiss and click!

Shags are largely resident, with little more than local dispersal from most colonies, so they must be sought near rocky coasts all year round.

■ *The dapper adult with its dark, oily green plumage, yellow gape, and comic, upturned crest is easily distinguished from the larger cormorant.*
■ *In flight they show proportionately shorter and less pointed wings than the cormorant, and more rapid wingbeats, with the neck usually fully extended. They also hug the sea more closely.*

Grey Heron
ARDEA CINEREA

LENGTH: 90–98CM **WEIGHT:** 1,100–1,700G **WHERE TO LOOK:** PONDS, LAKES, RIVERS, MARSHES AND OTHER FRESHWATER SITES, SOMETIMES SEEN AT COASTAL LOCALITIES, PARTICULARLY IN WINTER **NEST:** LARGE STICK CONSTRUCTION IN TREE-TOP COLONIES, ALTHOUGH OCCASIONALLY SINGLY OR ON GROUND **EGGS:** 4-5, PALE BLUE **FOOD:** VARIED, FISH, SMALL MAMMALS AND BIRDS **VOICE:** A LOUD, HARSH AND DISTINCTIVE *FRANK*; YOUNG BIRDS CHATTER OR GIVE A PIG-LIKE SQUEAL, ESPECIALLY BEFORE BEING FED

Adult

Juvenile

A heron standing motionless beside a river or pond is a very familiar sight, and the actions of a hunting bird that has succeeded in catching an eel are truly spectacular as this most accomplished of fisherman tries to swallow the most agile of fish. Frequently the eel actually knots itself around the heron's bill.

The grey heron population of England and Wales is probably better known than that of any other bird and now numbers some 4,000 breeding pairs (plus a further 1,000 or so in Scotland). The largest colony is at the RSPB Northward Hill reserve, Kent, where in most years the colony totals some 200 pairs.

If you visit the south coast of England and see what looks like a pure white heron, the chances are it is a little egret. Once rare in Britain, these elegant birds are now present year-round, with several hundred in the country at any one time.

■ *The large, dagger-shaped bill is a highly efficient tool for fishing. It is normally yellow, but turns bright pink when breeding.*

■ *In both flapping flight and when gliding and soaring, the heron is immediately identified by the broad, rounded wings, 'kinked' neck and long, trailing legs.*

■ *The claw on the third toe has a serrated edge, which enables the plumage to be preened clean.*

Bittern
BOTAURUS STELLARIS

A combination of the drainage of wetlands and human persecution in the 19th century has resulted in a very restricted bittern population, now probably numbering just 15 nesting pairs each year. The majority are confined to only two or three sites, and East Anglia is still the stronghold of the species.

The skulking and secretive nature of the bittern, the camouflage of the mottled and barred golden-brown plumage, together with the motionless stance, can make it extremely difficult to observe. Consequently, bitterns are most easily seen by birdwatchers in flight; hides at the RSPB's Leighton Moss reserve offer perhaps the best opportunities for observation.

The presence of bitterns in spring is best established by listening for the distinctive territorial 'booming' call of the male. This strange noise, although not loud, is far carrying and may be heard up to 4km away, most frequently at dusk in April or May.

Although a member of the heron family, when seen in flight the brown plumage with rounded wings can give the impression of a giant woodcock or owl.

LENGTH: 90–80CM **WEIGHT:** 900–1,500KG **WHERE TO LOOK:** REED BEDS, EXCEPT IN COLD WEATHER **NEST:** ON GROUND AMONGST REEDS **EGGS:** 5–6, OLIVE-BROWN **FOOD:** ALMOST EXCLUSIVELY FISH **VOICE:** MALE HAS A DEEP RESONANT BOOM, REPEATED 3–4 TIMES IN 5–6 SECONDS

Adult

Nest

Mute Swan
CYGNUS OLOR

LENGTH: 145–160CM **WEIGHT:** 8–13KG
WHERE TO LOOK: SHALLOW LAKES, SLOW
RIVERS, MARSHES, WET MEADOWS AND
SHELTERED COASTS **NEST:** BESIDE WATER,
HUGE HEAP OF VEGETATION WITH SHALLOW
DEPRESSION **EGGS:** 5–8, HUGE, CHALKY,
GREENISH, APRIL–JUNE **FOOD:** AQUATIC
VEGETATION OBTAINED BY DIPPING HEAD AND
NECK OR UP-ENDING; GRASSES TAKEN WHEN
GRAZING ON MEADOWS OR SALT MARSH;
SOME SNAILS, WORMS **VOICE:** HOARSE,
STRANGLED TRUMPETING, SNORTING AND
HISSING CALLS, WINGS NOISY IN FLIGHT.

Big white swans are symbols of grace, elegance and serenity, but also strength and power. Adult humans enjoy their beauty and shapeliness; children prefer to ask if it is really true that a swan can break a leg with one swipe of its wing! Probably not, but they are certainly big and impressive, and a very characteristic part of the British scene. Numbers have declined in central England where they seem most obviously at home.

Associated with an increase and spread in western Europe, mute swans in Britain became much more numerous early in the 20th century and by 1955/56 there were 3,500–4,000 breeding pairs and another 11,000 non-breeding birds. Hard winters, disturbance from boats and the effects of lead poisoning from lost fishing weights combined to cause a decline, though it has been most marked in central England and balanced by increases in the north. By 1983 there were 3,150 pairs and 12,600 non-breeders, but some of the most famous herds, on the Thames and at Stratford-upon-Avon, have declined almost to the point of disappearance.

Swans used to be kept for food, but their need for water and the problems associated with feeding, and then catching such big birds eventually caused a change-over to domestic geese.

Male mute swans can be very aggressive and will chase off intruders, flying and then swimming quickly towards them. They also perform a spectacular display known as 'busking' with arched wings, breast thrust forwards, head aimed back and neck feathers fluffed out; serious fights sometimes develop.

The adult pulls up food and passes it to a chick on one side, using the same action as in nest building; foot movements attract and stir up food particles for them.

Male
Female
Up-ending
Juvenile

Bewick's Swan
CYGNUS COLUMBIANUS

LENGTH: 115–125CM WEIGHT: 4–8KG WHERE TO LOOK:
FLOODED MEADOWS, SALT MARSHES, SHALLOW LAKES AND
RESERVOIRS FOOD: ROOTS, SHOOTS, AQUATIC PLANTS, GRAIN
AND WASTE POTATOES VOICE: VARIED SOFT OR LOUD AND
FAR-CARRYING, MUSICAL, BUGLING CALLS

Juvenile

Adult

Bewick's swans used to be common in west Scotland and rare in England, but since the 1930s the opposite has been the case. They breed in remote tundra at the far northern edge of Siberia, from which only a few thousand come to Europe each winter. In England the main flocks are found on the Ouse Washes and at Slimbridge, where artificial feeding brings them close to observation hides; normally they are very shy. Their appearance on these Wildfowl Trust reserves is predictable, but the big flocks remain spectacular. Elsewhere it is an exciting event to discover a newly arrived party of these wild and wonderful swans on a frosty November day.

They are noticeably smaller than other swans when seen side by side, but the shorter, straighter neck, black and yellow bill and shorter, less pointed and, when swimming, less elevated tail are the best distinctions from the familiar mute swan. Whooper swans are much more like them, but with a longer, flatter head profile and more yellow on the bill.

■ *Adults have rounded yellow side patches on an otherwise black bill; young birds are dingy grey with pink and black on the bill.*
■ *The typically thick goose-like neck can be raised erect, and then appears long and thin.*
■ *In flight Bewick's swans call loudly, but their wings simply 'swish', without the hum of the mute's.*

Whooper Swan
CYGNUS CYGNUS

LENGTH: 145–160CM; WEIGHT: 8–14KG WHERE TO LOOK: WET
MEADOWS AND STUBBLE FIELDS BY RIVERS AND ESTUARIES,
UPLAND POOLS, LARGE LOCHS. FOOD: LEAVES, STEMS AND
ROOTS OF AQUATIC PLANTS, WASTE GRAIN AND POTATOES –
ON DRY LAND IN MORE RECENT YEARS. VOICE: LOUD, TRUMPET-
LIKE OR BUGLING CALL, STRONGER THAN BEWICK'S.

Juvenile

Adult

Juvenile

Small, quiet lochs in the Scottish hills, grassy fields beside the mouth of a river, or wild, remote farmland with meadows and stubble not far from a lake make the ideal winter home for whooper swans. In some places, especially at the Wildfowl Trust reserve on the Ouse Washes, all three swans mix together in winter, but it is generally true to say that whoopers prefer the north and west of Britain to the softer south. Most of Britain's winter whoopers are from Iceland, where there are 5,000–7,000 birds, though only a small proportion nest in any one year. Like other swans and geese, the number here in any winter depends very largely on the breeding success of the previous season. Family parties will stay together all winter.

The weather in Iceland also plays a part in how many come to Britain and Ireland, as more will stay there in a mild winter, but a spell of bad weather even in mid-winter can trigger off a new movement south and flocks can cross to and from Iceland at almost any time from September to April. They can migrate at enormous heights, presumably in very cold air indeed. Very occasionally a pair or two of whooper swans will remain in Britain to breed, usually in the north or northwest of Scotland.

■ *Plumage is like Bewick's, but the longer bill and flatter forehead are obvious; notice that the yellow extends forward in a point in the side of the bill.*
■ *Whooper and Bewick's swans walk more freely than the waddling mute and are quicker to take to the air.*
■ *All swans are prone to reddish staining from oxides in water, but whoopers perhaps show it more often.*

Barnacle Goose
BRANTA LEUCOPSIS

LENGTH: 60-70CM **WEIGHT:** 1.5-2KG **WHERE TO LOOK:** MEADOWS AND STUBBLE BESIDE SALT MARSHES AND ON ISLANDS **FOOD:** LEAVES, STEMS, SEEDS AND ROOTS OF GRASS AND OTHER VEGETATION **VOICE:** SHORT, SHARP BARK, OFTEN REPEATED IN YAPPING CHORUS FROM FLOCKS

Adult

Juvenile

With its beautiful barring, glossy black chest and immaculate appearance, the barnacle is perhaps the most lovely of all geese. The neat little beak and, for a goose, rather long legs, add a distinctive touch at close range. Barnacles that breed in Greenland spend the winter in western Scotland, especially on the island of Islay, and in Ireland. There will usually be over 20,000 of them. Another group from Spitsbergen winters only on the Solway Firth; these have increased to over 10,000 birds. A third group breeds in the northern USSR and spends the winter in the Netherlands, but some reach England each winter. On Islay they have been the cause of great controversy, because they prefer to eat the rich, green grass of meadows improved for sheep rearing, to the detriment of the sheep. An RSPB reserve is managed in order to attract the geese away from other farms on the island, in an attempt to reduce the conflict.

■ *The young bird is duller than the adult, with mottled face and greyer chest.*
■ *In flight the black chest and white belly make an obvious contrast; from above, the rump is eye-catching.*

Brent Goose
BRANTA BERNICLA

LENGTH: 55–60CM **WEIGHT:** 1.2–1.5KG **WHERE TO LOOK:** MUDDY ESTUARIES AND ADJACENT SALT MARSHES AND PASTURES; SANDY BAYS **FOOD:** GRAZES AND UP-ENDS TO FEED ON EEL-GRASS, GREEN ALGAE, GROWING CEREALS AND MARSH PLANTS **VOICE:** DEEP, ROLLING BARK

On a dark, misty winter's day in southeast England, only the comfortable sounds of the Brents' deep, nasal, *rronk-rronk* calls, echoing around the marsh, may give them away. The flock may be hidden in the gloom, or tucked away in a muddy creek or out of sight behind a sea-wall, but these little geese are as much a part of the wilderness of Britain's low-lying coasts as the life-giving mud and marsh on which they live. They feed and roost in tight-packed groups, even when they fly to the fields, an increasing habit of recent years, so that counting them is a hard job. Dark-bellied birds come each winter from the northern tundra of the USSR, to feed in the southern estuaries; pale-bellied birds from Greenland visit Ireland, and others from Spitsbergen come to Lindisfarne. Both races are rare in world terms.

When ell-grass was reduced by disease in the 1930s, numbers of dark-bellied brents fell by at least 75 per cent. The population of this race is enormously variable depending on breeding success, but with careful protection has recently reached over 80,000, in turn renewing calls for their control.

■ *The black neck, chest, face, marked only on sides of neck, are unique; the juvenile has no neck patches at first, and barred wing coverts.*
■ *The dark birds are browner beneath, the black chest less contrasted than on the pale race; sometimes hard to tell the difference.*
■ *Though only as long as mallard, Brents look larger and heavier in flight, with their white rump obvious. Flocks are usually shapeless masses or lines, low and fast flying.*

Canada Goose
BRANTA CANADENSIS

LENGTH: 90–100CM WEIGHT: 4–5KG WHERE TO LOOK:
ORNAMENTAL LAKES, FLOODED GRAVEL PITS, RESERVOIRS, AND
NEARBY MEADOWS NEST: ON GROUND NEAR WATER, OFTEN
BELOW TREE OR BUSH; A PILE OF LEAVES, GRASS, REEDS EGGS:
5–6, CREAM OR WHITE, MARCH–APRIL FOOD: ROOTS, STEMS,
LEAVES AND FRUITS OF WATER AND WATERSIDE PLANTS; MOSTLY
GRAZES, ALSO UP-ENDS IN WATER VOICE: LOUD, RESONANT
HONKING CALLS, USUALLY OBVIOUS TWO NOTES – *GOR-RRONK*,
ETC. ALSO VARIOUS LOUD QUICKER AND SHORTER HONKING
AND TRUMPETING NOTES IN DISPLAY OR ALARM

Juveniles

In North America, the Canada goose is a highly migratory species with many distinct races and traditional migration routes and wintering grounds. It is odd that such a bird should be so successfully introduced to into Europe (to Britain in the 17th century) and remain content to live all year round on the lakes where its ornamental qualities were required. Nevertheless, the lakes and pools of Britain's stately homes, surrounded by ample flat, grassy expanses for easy grazing, proved ideal and the adaptable birds soon became established and familiar.

So long as food is readily available, Canada geese seem content to settle anywhere, even on a city-centre lake; if food is insufficient to support them, they simply fly elsewhere. By the late 1960s there were over 10,000 birds in Britain and their increase continues. In favoured sites in central England it is possible to find flocks of several hundred birds in late summer and autumn, which undoubtedly look spectacular and allow everyone to enjoy the sight and sound of 'wild geese', but they somehow lack the romantic associations and appeal of their truly wild relatives, which would not be seen dead in a town! Consequently, they are rather neglected – even despised – by many birdwatchers.

The Canada goose is easily recognised by the brown-barred back, creamy chest and black neck and head, with white 'chinstrap'. Winter flocks are well organised and often large, with considerable aggression being common between members of the group and towards threats from outside. Within the flock a hierarchy exists with large families dominating small ones; these in turn dominate pairs, with unfortunate single birds at the bottom of the 'pecking order'

■ As on other geese, the 'stern' is strikingly white – clearly an obvious mark for other birds to follow, especially in flight.
■ Both parents tend the young, which are able to feed themselves.
■ Chicks use frequent contact calls and perform greeting displays after accidental separation from the parents.
■ Chicks leave the nest on hatching and are vulnerable to predators; they fly after seven weeks.
■ Pairs – formed at about two years old – remain together for life; the young are tended by both parents but driven away the following spring.

White-fronted Goose
ANSER ALBIFRONS

LENGTH: 65–78CM **WEIGHT:** 1.5–2.5KG **WHERE TO LOOK:** MEADOWS IN BROAD RIVER VALLEYS, BESIDE ESTUARIES. VERY RESTRICTED, IN REDUCED NUMBERS, MOSTLY IN GLOUCESTERSHIRE, KENT, HAMPSHIRE. GREENLAND RACE IN WILDER PLACES, VERY RARE IN WALES, MORE WIDESPREAD IRELAND AND SCOTLAND **FOOD:** GRASS, ROOTS **VOICE:** MOST MUSICAL OF GEESE, WITH RINGING, LAUGHING, YODELLING QUALITY TO FLOCK CALLS; USUALLY HIGH-PITCHED *LYO-LYOCK; KLICK-KLEK*, ETC. HISSING AND YAPPING CALLS ON GROUND AND 'CREAKING' WINGS TAKING FLIGHT

Adult

Juvenile

To many people in the south of England this was once the most familiar of the wild 'grey geese', as greylags and pink-feet are more northerly in their distribution. Nowadays, however, flocks of introduced greylags are much more common, while, coincidentally, wild white-fronts have declined dramatically. Only in the North Kent Marshes, the Avon Valley of Hampshire, the Tywi Valley of Wales and on the Severn Estuary around Slimbridge, are there now regular flocks of birds from the Siberian tundra, and all have declined in numbers. In the north and in Ireland, darker birds from Greenland appear, around 20,000 all told in an average year.

White-fronts are fascinating to watch, like all geese, and the hides at Slimbridge in mid-winter offer the best views. They are noisy, busy and quarrelsome, quick to take alarm and difficult to approach except behind the Slimbridge screens. In flight, white-fronts en masse are unparalleled, as they cross the sky in huge 'Vs', lines and chevrons; in full voice they create a yapping, squeaking, babbling chorus that can be quite deafening from a really big flock – in the Netherlands it is often possible to see 10,000–15,000 together. In flight the white-front shows a white rump and some grey on forewing above. They are more agile in flight than greylags, especially when landing and taking off. The calls of geese are difficult for a beginner to identify, however the calls of white-fronts have a distinctive 'catch' to them.

■ *Immature birds are best recognised by their plain, brownish colour, orange legs and dull, pinkish bill.*

Bean goose
ANSER FABALIS

LENGTH: 65-80CM **WEIGHT:** 2–4KG **WHERE TO LOOK:** PASTURES AND ARABLE LAND **FOOD:** IN BRITAIN GRAZES MAINLY ON GRASSY FIELDS, BUT ON THE CONTINENT ALSO IN STUBBLE **VOICE:** GENERALLY QUIETER THAN OTHER GREY GEESE; RESEMBLES DEEP-VOICED PINK-FOOTED, WITHOUT THE HIGHER-PITCHED NOTES

Only in south-west Scotland, where a very few birds appear each winter, and in Norfolk, where a reduced but recently recovering flock can be found, are bean geese regularly seen in Britain. In most winters one or two will be found mixed with Russian white-fronts, but otherwise only irregular parties appear from time to time. At the traditional wintering places they are creatures of habit, seeking out the same preferred fields year after year. Choosing open spaces in winter, with a wide view, bean geese are shy and unapproachable birds.

Beans are big geese, though not so heavy as greylags, and their proportions – especially the neck – give them a special elegance. Adults are particularly cleanly barred above, but have none of the blue-grey cast so often evident on pink-feet, nor do they show the same fawn-buff colour on the breast.

■ *The bean has a longish, orange and black bill; the pink-foot has a short bill with pink band; the greylag has a paler head, and a massive orange bill with paler tip and no black.*
■ *Dark upperwings, a long, rather slender neck and deep calls are helpful distinguishing features in flight.*

Bean

Pink-foot

Greylag

Greylag Goose
ANSER ANSER

LENGTH: 75–90CM WEIGHT: 3–4KG WHERE TO LOOK: OPEN
ARABLE LAND, MARSHES AND LAKES. FERAL BIRDS IN MORE
ENCLOSED SPACES NEST: ON GROUND IN SHELTERED HOLLOW
OR IN REEDS EGGS: 4–6, CREAMY-WHITE, APRIL–MAY FOOD:
GRASS, SPILT POTATOES AND GRAIN; MOVING TO GROWING
CEREALS IN LATE SPRING VOICE: CLATTERING CLAMOUR IN
FLIGHT, LESS BUGLING OR TRUMPETING THAN OTHER GEESE,
MORE RATTLING IN EFFECT

Adult

The large, bright orange bill, generally pale appearance and loud, rather rattling calls (without the musical quality of many other geese) help to identity the greylag. Visiting birds in winter have pink legs, but some of the wild breeding stock, and some feral birds, have orange legs, although either colour may be hard to distinguish at a distance! Old birds have a few spots of black on the belly and chest, but never so much as a white-front.

All geese vary greatly in appearance according to light. Greylags are essentially pale birds, but strong sun can create sharply contrasting highlights and shadows, and swimming birds can often appear misleadingly dark-headed as their barred backs catch the light.

Britain's winter-visiting greylags – in record years there may be up to about 100,000 of them – come from Iceland in October, mainly to Scotland, where they need a safe, quiet roost on water and undisturbed feeding places. Wild breeding pairs frequent remote lochs; 'feral' birds, introduced but now living wild, may be tamer and breed on quite small, even well-wooded, pits in unlikely places.

The greylag is not generally long lived, studies showing that the average adult life expectancy is less than four years. Pairs form for life and will be together all year round, and families remain together during the winter within the spectacular flocks.

- Greylags are heavier and slower than pink-foots, with larger heads.
- Juveniles are duller and more irregularly barred above.

Pink-footed Goose
ANSER BRACHYRHYNCHUS

White-front

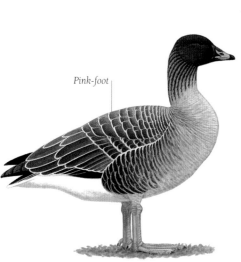

Pink-foot

Pink-foot

LENGTH: 60–75CM WEIGHT: 1.8–3.3KG WHERE
TO LOOK: ESTUARIES, SALT MARSHES, LAKES,
NEARBY ARABLE AND PASTURELAND FOOD:
GRASS, SPILT BARLEY AND OTHER GRAIN,
WASTE POTATOES VOICE: MUSICAL, DEEP
DI- OR TRI-SYLLABIC HONKING, ALSO HIGH-
PITCHED, SHARP *WINK-WINK*

In central and southern Scotland, where it mixes with greylags, and in northern England, especially on the Lancashire mosses, this is the most abundant winter goose. They come from Iceland and east Greenland and, like other northern geese, are very dependent on good weather during the short summer at such high latitudes. In a bad season they may rear virtually no young at all and fewer are seen in Britain as a result.

At places such as the north shore of the Solway Firth it is one of the great birdwatching experiences to stand between the inland feeding grounds and the estuarine roost at dusk, when stream after stream of noisy geese fly overhead. After many years with reduced numbers, the traditional Norfolk flocks have recently recovered, and it is now often possible to see several thousand there, too – much to the delight of more southern birdwatchers. The reason for the increase seems to be largely to do with improved food supplies and better refuges in Britain rather than changes in the breeding grounds, which are threatened with development.

This is perhaps the prettiest, most attractive grey goose. In flight, pink-footed geese have forewings that show blue-grey, more extensively than white-fronts but darker than greylags. The flight action is fast and aerobatic, while the head and neck look relatively small.

- The pink-footed goose has a barred, greyish back, pale buff fore body and very dark head and neck, with a rounded head, short, dark bill, and legs pale to deep pink.
- It may have white around the bill.

Shelduck
TADORNA TADORNA

Shelducks have startlingly white plumage, even on the dullest day; exaggerating their size and making them stand out from all the duller birds around. On a sunny day in summer the brightness of the bill is almost unreal, and the sharp, clean lines of the plumage are equally breathtaking.

Numbers have increased this century and today there are thought to be 12,000 birds nesting in Britain and Ireland. Because most of the shelducks of northwest Europe go to the same place to moult, this figure is small compared with the great gatherings in the Waddenzee. At least 100,000 gather there, safe for the dangerous period when they shed all their flight feathers at once – a characteristic of all ducks and geese – and are unable to fly. Their distribution abroad is quite wide, though largely limited in Europe to the coasts of France and those countries bordering the North Sea and the Baltic; but shelducks nest in scattered places in the Mediterranean and then eastwards beyond the Caspian into central Asia. This sporadic distribution shows a liking for rather warm climates and a need for productive shallow-water habits. In the past the range was probably more complete, and the isolated remnants have survived through their adaptability to changing conditions. It seems odd to find the same species on a cold Scottish mud flat and on a hot, reed-fringed Mediterranean marsh.

Although shelducks are primarily birds of the coast, they are quite frequent inland on migration or during harsh winter weather. They have even begun to breed inland, especially by flooded gravel pits.

LENGTH: 60–70CM WEIGHT: 1–1.8KG
WHERE TO LOOK: SANDY AND MUDDY SHORES, DUNES, FLOODED GRAVEL PITS, RESERVOIRS AND MARSHES NEST: IN BURROW, HOLE IN TREE, HAYSTACK EGGS: 8–10, WHITE, APRIL TO JUNE FOOD: MOLLUSCS, INSECTS, CRUSTACEANS DUG OR SIEVED FROM WET MUD OR FROM WATER VOICE: MALE WHISTLES; DEEP, QUICK QUACKS FROM FEMALE

Adult female

Adult male

■ *Flying birds show such a striking pattern that they are hard to miss.*
■ *Males in spring are glorious, with a brilliantly red bill topped by a large knob; females have no basal knob and show white facial marks, with less black below.*
■ *The broad sharp bill is ideally suited to sieving through wet ooze and dealing with molluscs.*
■ *The nest site is chosen by the female; she alone incubates the eggs.*
■ *Downy chicks start to cheep as they hatch; later they have high-pitched piping noises, with the same rhythm as the female's quack.*
■ *For 15–20 days the family stays in the feeding territory, then the chicks join with others in a crèche up to 100 strong. The crèche is often looked after by adults that have failed to breed.*
■ *An attacking bird chases others from its territory with head held low; the intruder runs off with its head raised and plumage sleek.*

Most pairs persist from year to year, and move to territorial feeding places on the shore by late March. At the same time they look for nest sites, often miles away, visiting them each morning. Nests may be close together, with no territories around them. When the young hatch, the family goes to a new, nursery area, with a 'mobile territory' centred on the chicks.

Juvenile

Wigeon
ANAS PENELOPE

LENGTH: 45–51CM **WEIGHT:** 600–900G **WHERE TO LOOK:**
SHALLOW, FRESH WATER WHEN NESTING, SALT MARSH OR
PASTURE IN WINTER **NEST:** ON GROUND IN COVER **EGGS:** 6–12,
PALE BUFF **FOOD:** VEGETABLE, MAINLY ALGAE AND EEL-GRASS
VOICE: WHISTLING *WHEE-OO*; GRATING *PURR*

Adult female

Adult male

The British breeding population of wigeon rarely exceeds 500 pairs, but in the winter months birds from Iceland, northern Europe and Russia move south, and as many as 200,000 are present during the January peak. The main wintering sites are coastal areas, apart from the Ouse Washes, where the creation of reserves to prevent disturbance, and the establishment of a water management regime on grazing meadows, has resulted in a dramatic increase to over 25,000 birds at a peak. The most evocative sound of a salt marsh is the whistle of a male wigeon. Feeding flocks move forward in dense groups; good sunlight reveals their beautiful colours.

The wigeon is a highly gregarious duck, between mallard and teal in size, with a short neck and tiny bill used for cropping vegetation.

■ *Note the small size and steep forehead; white and black undertail of the male; grey legs and small bill.*
■ *In flight, often with complex aerial manoeuvres, the distinctive whistle and prominent white patch on the upperwing of the male, plus the short pointed tail, are all distinguishing features. The overall impression is of a small, light duck with a dark head.*

Teal
ANAS CRECCA

LENGTH: 34–38CM **WEIGHT:** 240–360G
WHERE TO LOOK: SHALLOW WATERS **NEST:**
ON GROUND IN COVER **EGGS:** 8–11, OFF-
WHITE **FOOD:** SEEDS, INVERTEBRATES **VOICE:**
DISTINCTIVE HIGH-PITCHED, CHIRPING *KRICK*

In a group or 'spring', teal leap vertically from the water and then dash about the sky over a pool, so active that, although in shape they resemble small wigeon, they will often give the impression of a party of dark waders. By contrast, when walking they are, if anything, rather clumsy and less agile than the larger mallard. The smallest of the wintering ducks, and only a third of the weight of a mallard, the 100,000 or so that are present in December are to be found at both inland and coastal sites, with over 20,000 on the Mersey Estuary alone. The favoured areas are where shallow water only a few centimetres deep covers soft mud into which the birds can easily thrust their bills, for they rarely feed by up-ending, as do the larger species.

In areas where they are not disturbed, they become extremely tame and are often found feeding close to observation hides. Normally, however, because they are persecuted by hunters, they tend to be rather wary and difficult to see, looking very dark and dull except for the horizontal white bar across the males.

Adult male

Adult female

Mallard
ANAS PLATYRHYNCHOS

LENGTH 50–65CM **WEIGHT:** 950–1,300G **WHERE TO LOOK:**
ALMOST ANYWHERE WITH WATER **NEST:** USUALLY ON THE
GROUND, CAN BE HIGH IN TREE **EGGS:** 9–13, BLUISH-GREEN
FOOD: VARIABLE, OPPORTUNISTIC FEEDER **VOICE:** FEMALE GIVES
FAMILIAR *QUACK*, MALE A WEAK NASAL NOTE

Eclipse plumage

The commonest, most widespread of all ducks, the mallard needs no introduction, being encountered everywhere from the town park to the village pond, from the reservoir or gravel pit to the wildest sea loch or estuary salt marsh. Except for her yellowish bill and orange legs, the female is a rather undistinguished brown colour. This contrasts sharply with the male, with his striking bottle-green head and curled feathers above the tail. There are few sounds more familiar than the quack of the female mallard; the male has only a weak-rasping *raehb*.

During the summer months the male's plumage assumes an appearance similar to that of the female; this is called 'eclipse' plumage.

Highly adaptable, mallards often nest well away from water, high in a tree or on a building, and newly hatched young face a perilous journey. The British breeding population is difficult to estimate, but it could exceed 150,000 pairs, which together with an arrival of European birds, provides a winter count in excess of 700,000.

Mallard drakes tend to defend territories around a small headland or other landscape feature.

■ *Males have a dark green head, white neck ring, purple-brown breast and grey back.*
■ *Out of the water the birds walk easily, their bodies parallel with the ground. Both sexes have orange legs.*

Adult male

Adult female

Up-ending

Goldeneye
BUCEPHALA CLANGULA

Despite the recent welcome rise of the Scottish breeding population, the goldeneye is still best known as a winter visitor to Britain and Ireland. The peak winter population is 10,000–15,000 birds, widely distributed over inland waters (mainly large reservoirs) and also along the coast. The drakes are among the most handsome and distinctive of winter wildfowl, strikingly black and white, but the females and first winter birds are both less obvious and less distinctive, looking hunched and dark. Through the provision of large numbers of nest-boxes, goldeneyes have colonised Scotland in the last 20 or so years; in 1986 there were 44 successful nests, with 381 ducklings seen. Planned and supervised by the RSPB, this highly successful conservation operation also owes much to co-operative landowners. Look for a small, mainly grey duck, with or without a white collar below the brown head, showing a white flash on the side. Goldeneyes dive continually and are usually nervous and easily put up: watch for the white wing patches and listen for the distinctive wing noise.

great bird reserves

In addition to many nature reserves, there are 130 specialist bird reserves managed by the Royal Society for the Protection of Birds (RSPB), which are open to the public. These range from the reed-fringed meres of Leighton Moss on the Morecambe Bay coast of Lancashire, a haunt of the rare booming bittern, to the Abernethy Forest Reserve in Strathspey, where the fish-eating osprey successfully returned in 1959.

Islands provide some of the finest bird reserves, where huge populations of screaming sea birds roost and nest. Examples of these include the National Trust Island of Lundy off the north coast of Devon, where there are populations of puffins, guillemots, razorbills and kittiwakes; Skomer Island off the rugged coast of Pembrokeshire, which is known for its guillemots, kittiwakes, puffins and burrow nesting Manx shearwaters; and the Farne Islands off the Northumberland coast, which in addition to a fascinating bird life, have a large colony of grey seals.

Other coastal sites include perhaps the most famous is Minsmere in Suffolk, where you can find avocets, the elegant black-and-white wader which became the emblem of the RSPB after its successful return here, and the dizzy cliffs of Flamborough Head and Bempton on the Yorkshire's North Sea coast, where thousands of sea birds cling to the 400-feet (120m) cliffs and give out an unforgettable cacophony of sound.

Many of the larger reserves have information centres and hides where you can watch the wildlife in comfort, and at some you can hire binoculars for the day. Examples of these are at Loch Garten, where you can watch the Ospreys from a visitor centre, and Leighton Moss, where one of the hides even has easy chairs.

BELOW LEFT: THE STEEP VEGETATION COVERED CLIFFS OF LUNDY ISLAND. BELOW: THE SCRAPE AT MINSMERE IS AN AREA OF SHALLOW WATER, ISLANDS AND REED BEDS AND HOST TO THOUSANDS OF BIRDS.

Pintail
ANAS ACUTA

LENGTH: 51–66CM WEIGHT: 750–1,000G WHERE TO LOOK:
OPEN AREAS WITH SHALLOW WATER NEST: RARE, USUALLY IN
OPEN EGGS: 7–9, YELLOWISH FOOD: VARIETY OF PLANT AND
ANIMAL MATTER VOICE: QUIET WHISTLE FROM MALE, SHORT
QUACKS FROM FEMALE; SILENT IN FLIGHT

Adult male

Adult female

Subtlety of colour and an elegant form make the pintail one of the most attractive ducks. The gleaming, distinctive coloured, slightly off-white breast of the male is visible from a considerable distance when no other details may be obvious. In flight the shape is unmistakable; even the female shows a long pointed tail and long slender neck.

Fewer than 50 pairs breed in Britain, almost all confined to Kent and the fenlands of East Anglia, but, in winter, birds from Iceland, Scandinavia and Russia concentrate on some of the west coast estuaries, with counts of over 15,000 birds on the Mersey. Only here and on the Dee Estuary do counts regularly exceed 5,000. On these coastal sites they feed on tiny snail called *Hydrobia*, but increasingly the species has developed night flighting away from the more traditional coastal sites to exploit the stubble and potato fields of inland farms. They are much quieter birds than mallards and most people see them far less often, and usually in very small groups.

▨ *Female looks pale, greyish-brown with blue bill and pointed tail.*
▨ *The white stripe and breast of the male is distinctive.*
▨ *In flight, pintails look long and thin with pointed tail; the underside is pale and the upper wing dark with a pale line on the trailing edge.*

Shoveler
ANAS CLYPEATA

Swimming slowly forward, bodies almost awash, shovelers filter water through their big, broad bills, pushing it out through the sides and trapping food particles with the special serrations that line the edges. Feeding in this manner will often involve small groups, which appear to work in unison. To be successful this technique requires a rich food source – seeds and invertebrates – suspended in shallow water.

The male shoveler is distinctive both in shape and colour, while the brown-plumaged female shows the similar distinctive short neck and large bill. Both sexes show striking blue areas on the leading edge of the wing, although these are duller in the female. Especially as they take off, the wings of shovelers make a loud, deep 'woofing' noise, quite unlike mallards.

Something like 1,500 pairs may breed in Britain. They are mainly confined to the southeast, with the largest concentrations on the Ouse Washes. In the winter, populations from eastern Europe move westward and numbers as great as 10,000 reach Britain.

LENGTH: 44–52CM WEIGHT:
400–850GM WHERE TO
LOOK: SHALLOW WATER.
NEST: ON GROUND EGGS:
9–11, BUFF VOICE: QUIET *TUC*
BY MALE, FEMALE QUACKS

Adult female

Adult male

Eclipse male

▨ *In all plumages the body shape and size of bill is distinctive. Eclipse male differs from female in the redness of plumage.*
▨ *In flight the distinctive front-heavy look, with broad bill and tail-less shape, is apparent. The blue-grey forewing is also very obvious.*

Pochard
AYTHYA FERINA

Although one of the most familiar diving ducks, the pochard is actually a very scarce breeding bird in Britain. There are no more than 200–400 pairs, mainly in southeast England, with important concentrations in the North Kent Marshes and the Norfolk Broads. Most of the birds, which come to Britain and Ireland, are winter visitors from central Europe and as far away as the USSR. The wintering population may be as high as 80,000. About 85 per cent of their food is plant material, including many seeds, which is obtained by diving in shallow fresh water, hence the birds' preference for shallow and well-vegetated lakes and gravel pits. Reservoirs and other deep-water sites are more often used for roosting and nesting.

The males are usually unmistakable, but females sometimes cause confusion – especially when asleep. They have quite pale, greyish-brown bodies with pale marks at the eye and the base of the bill. The bill, when visible (pochards sleep for much of the day), has a broad pale band around the middle and a black tip.

LENGTH: 42–49CM WEIGHT: 800–1,200G
WHERE TO LOOK: WELL VEGETATED LAKES AND
POOLS IN SUMMER AND OPEN FRESH WATER IN
WINTER NEST: ON GROUND NEAR WATER
EGGS: 8–10, GREENISH FOOD: WATER PLANTS,
SEEDS AND INVERTEBRATES VOICE: HARSH
GROWLING NOTES

Adult female

Adult male

■ *Males have a reddish-chestnut head, black breast and vermiculated grey back.*
■ *In flight, the female looks very plain, but note the pale belly. Neither sex shows prominent wing markings.*

Ruddy Duck
OXYURA JAMAICENSIS

LENGTH: 35–43CM WEIGHT: 500–700G WHERE
TO LOOK: LAKES, PONDS, RESERVOIRS, GRAVEL
PITS NEST: WELL HIDDEN, NEAR WATER EGGS:
6–10, WHITISH FOOD: MAINLY INSECT LARVAE,
SEEDS. DIVES VOICE: LARGELY SILENT

Female

Summer male

Winter male

In the late 1950s, about 20 unpinioned young ruddy ducks escaped from the Wildfowl Trust reserve at Slimbridge. From their original strongholds on reservoirs in Somerset and Staffordshire, these North American 'stifftails' spread quite rapidly, having nested in the wild for the first time in 1960. There are now probably some 6,000 birds, mainly in the southern half of England, but with records from Wales (including Anglesey) and Northern Ireland. The species has also bred in one area in Scotland. Males in breeding dress are unmistakable, but winter males, females and immature birds need to be compared with various other ducks and also grebes which have dark crowns and white or pale cheeks. Look for the long tail, often held in a stiff cocked position, and the rather long, broad bill. When breeding, ruddy ducks prefer shallow waters with good surrounding vegetation, but in winter they use more open water and may occur in large flocks. Already several sites have become 'traditional' places and attract as many as 400 birds each year.

■ *The female has a brown cap with pale cheeks crossed by a dark stripe.*
■ *In summer the male is bright chestnut with white cheeks contrasting with black cap. Note the blue bill and stiffly cocked dark tail.*
■ *In winter, the male closely resembles the female, but still has clear white cheeks and a black cap. The large, broad bill becomes greyish. Note typical shape and posture (tail not always cocked). See Smew.*

Scaup
AYTHYA MARILA

Scaup are principally sea-ducks in winter, many of them coming to Britain's shores from Iceland. At present, probably only 5,000–10,000 winter here. Although widely scattered around the coast, they are most numerous in the Forth, the Dornoch Firth, Islay, the Solway, on the Cheshire Dee and at Carlingford Lough, Northern Ireland. Gone are the days when up to 30,000 could be seen in the vast flock which wintered off Leith in the Forth, attracted by waste grain from breweries and distilleries and by the small worms which lived on the raw sewage. Fewer grain discharges and better sewage treatment led to its abrupt disappearance. Males are easily distinguished from similar ducks. Females are not difficult, but beware of female tufted ducks with white face-marks; scaup are slightly larger and broader-looking, as well as much less dark in appearance. Their bills are longer and broader and, except on young birds, the white is always more extensive. Tufted ducks have broad black tips to their bills; scaup have only a narrow black mark, useful on dull-faced juveniles.

Male in eclipse

LENGTH: 42–51CM **WEIGHT**: 900–1,200G
WHERE TO LOOK: SHALLOW COASTAL WATERS, BAYS AND ESTUARIES. DOES NOT BREED IN UK **FOOD:** MAINLY MOLLUSCS, ALSO WASTE GRAIN **VOICE:** HARSH *KARR-KARR* WHILE FLYING

Adult female

Adult male

■ *The female scaup looks larger, broader and paler than the female tufted duck. It has a white patch on the face.*

■ *The male looks black fore and aft, and pale in the middle with white flanks and grey back: unlike tufted duck of either sex or any age.*

Tufted Duck
AYTHYA FULIGULA

LENGTH: 40–47CM **WEIGHT**: 600–1,000G
WHERE TO LOOK: AREAS OF OPEN WATER, INCLUDING RIVERS **NEST:** WELL HIDDEN, NEAR WATER **EGGS:** 8–11, GREENISH-GREY **FOOD:** SOME AQUATIC PLANT MATERIAL, BUT MAINLY MOLLUSCS, INSECTS ETC **VOICE:** VARIOUS HARSH GROWLING NOTES

After the ubiquitous mallard, the tufted duck is the most widespread and best-known duck, often occurring on park lakes and on rivers in towns and cities, where it soon becomes very tame. It is a remarkably successful species that has been quick to make use of the many new artificial water areas created by man, including gravel pits and reservoirs. In a mere 25 years the breeding population in mainland Britain has trebled to its present level of about 8,000 pairs; there are at least 2,000 more in Ireland. Similarly, the winter population has increased over the same period (by about 50 per cent) with a mid-winter peak of over 60,000 birds. Scottish birds are known to go to Ireland in winter, but those in Ireland and the rest of Britain apparently do not move far. Large numbers reach the British Isles from Iceland, northern Scandinavia and Russia, arriving from late September onwards to stay until early spring. Being so common and often so tame, tufted ducks can be watched and 'learned' thoroughly in all their plumages, which makes it that much easier for the birdwatcher when a scaup appears among them! They are livelier than nearby pochards during the day, as pochards are more nocturnal feeders. Tufted ducks are sociable, often displaying together in groups.

Adult female

Adult male

■ *Female tufted duck is a small, dark bird with pale flanks and always a suggestion of a crest. Some females show white on the face, but never as much as female scaup. A white undertail is not uncommon.*

■ *Dives normally last 15–20 seconds, generally to a depth of about 2.5m). Up to 100 dives per hour are common, with pauses of about 10 seconds between dives.*

Eider
SOMATERIA MOLLISSIMA

Adult female

Mature plumage

Piebald plumage

Adult male

Juvenile plumage

Even at very long range, an adult drake eider, uniquely white on top and black underneath, is easy to identify. Young males, passing through a variety of piebald plumages as they grow older, can be trickier, but at least the bill shape and their size and bulk are distinctive. Eiders are essentially birds of the northern and northwestern seaboards. They are usually close inshore, riding the swell in a sandy bay or out beyond the breaking waves on a rocky beach, often string out in long lines. The crèches of youngsters with their attendant 'aunties' may be seen running over mud in some northern estuaries, where they can be in danger of being snatched up by gulls.

Courtship begins in late winter, as with many wildfowl. The cooing and crooning calls of the beautiful drakes are familiar sounds along favoured coasts well into spring. Female eiders nest singly or in loose colonies, sometimes in quite open spots but often in a crevice between big rocks, occasionally in gull and tern colonies. Eiders are increasing, and perhaps as many as 30,000 pairs breed in Britain and Ireland, while the winter total is estimated at 72,000 birds. Eiders eat slow-moving, bottom-living creatures, mainly molluscs, which they take in dives from the surface. They use their feet to swim underwater, but half-open their wings as they roll forward to dive.

LENGTH: 50–71CM **WEIGHT:** 1,500–2,500G **WHERE TO LOOK:** COASTAL WATER, USUALLY CLOSE TO SHORE. **NEST:** ON GROUND, OFTEN EXPOSED. **EGGS:** 4–6, GREENISH-GREY. **FOOD:** DIVES (OR FEEDS FROM SURFACE) MAINLY FOR MOLLUSCS. **VOICE:** EXCEPT WHEN COURTING, RATHER SILENT.

▓ *The head profile and bill shape are important features in eider identification. Note the forehead-bill angle, and feathers reaching down the bill in a point.*
▓ *The female is best told by its rather plain, barred appearance, a pale line over the eye at close range, its size and distinctive bill.*

Velvet Scoter
MELANITTA FUSCA

The velvet scoter is both bigger and bulkier than the common scoter, with which it mixes, and is closer to an eider in size. Females and immature birds can be difficult to identify, especially at any distance, but at some stage the characteristic white wing patches will be seen. Eiders have different bill shapes and those which are as dark as velvet scoters will usually show much more white. The female's pale head markings are actually visible even at quite long range in reasonable light.

While individuals turn up quite regularly inland, most velvet scoters are seen on the sea, sometimes very close inshore, and are quite tame. They have been suspected of breeding in Britain in the past, but are essentially winter visitors from Scandinavia and western Siberia. Numbers are very variable from year to year: as many as 10,000 have been recorded, but the more normal total is probably 2,500–5,000. Recent work on winter sea duck populations has shown that the Moray Firth is as important for velvet scoters as it is for common scoters and long-tailed ducks. It is always a pleasure to watch a selection of these attractive marine species close to the shore.

LENGTH: 51–58CM **WEIGHT:** 1,200–1,800G **WHERE TO LOOK:** COASTAL WATERS, MAINLY NORTHEAST AND EAST. SOMETIMES OCCURS ON FRESH WATER INLAND. DOES NOT BREED IN BRITAIN. **FOOD:** DIVES; IN WINTER FEEDS MAINLY ON MOLLUSCS. **VOICE:** AWAY FROM BREEDING AREAS LARGELY SILENT.

Adult female

Adult male

Long-tailed Duck
CLANGULA HYEMALIS

Even where it is common and fairly easy to see, the long-tailed duck remains a blue riband species for the birdwatcher. Fortunately, despite plumage variations, it is not a difficult bird to identify. It occurs off many coasts in small numbers, wherever there are shallow waters offshore, but it is commonest from Northumberland northwards to Shetland, and in the Outer Hebrides. It can be seen close inshore in some areas, but often remains well out to sea, flying around a great deal. It is perfectly at home in the roughest conditions. It was only comparatively recently that realistic estimates of wintering numbers became available, following work on sea ducks in the Moray Firth area. This revealed that the Moray Firth regularly held 10,000–15,000 birds, which must be at least three-quarters of the total for Britain and Ireland. In the sandier inlets of the Firth, displaying groups in spring are at their liveliest and give the most delightful birdwatching.

LENGTH: 40–47CM WEIGHT: 600–800G WHERE TO LOOK: SEA COASTS. DOES NOT BREED IN BRITAIN FOOD: DIVES, MAINLY FOR ANIMALS, ESPECIALLY CRUSTACEANS AND MOLLUSCS VOICE: UNLIKE MANY SEA DUCKS, VERY VOCAL – DRAKES HAVE MUSICAL CALLS

Summer male

Winter male

■ *The winter male is a spectacular white bird with dark cheekmarks, and black on back, wings, breast and tail, which is very long. The small bill distinctly two-coloured – dark with pinkish band.*

Common Scoter
MELANITTA NIGRA

LENGTH: 44–54CM WEIGHT: 700–1,300G WHERE TO LOOK: COASTAL WATERS NEST: WELL HIDDEN NEAR WATER EGGS: 6–8, CREAM TO BUFF. RARE BREEDER FOOD: DIVES FOR MOLLUSCS

Adult female

Adult male

Common scoters breed on a few fresh-water lakes in Scotland and Ireland. In some areas, even in central England, they appear regularly on large reservoirs in late summer. Mainly, though, they are known as sea ducks, winter visitors from Scandinavia and Russia. There are big concentrations in the Moray Firth and Carmarthen Bay. It is often worth looking through flocks in the hope of discovering a few grebes, velvet scoters or long-tailed ducks. Scoters always give the impression of extraordinary buoyancy, and when the males raise their pointed tails and very slender necks, they belie their heavy build. On rare calm days the sounds of courting birds carry far across the water, a chorus of rippling, piping calls that spread infectiously through the flock.

Common scoters form close-packed, often very large, rafts on the sea, diving under frequently. They fly in long lines or dense packs.

■ *The female has obvious pale greyish cheeks but is otherwise rather uniform. No other duck – or grebe – showing pale cheeks is as dark.*
■ *The male is the only totally black duck. Its black and yellow bill can often be seen at very long range.*

Red-breasted Merganser
MERGUS SERRATOR

Although they now breed in northwestern England and in parts of Wales, mergansers are most commonly associated with Scotland and Ireland. While many nest well inland on lochs and rivers, the majority breed along the coast, especially in inlets and sea lochs with an abundance of small islands. Some remain on fresh water in winter, but most move to coastal waters, occurring right around the eastern and southern coasts of England as well as their western and northern haunts. The total winter population is perhaps as high as 11,000 birds.

Seen well, males are unlikely to be confused with other sawbills, but 'redheads' (females and immature birds) can be tricky; they are always thin-billed, darker and generally lacking the clear-cut markings of the latter. The facial expression is different, with almost a 'smile' compared with the stern goosander.

LENGTH: 52–58CM WEIGHT: 900–1,200G WHERE TO LOOK: INLAND LOCHS, RIVERS ALSO COASTAL WATERS NEST: ON GROUND, WELL HIDDEN EGGS: 8–10, BUFF TO OLIVE FOOD: AS OTHER SAWBILLS, FISH CAUGHT BY DIVING AND PURSUIT UNDER WATER VOICE: MOSTLY SILENT

Adult female

Adult male

■ *Female is smaller, darker and more obviously crested than goosander. Note lack of clear-cut division between head colour, throat and neck.*
■ *Male unmistakable – fine red bill, wispy crest, white neck-band, orange-brown breast.*
■ *Males have spectacular displays, often performed in late winter.*
■ *A rakish flight outline, with white inner wing on the drake and a patch on the female.*

Goosander
MERGUS MERGANSER

LENGTH: 58–66CM WEIGHT: 1,100–1,700G WHERE TO LOOK: FRESHWATER LAKES AND RESERVOIRS, LOCALLY ON SHELTERED COASTS NEST: USUALLY HOLE IN TREE, ALSO IN GROUND OR NEST-BOX EGGS: 8–11, WHITISH FOOD: FISH VOICE: SILENT, EXCEPT DURING DISPLAY

Adult female

Adult male

The goosander is the largest of the three sawbills found in Britain and Ireland; there is little risk of confusion with smew, the smallest species, but 'redhead' (female and immature) goosanders and red-breasted mergansers require care. With practice, they are not actually too difficult to identify and the goosander's clear preference for inland fresh water in winter is a useful extra clue. It haunts fish-rich lochs, lakes and rivers in the breeding season and is very much a bird of large areas of open water, including reservoirs, in winter. Only locally (such as in the Beauly Firth, where there may be as many as 1,500 birds) does it winter regularly on sheltered coasts. Not long ago, the goosander bred only in Scotland, but it is now established in parts of northern England and has also colonised Wales and Ireland in very small numbers. The population appears to be fairly sedentary and, except when hard weather brings influxes from Europe, is not added to by migrants. About 8,000 spend the winter here. They are best sought on traditional sites, albeit often rather modern reservoirs, and are relatively rare away from these regular wintering places.

■ *The male – black, white and pink – is unmistakable.*
■ *The female goosander is rather larger than the female merganser and much more uniformly grey, with clearly demarcated red-brown head and neck, well-defined white chain and throat and less wispy crest. The immature is similar.*
■ *Large, long and rakish in flight, the drake is very white with a dark head. The 'redhead' is more uniform, but with darker head and white wing patches.*

Golden Eagle
AQUILA CHRYSAETOS

Soaring majestically on outstretched wings over a wild, mountainous landscape, the golden eagle is a genuinely thrilling sight. Like many of Britain's rarer raptors, its home is in Scotland, where it nests on crags and hunts over moorland and bare hillsides. Therein lies one of the main threats to its future, for such areas are becoming the target for forestry plantations. As blanket coniferous forests start to swathe the Scottish glens and moors the eagle's vital feeding grounds are lost.

Around its eyrie, a golden eagle hunts over a 'home-range', which can vary from 3,000–7,000 hectares. Much of its food is carrion, particularly in winter when dead sheep can form nearly half its diet. Otherwise it feeds on medium-sized mammals and birds, notably mountain hares and red grouse.

The eagle has declined in many countries and Scotland is no exception. During the last century it was intensely persecuted; during World War II numbers rose, only to be reduced again by killing on grouse moors. Then followed reduced breeding success, through eating sheep carrion contaminated by dieldrin sheep dip.

Today the illegal use of poisonous baits is almost certainly having its effect on the eagle population, and nests are still robbed by egg collectors. Scotland has 420 pairs of golden eagles, one of the highest numbers in Europe. This gives Britain an international responsibility to ensure than poisoning, egg collecting and, particularly, blanket afforestation are kept in check.

Seen in flight, an adult golden eagle appears rather uniform in colour. Juvenile birds, on the other hand, show a lot of white on the wings and base of the tail, leading to possible confusion with the white-tailed eagle. The latter's broad-winged silhouette, however, is distinctly different.

White-tailed Eagle
HALIAEETUS ALBICILLA

White-tailed eagles have been successfully reintroduced to Scotland after an absence of more than 50 years. They are found almost exclusively in coastal areas, their broad wings giving them a characteristic 'barn-door' appearance in flight, unlike that of the golden eagle.

Adult brown with white tail, variable whitish feathers on head and upper breast, yellow bill. Juveniles harder to identify, lacking obvious tail of adult.

Juvenile plumage

Adult plumage

Plumage development

LENGTH: 75–85CM **WINGSPAN:** 200–220CM **WHERE TO LOOK:** WILD MOUNTAINOUS COUNTRY IN SCOTLAND; WITH LUCK IN THE LAKE DISTRICT **NEST:** REMOTE CRAGS, OCCASIONALLY SCOTS PINE. EYRIE WITH EXTENSIVE VIEWS; PAIR OFTEN HAS 2–4 ALTERNATE NEST SITES. BULKY NEST OF BRANCHES LINED WITH GRASSES **EGGS:** 1–3 (USUALLY 2), WHITISH OR BLOTCHED RED-BROWN **FOOD:** HARES, RABBITS AND GROUSE, ALSO CARRION; HUNTS OVER VAST AREA ('HOME RANGE') **VOICE:** THIN YELP AT NEST AND WHISTLING *TWEEOO* ALARM

■ *Britain's largest bird of prey, with a 2-metre wingspan.*
■ *When seen close to, the massive bill, accentuated by the flat crown, is impressive. The crown and rather shaggy hind neck are washed golden-yellow.*
■ *Golden eagles and buzzards both soar on raised wings, so caution is needed at a distance. The eagle is much larger with a more protruding head; longer wings are often 'pinched-in' at the body.*

Buzzard
BUTEO BUTEO

LENGTH: 50–55CM **WINGSPAN:** 115–130CM **WHERE TO LOOK:** HILLY COUNTRY AND WOODEN FARMLAND **NEST:** TREES AND CRAGS, BULKY **EGGS:** 2–3, WHITE OR BLUISH, WITH REDDISH-BROWN BLOTCHES **FOOD:** RABBITS, EARTHWORMS, CARRION **VOICE:** MEWING *PEEIOO*

The buzzard is the commonest large bird of prey to be seen in western Britain, the Lake District and Scotland. The fate of the buzzard in Britain has been dictated by two main factors: gamekeepers and rabbits. At the turn of the century it was a relatively rare bird, but with a decline in persecution and in the collection of specimens and eggs, and with rabbits still common and widespread, an increase took place up to the 1950s. An interesting aspect of this was the way buzzards spread eastwards during the two world wars – when keepering was reduced or non-existent in many areas. Between 1952 and 1955 myxomatosis struck Britain's rabbits, resulting in their near elimination. This in turn had a drastic effect on buzzards, which depend largely on rabbits during the breeding season. The buzzard population may have been reduced in half, but today there are signs that it is spreading its range once again. However, it is particularly vulnerable to poisoned baits – there are more buzzards killed in this way than any other raptor in Britain.

The buzzard is compact, well proportioned, with broad head and thickset neck.

The adult has a dark band on the rear of the wing and tail, this is absent in the juvenile. The tail may have a faint orange hue.

From below buzzards can be highly variable – from largely dark to largely white – though in Britain most are brownish with pale, lightly barred flight feathers.

In flight, it circles effortlessly over hillsides, rising in the updraught or in a hot air thermal. Wings are raised when soaring but flat in glides – soars with tail fanned.

Honey Buzzard
PERNIS APIVORUS

The honey buzzard is one of the commonest large raptors breeding in Europe, so why is it so rare in Britain? Part of the answer must lie in its diet of bee, wasp and insect larvae – the numbers of which can be seriously affected by the wet summers of Britain's Atlantic climate. Another factor is its type of migration. Honey buzzards spend the winter in Africa and do not like making the long sea crossing, so they migrate where the sea is at its narrowest – places in Europe like the Bosporus and Gibraltar. The English Channel, therefore, could act as a serious barrier to those that might otherwise reach our shores.

The few that nest in Britain do so from Hampshire to Scotland, but the population is probably less than 30 pairs. They can occasionally be seen on migration in late spring and autumn when care should be taken not to confuse them with the commoner buzzard: note the honey buzzard's small protruding head and neck, long tail, flat wings when soaring and characteristic tail and wing pattern.

LENGTH: 50–60CM **WINGSPAN:** 135–150CM **WHERE TO LOOK:** UNCOMMON MIGRANT IN SOUTH AND EAST. RARE BREEDER IN MIXED OPEN MATURE WOODLAND **NEST:** IN LARGE TREE, OFTEN BUILT ON AN EXISTING NEST **EGGS:** 2, WHITISH WITH RED OR CHOCOLATE MARKINGS **FOOD:** BEE AND WASP GRUBS, OTHER LARGE INSECTS, SMALL MAMMALS

Varies in pattern below from whitish through to chocolate brown. Typically barred with dark patches on forewing and characteristic lines on flight feathers. Bars on tail also a clue to identification. Note well-protruding cuckoo-like head, long tail and narrower wings.

Rough-legged Buzzard
BUTEO LAGOPUS

The rough-legged buzzard is an uncommon winter visitor. Its long wings, white tail-base and habit of frequently hovering are good identification clues.

Marsh Harrier
CIRCUS AERUGINOSUS

Adult male

Adult female

Like many raptors, the marsh harrier suffered from persecution in the last century and actually became extinct as a breeding bird. Then, just before World War I, a pair nested and heralded the recolonisation of Britain. At first this was slow, but with increased protection in the 1950s numbers grew to 15 pairs in 1958. This success was short-lived, however, because they succumbed to pesticides, and the population crashed to just one pair in 1971.

Subsequently, with voluntary bans imposed on the use of the more persistent kinds of pesticides the situation greatly improved, and a quite dramatic recovery took place, with over 30 pairs raising nearly 100 young each year in the late 1980s. Furthermore, birds are spreading from their traditional nest sites in East Anglia, though the best chance of seeing this grand bird of the reed beds is still at RSPB reserves such as Minsmere in Suffolk and Titchwell in Norfolk.

■ *The dark brown female usually has a creamy crown, throat and shoulders. The brown tail is unbarred.*

■ *Note the tricoloured wings of the male (pictured); below it has a russet-streaked body, whitish underwings with black tips.*

■ *Flight is leisurely, with glides on raised wings.*

LENGTH: 55CM **WINGSPAN:** 115–130CM **WHERE TO LOOK:** REED BEDS, THOUGH OFTEN HUNTS OVER NEARBY FIELDS. **NEST:** BULKY, AMONG REEDS AND VEGETATION IN WATER **EGGS:** 4–5, BLUISH-WHITE, OFTEN STAINED **FOOD:** MAINLY FROGS, BIRDS AND SMALL MAMMALS **VOICE:** A PLAINTIVE SHRILL *KWEEOO*

Red Kite
MILVUS MILVUS

Colouration above

Colouration below

LENGTH: 60–65CM **WINGSPAN:** 175–195CM **WHERE TO LOOK:** MATURE OAK WOODS IN STEEP VALLEYS AND NEARBY HILL COUNTRY IN CENTRAL WALES. **NEST:** OF STICKS AND MUD IN TALL TREES. **EGGS:** 3–4, WHITISH, VARIABLY MARKED. **FOOD:** SMALL MAMMALS, BIRDS, WORMS, CARRION **VOICE:** SHRILL, QUAVERING *WEEO-WEOO-WEOO*

Strict security surrounds Britain's red-kite breeding area in central Wales. Once a common scavenger (even in towns), its population gradually dwindled as hygiene improved and fewer animals died to provide it with carrion. Persecution also took its toll. The Welsh population now numbers nearly 90 pairs, and under careful protection has slowly increased from just 12 birds at the turn of the century.

What problems does it face now? Several succumb each year to the illegal activities of egg collectors, and for this reason nests are guarded. Poison continues to produce victims: poison baits set for crows and foxes (an illegal act in itself) are indiscriminate and can easily kill kites.

On one occasion two were found dead on a poisoned carcass. Sadly, about two-thirds of all known kite deaths that have been investigated have been directly attributable to human action.

A natural hazard is bad weather in May, which can seriously affect chick survival. The hanging oak woods in which it nests will remain vital.

■ *Distinctive colouration below with rusty body and underwing coverts; whitish head, reddish tail, noticeable white wing-patches and black wing tips.*

■ *In good light, the rusty-red tail is very obvious. Note the distinctive buff band on the upperwing.*

■ *It soars on slightly bowed wings held forward. Flight is graceful, with the forked tail constantly manoeuvred.*

Hen Harrier
CIRCUS CYANEUS

LENGTH: 45–50CM **WINGSPAN:** 100–120CM
WHERE TO LOOK: MOORLAND AND BRACKEN-
COVERED HILLS, NEWLY AFFORESTED AREAS,
BUT MARSHES AND FARMLAND IN WINTER
NEST: ON GROUND IN HEATHER, LINED WITH
RUSHES AND GRASSES **EGGS:** 4-5, BLUISH-
WHITE, OCCASIONALLY WITH REDDISH
MARKS **FOOD:** SMALL BIRDS AND MAMMALS
VOICE: RAPID, CHATTERING *KE-KE-KE-KE* IN
NESTING AREA

Adult male

Harriers fly low and more quickly than often imagined over open ground, wings often held up in a slight 'V'. Female and young hen and Montagu's harriers are very similar and, in spring and autumn when they are most likely to overlap, many are simply noted as unidentified 'ring-tails'. The hen harrier is the larger of the two, broader in the wing (especially near the tip which is particularly long and slender in Montagu's) and the head pattern is a little different with a less bold cheek patch on the hen harrier. Juveniles look like females except that young Montagu's have unmarked rufous underparts – a useful point.

Many hen harriers breed on heather moorland and come into conflict with shooting interests because grouse can form an important part of their diet. Whether they cause any reduction in the numbers of grouse available for shooting is a matter of debate, though certainly where grouse numbers are healthy, scientists have shown hen harriers have little or no effect on the population.

Most birdwatchers see hen harriers as winter visitors, which particularly favour the coastal areas of south and east England.

■ *The male is pale grey, white and black below. Note the grey hood and dark trailing edge to the wings.*
■ *Female very similar to female Montagu's, but larger with different head pattern: compare the two. Juveniles are similar to females.*
■ *Flight includes dramatic switchback displays over the breeding area.*

Montagu's Harrier
CIRCUS PYGARGUS

Wintering in Africa, Montagu's harriers arrive on their breeding grounds in April and May. They are not uncommon on the continent, with perhaps 1,000 pairs in France and 6,000 in Spain, but in Britain they are rare birds. The highest numbers this century were in the 1950s, when some 40 pairs bred, mainly in Devon and Cornwall. A period of decline followed with a 'low' in 1975 when none bred. There has been an improvement since and now several pairs regularly nest in southern England. But there has been a change of habitat. Traditionally they nested on heaths, reed bed fringes and new conifer plantations, but now all the nests are in corn or rape fields. Therein lies a problem. When the fields are to be cut, the young are still in the nest and earlier spraying operations can flatten them. Thus, nests have to be located and protected from certain farming activities and, if necessary, an area around them left uncut until the young fly. This is a case where farmers and conservationists have worked closely together.

LENGTH: 40–45CM **WINGSPAN:** 105–120CM
WHERE TO LOOK: CEREAL AND RAPE FIELDS IN
SOUTHERN ENGLAND, PREVIOUSLY IN REED
BEDS, MOORLAND AND YOUNG FORESTRY. A
VERY RARE SUMMER VISITOR **NEST:** IN CROPS,
LINED WITH GRASSES ETC **EGGS:** 4–5, PALE
BLUISH-WHITE WITH OBSCURE RUSTY
MARKINGS **FOOD:** SMALL MAMMALS AND
BIRDS **VOICE:** HIGH-PITCHED *YIK-YIK-YIK* OVER
BREEDING AREA

Adult female

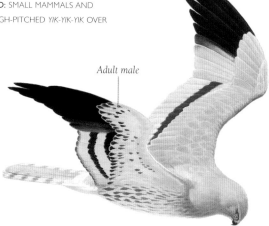

Adult male

■ *The female Montagu's and hen harrier are similar, with a white band at the base of the tail. A 'ring-tail' from November to late March is seen only on the hen; in summer both species display this feature – take care!*
■ *The main features to look for on the male are dirty-grey plumage, black wing tips and bars on the underwing.*

Osprey
PANDION HALIAETUS

LENGTH: 55–60CM **WINGSPAN:** 145–170CM **WHERE TO LOOK:** BY OPEN WATER STOCKED WITH FISH. SUMMER VISITOR TO SCOTLAND AND UNCOMMON PASSAGE MIGRANT IN SPRING AND AUTUMN. WINTERS IN AFRICA **NEST:** NEAR WATER, USUALLY IN CONIFER-TOP, BUT ALSO ISLAND RUINS. SAME EYRIE OF STICKS (LINED WITH GRASSES AND FINER MATERIAL) USED ANNUALLY AND ADDED TO UNTIL LARGE SIZE; BUT REMAINS INCONSPICUOUS IN TREE TOP **EGGS:** 2–3, WHITE, BOLDLY BLOTCHED DEEP CHOCOLATE OR REDDISH-BROWN **VOICE:** REPEATED, SHORT, SHRILL, WHISTLE *TCHIP TCHIP TCHIP*

The osprey was formerly a common breeding summer visitor to Scotland, but persecution by egg collectors and trophy hunters at the turn of the century brought it to extinction in Britain. No more that spectacular dive into a loch to emerge holding a pike or trout torpedo fashion to carry off to its eyrie high in a pine. No more, that is, until 1955 when a pair returned to nest at Loch Garten. Immediately protected by the RSPB, a success story followed, with these birds or their future offspring showing off their families to over a million visitors, while at the same time increasing to over 40 pairs. Since their return nearly 600 young have been raised.

Ospreys migrate to West Africa, where they spend the winter in tropical climes; summer in the pines among lochs, winter in the palms along rivers with hippos, or by golden Atlantic beaches.

What of the future? They continue to increase in Scotland, and with the help of artificial nesting platforms might well be encouraged to start breeding in England. However, they will always face danger on migration.

■ *Long-winged with a shortish tail. In most positions the wings are decidedly angled which, with colouration, gives the appearance of a large gull.*

■ *It has a small head and relatively small bill, with a long hook for dealing with bony fish. The white head, with brown eye stripe, contrasts with the all-brown upperparts.*

■ *Unmistakable from below, the white body and wing linings contrast with the greyish flight feathers and black wrist patches. Note the breastband.*

■ *When hunting, circles or hovers over water then dives feet first when fish is sighted.*

■ *Fish are held headfirst in torpedo-like manner. It is possible that prey up to 3kg in weight might be carried by adult. Occasionally two fish are caught in one dive.*

■ *Adaptations for capturing fish include strong legs and feet, long claws, spiny scales on underside of toes and a reversible outer toe.*

Sparrowhawk
ACCIPITER NISUS

LENGTH: 30–40CM **WINGSPAN:** 60–80CM **WHERE TO LOOK:** WIDESPREAD RESIDENT, BUT LESS COMMON IN SOUTHEAST ENGLAND; CONIFEROUS AND MIXED WOODLAND, FARMLAND WITH HEDGEROWS; LOOK FOR DISPLAYING BIRDS IN SPRING, OR SOARING BIRDS AT ANY TIME **NEST:** BUILT OF STICKS, SOMETIMES USES FOUNDATION OF OLD NEST OF ANOTHER SPECIES, HIGH IN CONIFER NEAR TRUNK **EGGS:** NORMALLY 4–5, WHITISH, MANY WITHOUT MARKINGS **FOOD:** SMALL BIRDS CAUGHT ON THE WING IN SWIFT DASHES **VOICE:** HARSH *KEK-KEK-KEK-KEK*

The sparrowhawk is Britain's second commonest bird of prey. It is fairly widespread, but commoner in the north and west. Its long legs and long central toe – for catching and holding prey – indicate the sparrowhawk is a bird eater, and birds form almost its entire diet. Prey is caught by surprise attack either from a concealed perch or flight close to a hedgerow or woodland edge. Very rarely will it 'stoop' on its prey. Sparrowhawks can carry prey as heavy as themselves.

Like most raptors, sparrowhawks were seriously affected by the introduction of DDT and other chemicals, such as dieldrin and aldrin, to control insects and other invertebrates that are harmful to agriculture. During the late 1950s and early 1960s a population decline started and sparrowhawk numbers were reduced by 50 per cent in western Britain. In the east, where agriculture was more intensive, the bird was practically wiped out. With the voluntary and legal bans on the use of pesticides the situation is now improving. Once again, sparrowhawks can be seen over the woods and fields of East Anglia, Kent and Sussex; indeed in some areas they may be as common as kestrels, though few would realise this because of the sparrowhawk's secretive behaviour. A woodland dweller, it spends most time perched in thick cover. It's wing and tail shape are adapted for flying between trunks and branches.

The female is much larger than the male and double its weight. She is duller and browner than the male with grey brown barring below and grey brown above, not so bluish as the adult male. Her eye is yellow, whereas that of the male is orange.

Goshawk
ACCIPITER GENTILIS

LENGTH: 50–60CM **WINGSPAN:** 95–125CM **WHERE TO LOOK:** EXTENSIVE PINE OR BEECH WOODLAND. SHY AND QUITE RARE **NEST:** SUBSTANTIAL, OF STICKS IN TREE **EGGS:** 3–4, BLUISH-WHITE **FOOD:** SQUIRRELS, PIGEONS, JAYS ETC **VOICE:** ONLY AT NEST, RAPID HOARSE *GEK-GEK-GEK-GEK*

For the birdwatcher, the goshawk presents a problem: it is easy to confuse the smaller male with a female sparrowhawk. Note carefully the goshawk's shorter tail with a rounded (not square) end, longer, broader wings with a more 'S'-shaped rear edge, bulkier size and slower wingbeats.

Goshawks probably became extinct in Britain in the early part of the century, but in the early 1960s they started to breed again. There was initially some debate as to their origin, but it is now generally accepted that the recolonisation was the result of falconers' birds escaping or being deliberately released. Now the population of this shy forest dweller could number over 200 pairs, yet such a figure will never appear in national reports, for most birdwatchers or recorders are reluctant to submit their observations. Understandably they are concerned that publication – however vague – may result in sites becoming known, which could lead to an increase in egg collecting or robbery of the young (for falconry), two activities that seriously affect the goshawk population in the best-known localities.

It has a protruding head, conspicuous stripe above the eye and noticeably banded tail.
The female is much larger than male, approaching the size of a buzzard. Upperparts are dark brown and underparts are whitish and barred.
The male is distinguishable from a female sparrowhawk by its bulkier size, relatively longer, more 'S'-shaped wings and shorter, rounded tail.
In flight, soars and glides on flat wings.

Kestrel
FALCO TINNUNCULUS

LENGTH: 33–36CM **WINGSPAN:** 70–80CM **WHERE TO LOOK:**
MANY PLACES EVEN IN CITY CENTRES; CAN BE MOST EASILY
OBSERVED OVER ROADSIDE VERGES. MOST WIDESPREAD BIRD OF
PREY IN BRITAIN **NEST:** HOLE IN TREE, CREVICE IN WALL OR CLIFF
FACE, LEDGES (EVEN ON BUILDINGS) AND OTHER STRUCTURES;
MAY USE OLD CROW'S NEST **EGGS:** 4–5, WHITE WITH RED-
BROWN MARKINGS, LAID IN MID-APRIL IN SCRAPE WITH NO
LINING **FOOD:** USUALLY FIELD VOLES, MICE, INSECTS, WORMS;
URBAN KESTRELS, ESPECIALLY, TAKE SMALL BIRDS. HUNTS BY
HOVERING OR PERCHING IN READINESS TO POUNCE ON PREY
VOICE: *KEE-KEE-KEE-KEE* GENERALLY AT NESTING AREA

Adult male

Adult female

Few people can fail to notice kestrels hovering over roadsides and, particularly, motorway verges. This, Britain's commonest and most familiar bird of prey, can be seen on most days by anyone with the opportunity to look for it. Kestrels require open areas to hunt over, particularly grassy meadows and banks; and safe nest sites, such as holes in trees and quarry ledges. They readily take to nest-boxes and are also venturing into towns where they nest on ledges on buildings. The RSPB knows that a number of kestrels are taken illegally each year as chicks that are then reared in captivity. The would-be falconers may attempt to fly the birds, but more often the birds are abandoned and this inevitably means that they will die.

Pesticides have less affected kestrels than other raptors, but nonetheless they became scarce in the intensively farmed arable land of eastern England during the late 1960s and early 1970s. Numbers are back to their former levels, and the population is estimated at about 70,000 pairs. Now that the pesticide problem seems to be under control, the future conservation of the kestrel lies with the maintenance of its food supply, notably voles and mice. Conversion of rough grazing land to cereals, and stubble burning, can seriously affect the abundance of these small mammals.

■ *The handsome male has chestnut back and wings spotted black, a blue-grey head and a faint black 'moustache'. Below it is deep or pale buff, spotted lightly with black. The blue-grey tail has a conspicuous black band.*
■ *The female is much duller than the male, being muted chestnut brown above, heavily barred blackish. The colour is relieved sometimes by a tinge of grey on head and tail.*
■ *Juveniles are similar to the female but never show grey in the tail.*
■ *A kestrel's pointed wings and hovering flight when hunting instantly distinguish it from the sparrowhawk, the second commonest raptor in Britain. Black flight feathers contrasting with chestnut upperparts are a good feature at a distance.*

Female

Merlin
FALCO COLUMBARIUS

The tiny merlin has a certain dash and energy about it which gives it a special appeal. It is Britain's smallest falcon and a bird of the upland heather-covered moors, and therein lies one of the main problems it faces. These areas are under threat from forestry planting or conversion to grass through sheep grazing or re-seeding. True heather moors are disappearing at an alarming rate and their future protection as a habitat for the merlin is closely connected with the continuation of grouse shooting. But grouse numbers are falling and this, coupled with the high cost of running moors, is encouraging some owners to move towards an income from trees and sheep – two factors definitely detrimental to merlins.

Merlins are not persecuted, and keepers enjoy having them on their moors as much as birdwatchers do. Problems through the use of pesticides are probably largely over and so habitat destruction is almost certainly the major cause of their decline.

◼ *The male is pale rusty below with dark streaks, underwing coverts are whitish-buff streaked reddish brown and the flight feathers are whitish with dark bars.*
◼ *Females are brown above and creamy-white below, heavily streaked reddish brown.*

Adult female

Adult male

LENGTH: 27–32CM WINGSPAN: 50–70CM WHERE TO LOOK: UPLANDS, ESPECIALLY MOORS AND FELLS IN SCOTLAND, NORTHERN ENGLAND AND WALES. QUITE RARE. IN WINTER, COASTAL MARSHES AND FARMLAND NEST: SCRAPE IN COVER OF HEATHER ON LOWER SLOPE OF MOOR. WILL USE OLD NEST OF CROW EGGS: 3–6, USUALLY 4, CREAM STIPPLED WITH RED-BROWN SPOTS FOOD: SMALL BIRDS, ESPECIALLY MEADOW PIPITS, CHAFFINCHES AND TITS, WHICH ARE CAUGHT IN FLIGHT VOICE: A RAPID, GRATING CHATTER, *QUIK-IK-IK-IK*, WHEN NEST SITE INTRUDED UPON

Hobby
FALCO SUBBUTEO

The graceful hobby is a trans-Saharan migrant that spends the winter in Africa and is present in Britain for about five months in the summer. Mostly confined to southern England, it is thus only likely to be confused with the kestrel as there is no other similarly shaped raptor present. It arrives in May, and the breeding season is late, with young in the nest from mid-July onwards, coinciding with the appearance on the wing of young swifts, swallows and martins, which are easily caught by the parent hobbies. Look for hobbies over heathland, gravel pits and farmland with conifer clumps, and at swallow and martin roosts in early autumn. In addition, dragonflies and other insects are taken in flight – dextrously grasped in an outflung talon, they are quickly transferred to the bill for devouring.

Hobbies are secretive and a nesting pair can easily go undetected, especially on farmland. As a consequence, informed opinion now believes the population may be as high as 500 pairs, well above the often-quoted figure of 100–150 pairs. Unlike many of Britain's birds of prey, the hobby does not seem to be under threat from habitat destruction, pesticides or human persecution, though a few clutches are lost to egg collectors each year.

LENGTH: 30–35CM WINGSPAN: 70–85CM WHERE TO LOOK: HEATHS AND DOWNS IN SOUTHERN ENGLAND, ALSO FARMLAND NEST: OLD CROW'S NEST, DOES NOT BUILD EGGS: 2–3, YELLOWISH WITH RED-BROWN BLOTCHES FOOD: BIRDS, ESPECIALLY MARTINS, INSECTS VOICE: RAPID *KEW-KEW-KEW*, MUSICAL FOR FALCON

◼ *The hobby is dark slate-grey above with a prominent black 'moustache' on whitish cheeks. Its rusty-red undertail coverts are important field marks. The whitish underparts are broadly streaked black. It has fairly uniformly chequered underwings and is lightly barred under the tail.*
◼ *In flight the hobby is swift and agile, with fast, stiff wingbeats, interspersed with short glides when hunting. At other times, the wingbeats are relaxed.*

along the coast

Both for scenic beauty and for wildlife interest, the British coastline is outstanding. It has everything from towering cliffs to shallow estuaries, shingle beaches and sand dunes. The variety and richness in both habitat and wildlife is often stunning and, whatever the season, there is always something to see. Many of Britain's best sites for birdwatching are on the coast, including the Farne Islands, and the RSPB reserves at Minsmere on the Suffolk coast, Titchwell in Norfolk, and Leighton Moss in Lancashire. From April until July, the cliffs of Britain are home to vast numbers of breeding seabirds, particularly to the north and west – a notable exception is Bempton Cliffs on the east coast, famous for its nesting gannets. Watch a seabird colony for even a short time and it soon becomes apparent that each species has its own special nesting requirements. Razorbills prefer crevices and boulders close to the sea; shags and fulmars nest on broad ledges; while kittiwakes and guillemots are often densely packed on narrow ledges overhanging sheer drops. Puffins dig burrows into the grassy slopes higher up the cliffs, while herring gulls and lesser black-backed gulls are found in loose colonies among the tussocks of vegetation.

Estuaries and mudflats found all around the coast provide superb opportunities for birdwatching throughout the year. The estuaries are important staging posts for migrants, and from autumn to spring vast numbers of migrant birds may be seen enjoying these rich feeding grounds. One of the most conspicuous birds of the coast is the redshank. Often called 'the sentinels of the marsh', these red-legged waders are alert and quick to utter their alarm call. This brings potential danger to the attention of other wading birds such as dunlins, ringed plovers, grey plovers, knots, curlews and godwits. Shelducks are conspicuous mudflat inhabitants, together with teal and wigeon. In some areas they feed alongside Brent geese, which are winter visitors to the south- and east coast estuaries from their winter breeding grounds in the high Arctic. All these birds visit the estuaries to feed: huge concentrations of invertebrate life – molluscs and crustaceans in particular – live in the surface layers of the mud.

Beaches and sand dunes, especially in southern Britain, suffer more than most habitats from human disturbance. Nesting birds also suffer, and it is only in certain protected areas in England that terns, oystercatchers, ringed plovers and black-headed gulls can rest in peace. Further north in Britain the beaches are less disturbed and you are more likely to encounter nesting birds. Always be on the lookout for signs of alarmed or distressed birds in these areas during the breeding season.

Peregrine
FALCO PEREGRINUS

The life and times of the peregrine are among the best documented of any bird. Before World War II it was heavily persecuted by keepers and collectors; during the war it was shot to protect pigeons carrying messages; after the war it was hit by pesticides and then subjected to high levels of theft of its eggs and young. It was the use of pesticides that was the most damaging, reducing the population to an all time low in the early 1960s. Quick action by conservationists in studying just why peregrines were starting to lay thin-shelled eggs (which therefore broke) or failing to raise young resulted in the discovery that levels of pesticides were building up in their tissues through eating prey that had fed on contaminated insects. Being persistent, these chemicals accumulated in 'top' predators like the peregrine. Once discovered, action was swift and voluntary bans on the manufacture and use of these dangerous substances were introduced. So, in many ways, the peregrine was a barometer of the health of the environment, and for that we should be grateful.

The peregrine is a large, powerful falcon, with the female noticeably larger than the male. A peregrine requires about 100g of food a day. Its prey includes game birds, waders, pigeons and other medium-sized birds, such as thrushes. On an estuary in winter the falcon's presence will cause alarm to wildfowl and waders.

These days, the best places to look of peregrines include the rocky west coasts of England and Wales and in Scotland. Resident pairs of adult birds are often present in the same location throughout the year, while juvenile birds tend to wander further afield. At Symonds Yat Rock in Gloucestershire there is a public viewpoint each summer. To this day peregrine nests are still robbed of eggs and young, and vigilant wardens guard many during the breeding season.

▨ *Adult peregrines are dark bluish-grey above; underparts are white to warm buff, densely barred black, but the white chin and cheeks have a conspicuous black lobe-like strip from beak to eye. The underwing is lightly barred, with little contrast between coverts and flight feathers.*

▨ *Juvenile birds are dark brown above, rusty-buff below, streaked (not barred) dark brown, with a 'moustache' thinner than an adult's.*

▨ *A peregrine is powerful, swift and agile in flight with stiff, shallow wingbeats and occasional short glides. It stoops on prey from a height on nearly fully closed wings. The actual speed of the stoop – by which its prey is caught – is the subject of much debate, but can reach between 160 and 320kph.*

▨ *In silhouette note the compact shape, broad-based pointed wings (wings often appearing triangular-shaped) and square-cut or slightly tapering medium-short tail.*

LENGTH: 40–59CM **WINGSPAN:** 80–115CM **WHERE TO LOOK:** MOUNTAINS, MOORLAND AND SEA CLIFFS, BUT NOT IN SOUTHEAST ENGLAND IN BREEDING SEASON. ESTUARIES AND COASTS IN WINTER **NEST:** LEDGE OR CREVICE ON CLIFF OR QUARRY FACE; MAY USE OLD RAVEN'S NEST **EGGS:** 3–4, LIGHTLY DAPPLED TAWNY TO REDDISH BROWN, LAID IN BARE SCRAPE **FOOD:** MEDIUM-SIZED BIRDS SUCH AS PIGEONS, CROWS, SEABIRDS, GROUSE; TAKEN ON WING IN POWERFUL STOOP; ALSO MAMMALS **VOICE:** IN BREEDING SEASON A SHRILL CHATTERING *KEK-KEK-KEK-KEK*, HARSH *KAARK*

Red Grouse
LAGOPUS LAGOPUS SCOTICUS

LENGTH: 37–42CM **WEIGHT:** 550–690G **WHERE TO LOOK:**
MOORLAND WITH GOOD COVER OF HEATHER; ALSO ON DAMP
COTTON-GRASS OR SEDGE **NEST:** ON GROUND **EGGS:** 4–9,
CREAM, BLOTCHED BROWN **FOOD:** HEATHER, SEEDS, BERRIES
VOICE: EXPLOSIVE, RAPID BARKING NOTES

Adult female

Adult male

The head-to-toe feathering of the red grouse enables it to withstand the frequently appalling weather conditions of Britain's moorlands. Regularly feeding beneath snow, this dark, rusty-coloured bird avoids its predators – peregrines and eagles – but faces months of hardship. The closely related willow grouse, of Scandinavia, actually changes to white plumage in winter like the ptarmigan.

The red grouse was once unique to Britain, but has been introduced to other parts of the world; it has also lost its status as Britain's only unique species, being reclassified as a race of the willow grouse. The 'Glorious Twelfth' is 12 August, the start of the grouse shooting season, and most grouse are on ground maintained by keepers. Management of heather by burning allows fresh new growth with succulent shoots – ideal food – but over-burning and over grazing destroy the heather, which the grouse rely on. When flushed, the grouse utters a rapid staccato call which changes to a distinct 'go-back-go-back' – the sound is evocative of the wild habitat and, taken literally, probably good advice as the mist and clouds roll in over the high, exposed moor.

▓ *Males are rustier-red than the buff-speckled females.*
▓ *It flies with whirring wings and short glides, accompanied by abrupt, cackling calls; note the dark wings and tail.*
▓ *Although mostly on open moors, the red grouse will take grit from edges of roads to help digest heather.*

Ptarmigan
LAGOPUS MUTUS

LENGTH: 34–36CM **WEIGHT:** 400–600G **WHERE TO LOOK:**
SCOTTISH MOUNTAINS, LOWER IN EXTREME NORTH **NEST:** ON
GROUND **EGGS:** 5–9, CREAM WITH BROWN SPOTS **FOOD:**
HEATHER, OTHER PLANTS **VOICE:** QUIET, RATTLING
KARRRAKAKAKA, BELCHING *AAR-AA-KA-KA*

Adult male

Adult female

Winter adult

The snow lies thick on the high Scottish mountains for three months or more and the ptarmigan in their smart white winter dress crouch unnoticed. As spring begins to melt the snow, and rocks and vegetation show again, they develop mottled plumage to merge with the new background. When all the snow has gone in mid-summer, ptarmigan disappear against the lichen-covered rocks with their grey-brown and black plumage patterns. These mountain grouse really are masters of disguise, but despite their superb camouflage many still fall prey to the golden eagle.

In late autumn and winter large parties of ptarmigan may gather, using the theory that many pairs of eyes are better than one. The largest flock recorded in Scotland was of 470 birds! Normally, flocks number several dozen at most, with males and females in different groups. The males put themselves in the front line against predators and harsh weather by feeding in the more exposed places. If many males die, the remainder become highly polygamous in the following spring, often having three or more mates. Ptarmigan seem to be oblivious to humans and are often surprisingly approachable.

▓ *It has a black tail and white wings all year; only the body feathers change colour. Never so rich brown as red grouse; males are often quite grey or patchy in summer, females more buff. In winter all white except for the tail. The male has red wattle and a black eye patch.*
▓ *Perfectly hidden on mountain screes, only movement and blinking white eyelids give them away. Rarely seen below 600m except on northern coastal hills.*

Black Grouse
TETRAO TETRIX

As a silvery dawn breaks, with dew heavily on the ground, male black grouse gather to display at favoured, traditional sites called leks. In Britain, groups may number up to 40 birds, but in the USSR leks may hold 200. The curious ritual is practiced throughout the year except for a break in late summer and autumn, when the birds are moulting. Males fluff up their white undertail coverts and raise their lyre-shaped tails, inflate their blue necks and make a bubbling, dove-live cooing in a regular pattern. The males – blackcocks – bustle about in mock fights, while the females – greyhens – watch nearby. The display will continue even without greyhens present – and so vain are the blackcocks that they will even strut about alone! Although the black grouse has disappeared from many of its old haunts, due to over-shooting and loss of habitat, its population is increasing in a few parts where new conifer plantations provide temporary havens.

Adult male

Adult female

LENGTH: 40–55CM **WEIGHT:** MALE 1,300G FEMALE 1,000G **WHERE TO LOOK:** TYPICALLY EDGES OF MOOR ON HEATH NEAR TREES, BOGS, PLANTATIONS **NEST:** ON GROUND IN LONG GRASS **EGGS:** 6–10, BUFF WITH BROWN SPOTS **FOOD:** BUDS, SHOOTS OF BIRCH, PINE **VOICE:** FAR-CARRYING DOVE-LIKE BUBBLING; HISSING SNEEZE

Capercaillie
TETRAO UROGALLUS

Adult male

Adult female

LENGTH: 60–87CM **WEIGHT:** MALE 4KG **WHERE TO LOOK:** OLD CONIFER FORESTS OF NORTH SCOTLAND **NEST:** ON GROUND NEAR TREE **EGGS:** 5–8, BUFF-SPECKLED BROWN **FOOD:** PINE NEEDLES, BUDS, ALSO SEEDS, BERRIES **VOICE:** MALE – CLICKING SONG; FEMALE – PHEASANT-LIKE CROW

These giants of the forest, though the size of turkeys, can be elusive, disappearing into the pines away from a frustrated observer – either clattering through the branches of creeping silently away on the ground. A quiet onlooker may be lucky enough to see one crash out of a tree to fly off on large, rounded wings. In the early spring, dripping water may stimulate the male's song, which starts with a similar *pelip-pelip* sound and continues into a fast *plip-plip-plip-itit-t-t klop*! The last note sounds like a cork popping from a bottle. The turkey-like display attracts females and keeps other males at bay, indeed even other animals. Occasionally an unpaired male will display to anything that moves – even people have been attacked by raving male capercaillies. The species became extinct in Britain in the late 18th century due to over-hunting and loss of habitat. Today's population of several thousand birds has built up from a few birds introduced from Sweden in the 1830s. Most are found north of the River Forth, generally preferring old forest to plantations.

■ The cock's black and brown plumage glistens green in good light. The white shoulder patch and pale bill are often obvious.
■ The hen's large size and broad, fanned tail separates it from other grouse; note the orange breast and richly coloured plumage with many black bars. The male is unique.
■ Capercaillies may be flushed from clearings in forests where juniper and bilberry provide good feeding.

Pheasant
PHASIANUS COLCHICUS

The vivid plumage of the splendid male serves to attract females – up to 18 have been recorded in one harem. The male scuttles around each hen, trailing the near wing, twisting over his tail and inflating his facial wattles to show off his finery. Once the females have settled down on a nest, the male appears to ignore them. This is for the best – his colours would soon attract the attention of predators such as fox or stout, whereas the female and young are well camouflaged. Although introduced to Britain, probably before the Norman Conquest, pheasants are now a familiar and characteristic part of the British landscape – even favourite Christmas card birds! It seems odd to think that they are not 'British' at all.

LENGTH: 53–90CM **WEIGHT:** 1–1.5KG **WHERE TO LOOK:** WOODS, AGRICULTURAL LAND WITH DENSE COVER, MARSHES **NEST:** ON GROUND, WELL HIDDEN **EGGS:** 8–15, OLIVE **FOOD:** GRAIN, SEEDS, BERRIES, INSECTS; EVEN LIZARDS, MICE **VOICE:** LOUD CROW AND SHORTER *HIC-UP*

Adult male

Adult female

■ *The long-tailed male is quite unlike any other British bird, and is more likely to run than fly from danger.*
▨ *The smaller, short-tailed female resembles a large partridge, but its pointed tail is never rusty. Beware half-grown young birds that can already fly, thus causing confusion.*

Quail
COTURNIX COTURNIX

LENGTH: 16–18CM **WEIGHT:** 70–150G **WHERE TO LOOK:** ARABLE LAND ON LIMESTONE OR CHALK, OPEN DOWNS **NEST:** SCRAPE ON GROUND **EGGS:** 7–12, BUFF, VARIABLY BLOTCHED BROWN **FOOD:** SHOOTS AND SEEDS, ALSO INSECTS **VOICE:** LOUD, LIQUID *WHIC WHIC-IC*; DOLL-LIKE *MAMA*

A rare breeding bird, appearing sporadically, mainly in southern counties, the quail has periodic 'good years', which bring more to nest here. A decline noted during the early years of this century was thought to be due to over-persecution by egg collectors and shooters rather than any agricultural changes. Today it is much more a characteristic bird of rolling cereal fields shimmering in the heat of Spain or southern France, where the dawn and dusk chorus of penetrating, triple calls can be quite dramatic. If flushed – not an easy thing to accomplish – the quail flies on relatively long, narrow wings before dropping back into the vegetation with a lark-like flutter, as much like a big lark or small snipe as a partridge. Usually quails will scurry away through vegetation without ever being detected, and they are nearly always 'heard but not seen'. This is Britain's only migrant gamebird, and most move to central and southern Africa after the breeding season. On migration European quails suffer enormous losses at the hands of trappers and gunmen in North Africa, especially Egypt and Libya. It is difficult to judge just how damaging this is to the long-term wellbeing of the quail population.

These days, quails in Britain seem to prefer barley fields, especially where strips of set-aside lie adjacent to the crop.

Adult male

Adult female

■ *The female lacks the facial markings and chestnut streaks of the male.*
▨ *Short, quick flights on rather long wings are characteristic.*
▨ *Its small size makes confusion unlikely with other gamebirds except half-grown, but flying, young partridges which have rusty tails. Quail usually crouch, but they may stand higher to peer over short vegetation.*

Red-legged Partridge
ALECTORIS RUFA

LENGTH: 32–34CM **WEIGHT:** 500G **WHERE TO LOOK:** OFTEN-DRIER ARABLE LAND, HEATHS AND DUNES **NEST:** ON GROUND IN DENSE VEGETATION **EGGS:** 10–15, SPOTTED BROWN **FOOD:** SHOOTS, SEEDS; ALSO SLUGS, INSECTS **VOICE:** HARSH, LOUD, CHUFFING *CHUKAARR… CHUKAARR*

Adult male

Adult female

There are as many red-legged partridges as there are grey, but the red-legs are less widespread. Red-legs are much easier to see, as flocks up to 20 strong wander over ploughed fields and open pastures. Despite their rather bright colours, however, they can conceal themselves remarkably well even on open ground. Crouched low into a depression, the black and white face and striped flanks help to break up the outlines of the birds and make them less eyecatching. When approached, they will run away rather than fly, but if taken by surprise at close range they burst into the air with whirring wings then glide down to the ground before scampering away on bright-red legs. Watch them walk over rough ground and you will see that the head remains very steady while the legs and body act as a 'suspension' absorbing all the irregularities – better for seeing food and possible danger. Red-legs often perch on high objects – walls, haystacks; even old farm buildings; a grey partridge is unlikely to do this. The 'French partridge' is often more familiar that the grey these days.

▓ *Its uniform buff-brown back, well-marked face and red bill and legs are all distinctive.*
▓ *It flies with long glides between bursts of whirring wingbeats, showing rusty tail and plain sandy-buff upperparts.*
▓ *The crouching bird looks like a clod of earth, and is surprisingly large when seen well.*
▓ *Red-legs are found particularly in southern and eastern England.*

Grey Partridge
PERDIX PERDIX

Adult male

Adult female

LENGTH: 29–31CM **WEIGHT:** 350–400G **WHERE TO LOOK:** ARABLE LAND, LOWER MOORLAND EDGES AND ROUGH PASTURE **NEST:** IN THICK COVER **EGGS:** 12–19, OLIVE-BUFF **FOOD:** MOSTLY VEGETABLE, BUT CHICKS EAT INSECTS **VOICE:** LOUD, LIKE CREAKY, RUSTY GATE *SKERRR-IK; IK-IK-IK* IN FLIGHT

Although feeding predominantly on plants, insects form a vital part of every partridge's diet during the first few weeks of its life. A mixed diet of animal and vegetable helps chicks to develop more quickly. Unfortunately, many of the insects they eat are crop pests, like aphids, weevils and sawfly larvae. In cereal crops these have been greatly reduced by effective use of pesticides – and so the partridge has declined. Other changes in farming practice have not helped. Loss of hedges reduces nesting places, herbicides kill off food plants like grasses and chickweed, and more efficient harvesting leaves less waste grain in fields. Because the numbers have declined many have been imported from Europe for shooting and in some places so many have been released that it is difficult to class the bird as 'native'. Other species of partridge, especially the chukar, have also been introduced in hundreds – surely not the best way to protect wild birds that are already under pressure. Autumn coveys (or flocks) give an idea of the breeding success – up to 20 birds at times, but after a bad year as few as three or four. Without its partridges, the countryside would be the poorer.

▓ *It is smaller than the red-legged, with orange face, speckled upperparts and less bold flank stripes. Its creaky calls are quite different.*
▓ *The male has a more obvious horseshoe mark on its belly than the female.*
▓ *Whirring flight, frequent glides; streaked back, rusty tail.*
▓ *It takes to flight rather than running if threatened, usually with short, clicking calls.*

Water Rail
RALLUS AQUATICUS

LENGTH: 23–28CM **WEIGHT:** 90–150G **WHERE TO LOOK:** THICK REED BEDS AND MARSHES; ALSO OVERGROWN DITCHES, OLDER THICKETS **NEST:** IN VERY DENSE COVER OF DEAD REEDS AND OTHER AQUATIC VEGETATION **EGGS:** 6–11, BUFF, WITH A FEW GREY OR BROWN SPOTS AND BLOTCHES **FOOD:** MOSTLY INSECTS AND GRUBS, BUT ALSO BERRIES AND SEEDS. LARGER PREY SUCH AS FISH, SMALL MAMMALS, EGGS, BIRDS AND CARRION ALSO EATEN **VOICE:** VARIED PIG-LIKE SQUEALS AND GRUNTS; OTHER CALLS INCLUDE WHISTLES, SQUEAKS AND HISSES

A winter cold spell of four or five days' duration is usually enough to drive this normally very secretive bird out of a frozen reed bed to areas of unfrozen running water. The true shape of the water rail cannot be appreciated during winter as it fluffs up its striped flanks to retain body heat. The skeleton illustrates how incredibly slim it really is; looking almost as though it has been squashed from both sides, it enables the bird to slip between reed stems quickly and quietly.

The long red bill is used to probe into mud or shallow water for grubs, but can be turned on unsuspecting small birds and mammals with deadly accuracy. Water rails have been observed eating large dead birds, like moorhens, which had probably frozen to death.

Flying as a last resort, water rails will normally dart into a clump of vegetation and will only move when virtually stepped on. Sometimes one gives an unexpectedly clear view when it hides its head behind a stem, leaving the rest of its body exposed!

■ The buff undertail is shown when the tail is jerked up. Brown horizontal streaks on upper parts and vertically striped flanks help to hide the bird in vegetation.
■ Its slim body glides between reed stems without touching them, so that not even a twitching reed head will point a hungry marsh harrier in the right direction.
■ Long toes prevent feeding birds sinking into deep mud.
■ More often heard than seen, the strange squeaks, hisses and squeals will give away its presence. These noises inform other water rails of its position.

Corncrake
CREX CREX

LENGTH: 27–30CM **WEIGHT:** 150–200G **WHERE TO LOOK:** HAYFIELDS, IRIS BEDS. FORMERLY COMMON THROUGHOUT BRITAIN, NOW RARE **NEST:** HIDDEN IN DENSE TUSSOCK **EGGS:** 8–12, CREAMY WITH BROWN BLOTCHES **FOOD:** MOSTLY INSECTS, WORMS; A FEW SEEDS **VOICE:** DISTINCTIVE, REPEATED *CREK-CREK*

The future of the corncrake in Britain seems now to be in the hands of farmers. Strangely, it was the farmers who first helped it spread its range. As forests were felled centuries ago, giving way to cultivated grassland, corncrakes rapidly moved in, taking advantage of the newly created habitat. The introduction of mechanical grass cutters and the repeated cuts of grass to make silage have forced the corncrake out of many areas in recent decades; changes in Africa's climate may also have been disastrous though the habitat remains good.

The rasping call would have been familiar to all county dwellers in the early 1900s. Today it is only a few crofters farming in traditional ways in western Ireland and the Hebrides who hear the corncrake summoning spring after its long-distance migration from wintering grounds in central Africa. The call, which gave the corncrake its Latin name, is likened to the teeth of a comb being drawn rapidly across the edge of a matchbox twice, but at close range is a much louder, harder sound. In the autumn, corncrakes are occasionally seen along the south coast, especially if unfavourable weather halts their migration southwards.

■ Also called the landrail, the corncrake resembles a moorhen in shape, but its striped buffish plumage with greyer head and its habitat (especially hay meadows) are good clues to identification.
■ Very skulking, but easier to see soon after its arrival in May when vegetation is still low.

Moorhen
GALLINULA CHLOROPUS

LENGTH: 32–35CM **WEIGHT:** 200–400G **WHERE TO LOOK:**
FRESH WATER FROM SMALL POOLS TO LARGE LAKES OR RIVERS,
ALWAYS REQUIRES GOOD PLANT COVER. FEEDS ON WET
MEADOWS **NEST:** FLOATING HEAP OF VEGETATION, OR UP TO
5 METRES HIGH IN TREES OR BUSHES BESIDE WATER **EGGS:** 5–11,
GLOSSY BUFF WITH BROWN AND BLACK BLOTCHES **FOOD:**
WATER WEEDS, SEEDS, FRUIT, GRASSES, INSECTS, WORMS AND
LARVAE **VOICE:** VARIABLE, OFTEN URGENT *KITTIK*, A LOUD,
ABRUPT OR METALLIC *KAAK* AND *KIC-KIC-KIC*

Juvenile

Adult male

Moorhens are very adaptable birds, being able to climb trees, walk or run on flat ground, swim, wade and clamber through undergrowth. Yet they never appear to be quite at home, often moving awkwardly or cautiously with their big feet getting in the way. The long, spread toes enable them not only to wade on marshy ground without sinking, but also to swim confidently – they are among the few British birds able to swim well without webbed or lobed toes. Jerky movements and frequent stops to survey the surrounding land exaggerate their cautious nature. At the first sign of danger the tail is flicked to warn other birds, before an ungainly waddling exit, with head held low, into the nearest area of dense cover. A moorhen caught out by a predator on open water will dive and stay submerged by clasping on to underwater plants until the threat has gone. Two or three broods are reared each year. The black, downy young follow their parents persistently, waving tiny wings as though rowing through the air, trying to attract attention.

▧ *At close range the bright bill, brownish back, black head and slatey underside look very different from the 'black and white' of a distant bird.*
▧ *Juveniles have browner backs, buff underparts and a greenish bill (quite unlike adult).*
▧ *When swimming, the bird's tail is held nearly as high as the head, unlike the more horizontal body of the coot. Notice the flank streaks.*
▧ *Dangling legs and rather bowed wings are characteristic in flight, which is usually only over short distances.*

Coot
FULICA ATRA

LENGTH: 36–38CM **WEIGHT:** 400–800G **WHERE TO LOOK:**
LARGER AREAS OF OPEN WATER WITH PLENTY OF VEGETATION.
ALSO TOWN PARK PONDS **NEST:** AQUATIC PLANTS, FLOATING,
BUT ANCHORED TO SAFE FOUNDATION **EGGS:** 6–9, BUFF
WITH SMALL DARK SPOTS **FOOD:** SHOOTS OF REED, ROOTS,
ALGAE; ALSO INSECTS, EGGS **VOICE:** *KEP* OR *COOT* CALL, LOUD
AND ABRUPT

Large, lobed feet

During the breeding season coots do not tolerate each other's company, often fighting viciously with their long, sharp claws. With head almost flat on the water and wings bunched high over its short tail, a coot will drive off birds much larger than itself – even swans and geese. Noisy calls and splashing fights are frequent in summer wherever there are coots.

Large winter flocks, often several hundred strong, will gather on favourable waters to dive for food. When on the surface the broad body appears unsinkable, but air is pushed out of the feathers by flattening them and a leap well clear of the water before submerging helps the coot dive to depths of 7m. The huge lobed grey feet are quite unlike the moorhen's and enable it to swim and dive very efficiently.

Coots spending the winter on ponds near humans will become very tame, even taking food from the hand. Their urge to feed will often lead to a squabbling mass of black and white as they clamber over each other. Moorhens are always far more timid, pushed out to the edge of the bustling, self-important coots. The two species are, however, seldom seen without each other's company.

▧ *The silky black plumage helps to show off the white bill and frontal shield; the glowing red eye is a common feature of nearly all European crakes and rails.*
▧ *Downy black and red chicks pester the adults continuously for food; older juveniles are grey with white face and breast.*
▧ *Wings raised to make it look bigger, an aggressive coot will menace an intruder by showing its white bill and shield. This is turned away in courtship.*

Oystercatcher
HAEMATOPUS OSTRALEGUS

LENGTH: 40–46CM WEIGHT: 500–600G WHERE TO LOOK: ON
ALL COASTS, SOME ON COASTAL FIELDS. ALSO BREEDS IN RIVER
VALLEYS NEST: SIMPLE SCRAPE EGGS: 2–3, PALE BUFF, SPOTTED
BROWN FOOD: MUSSELS, COCKLES, RAGWORMS; WORMS
INLAND VOICE: CLEAR, SHARP *KLEEP*

This big, boldly coloured bird is a familiar sight on estuaries and rocky shores all around the coast, equally characteristic of cold, bleak mud flats, sunny sandy beaches, beautiful Scottish sea lochs and tangy mussel beds. After a steady rise in numbers, at least 280,000 now spend the winter in Britain, many from the Faroes, Iceland and Norway, although 40,000 pairs breed here. Some winter concentrations are huge – in Morecambe Bay alone there can be 50,000 – and to see them pouring in to their high-tide roost, landing on the run and crashing into those already settled, is a noisy experience. Numbers in an estuary vary according to the food supply – a good cockle year means more oystercatchers. Unlike most waders, the oystercatcher collects food and takes it to its chicks, because they have yet to learn the specialist feeding techniques that make this bird so successful. Many stalk their prey, waiting for a chance to strike the bill into an open shell; others simply find a shellfish and hammer it open with the powerful, chisel-tipped orange bill.

The majority of British oystercatchers breed around the coast, favouring sandy or shingle beaches. Not surprisingly, perhaps, pressure from human visitors effectively excludes them from most areas of south and east England, unless specially protected. The west coasts of England and Wales are much more suitable for breeding oystercatchers and in Scotland they are widespread, even at inland sites.

Summer plumage

Winter plumage

■ *The black and white plumage is striking even at a distance. The white patches make a dazzling pattern in flight.*
■ *In summer the bird is glossy black above, but in winter duller with a white collar.*
■ *It is large, with a heavy orange bill, red eyes and stout, pale pink legs.*
■ *The chick is well camouflaged against pebbles and lichen-covered seashore rocks.*

Avocet
RECURVIROSTRA AVOSETTA

LENGTH: 42–45CM **WEIGHT:** 300–400G **WHERE TO LOOK:**
MUDDY COASTS IN SOUTH AND EAST ENGLAND; BREEDS
MAINLY ON EAST ANGLIAN COASTAL LAGOONS **NEST:** SCRAPE,
LITTLE LINING **EGGS:** 3–4, BUFF, SPOTTED **FOOD:** SMALL SHRIMPS
AND WORMS **VOICE:** *KLUTE*

Plumage development

Nest

Active protection and habitat management are the main reason why the avocet has managed to gain a strong foothold in Britain. In 1947 two groups totalling 28 pairs were discovered breeding on land flooded as part of wartime defence measures. It is thought that inadvertent protection afforded to Dutch and Danish birds during wartime allowed numbers on mainland Europe to build up. This made colonisation of suitable areas in England more likely. The areas were purchased by the RSPB and sophisticated systems were developed to improve the nesting and feeding conditions, including the salinity of the water. Those areas, Minsmere and Havergate Island, remain the principal breeding places, although birds have spread to many other areas, particularly in north Norfolk. The total number of pairs in Britain is now over 400 and rising.

They require brackish water, which can support very high numbers of small shrimps, the main food in summer. Up to 300 avocets remain in southern England during the winter, mainly in Havergate, or on the Exe and Tamar estuaries in Devon. Avocets often swim, up-ending to catch their food and looking remarkably like shelducks or gulls. In some places they even roost on the water like ducks. Despite their fragile bills and delicate build, they are very aggressive near the nest, viciously attacking intruding shelducks.

Perhaps because of the attractive appearance or their rarity value, avocets still suffer from persecution from egg collectors. A careful watch is therefore maintained at nesting sites throughout the breeding season.

▨ *The upcurved bill of the avocet is unmistakable. A tall, elegant eye-catching bird, among gulls it looks smaller and pure white. Its legs are often hidden in water.*
▨ *It appears very white in flight with flickering black wingtips. Its legs trail behind and the neck protrudes in front, which makes it look long.*
▨ *The juvenile is like the adult, but black areas are dull brown.*
▨ *Typically, feeding action is a distinctive sideways sweep of its bill through watery mud.*
▨ *Breeding birds sit conspicuously on rudimentary nests on muddy islands in a few coastal reserves.*

LEFT TO RIGHT: AN EXOTIC SOUTHERN AUSTRALIAN WEDGE TAILED EAGLE; FALCONRY DISPLAY AT NATIONAL BIRD OF PREY CENTRE; AN EAGLE OWL AT NBPC; GOLDEN EAGLE

where to see birds of prey

Birds of prey (raptors) are the most difficult groups to identify. Views may only be brief or distant. This makes familiarity hard to achieve. Wing shape and position, and tail length are important to distinguish families, but then one should concentrate on plumage, especially wing patterns. Britain's has a wide range of birds of prey parks and reserves, where you can see native and more exotic birds of prey as well as watching flying displays and get tuition in handling raptors.

WHERE TO SEE THEM

The Cornish Birds of Prey Centre
Meadowside Farm. Winniards Perch,
St Columb, Cornwall TR9 6DH
01637 880554
www.cornishbirdsofprey.co.uk

The centre includes 50 birds of prey, many of which take part in regular flying displays. The centre also includes one of the largest collections of peacocks in the southwest.

The New Forest Owl Sanctuary
Crow Lane, Crow, Ringwood,
Hampshire BH24 1EA
01425 476487
www.newforestowls.co.uk
Here you can see 350 owls, birds of prey and other wildlife as well as spectacular flying displays daily.

The National Birds of Prey Centre
Newent, Gloucestershire GL18 1JJ
0870 9901992
www.nbpc.co.uk
The centre houses approximately 250 birds and over 85 species with daily flying displays. The centre promotes the conservation of birds of prey through education, captive breeding and research.

Eagle Heights
Lullingstone Lane, Eynsford, Kent
DA4 0JB
01322 866466
www.eagleheights.co.uk
The centre's primary objectives are conservation, education, recreation and sanctuary. There are daily flying displays.

Lincolnshire Birds of Prey Centre
Long Sutton, Spalding, Lincolnshire
PE12 9LE
01406 363833
www.butterflyandwildlifepark.co.uk
Set in the Butterfly and Wildlife Park, you can see plenty of species and twice daily flying displays.

Birds of Prey Centre
Sion Hill, Kirby Wiske, Thirsk, North
Yorkshire YO7 4EU
01845 587522
www.falconrycentre.co.uk
Flying displays of hawks, buzzards, eagles, falcons, kestrels and owls.

Highland Falconry
Auchingarrich Wildlife Park, Comrie,
Perthshire PH6 2JS
01764 679056
highlandfalconry.scotlandrocks.co.uk
Situated within the award winning Auchingarrich Wildlife Park you can see a number of different species including hawks, eagles and falcons as well as twice daily flying displays.

LEFT: GOSHAWK HANDLER AT NBPC, NEWENT

Ringed Plover
CHARADRIUS HIATICULA

Adult male

Juvenile

LENGTH: 18–20CM **WEIGHT:** 56–70G
WHERE TO LOOK: SANDY PARTS OF ESTUARIES,
BEACHES, GRAVEL PITS **NEST:** SCRAPE, LITTLE
LINING **EGGS:** 3–4, BUFFISH OR BLUISH,
SPOTTED; APRIL–AUGUST **FOOD:** SMALL
SHRIMPS, SNAILS, WORMS AND INSECTS
VOICE: MELLOW, RISING *TOO-LI*

The very distinctive stop-go action when feeding provides an easy way of separating this species from other small coastal waders. Like other plovers, it uses sight to locate prey moving on the surface of the sand. For this reason strong winds, heavy rain or very cold weather make finding food difficult. When feeding in slightly muddier areas it often trembles a foot; this disturbs invertebrates — which then reveal them. About 8,600 pairs breed in Britain; the greatest concentration is on the sandy agricultural land (the machair) of the Western Isles, where over a quarter of the total is found. Elsewhere they are mainly on coastal beaches, but increasingly inland on reservoirs, gravel pits or rivers in northern Britain. Males have a striking display flight in which they hold their wings stiffly and flap slowly, calling loudly with continuous, piping leea. In winter some 23,000 are present in Britain, most of which are native breeders and their young.

▨ *Small, chunky wader with a stubby, yellow and black bill, and orange legs. Rather chubby, and a fraction larger than dunlin.*
▨ *Adults have a clear black breastband and face mask; in females it is washed slightly browner. Thin orange rings around the eyes.*
▨ *Characteristic 'stand-watch-run-pause-bob-down' feeding action.*
▨ *Juvenile has a brown band through its eye and a brownish, sometimes incomplete breastband. Streak of white over eye. Looks pale.*

Little Ringed Plover
CHARADRIUS DUBIUS

Adult male

Juvenile

LENGTH: 14–17CM **WEIGHT:** 35–45G
WHERE TO LOOK: INLAND WATERS; SCARCE
ON MIGRATION ON COASTAL LAGOONS
NEST: SIMPLE SCRAPE **EGGS:** 3–4, APRIL–JULY;
BUFF TO GREEN-BLUE WITH SMALL SPOTS
FOOD: INSECTS, OTHER INVERTEBRATES
VOICE: A CLEAR *PEEOO*, SHARP *PEW*

The expansion in gravel extraction over the last 40 years has aided this species considerably. Breeding was first recorded in Britain at Tring Reservoirs, Hertfordshire, in 1938. Since then the numbers have rapidly increased so that in 1984, over 600 pairs bred. Initially, nearly all birds were in south and east England, but they have now spread into Wales and Scotland. The majority breed on gravel pits and banks of reservoirs, but some do so on their typical continental habitat of shingle riverbeds. As ringed plovers increase inland, it seems that little ringed plovers find it difficult to compete with the more aggressive, larger species and are being forced away from traditional sites. The two look very similar at first sight, but careful observation will reveal differences. Sometimes this species can be picked out first by its slightly faster feeding action and relatively small size, and then positively identified by its thin, mostly black bill and clear, yellow eye-ring. In flight, the dark wing without a white wingbar and sharp calls would dispel doubts. It is an early summer migrant, returning in March and April from wintering grounds in tropical Africa and quickly settling into nesting territories.

▨ *Very bold, yellow eye-ring is characteristic in adults; single black breastband.*
▨ *Similar to the ringed plover, but subtly different. Slightly smaller, longer, slimmer. The bill is thinner, mostly black; the legs are longer, more yellow or pinkish; and the breastband is narrower.*
▨ *In flight it looks small and dark.*

Golden Plover
PLUVIALIS APRICARIA

LENGTH: 26–29CM **WEIGHT:** 150–250G **WHERE TO LOOK:**
WINTER – ON PERMANENT GRASSLAND, CULTIVATED LAND;
SUMMER – ON MOORLAND **NEST:** DEPRESSION IN PEAT **EGGS:**
3–4, BUFF, BLOTCHED BROWN, APRIL–JUNE **FOOD:** INSECTS,
SOME SEEDS **VOICE:** CLEAR, WHISTLED *TOOEEE*

Summer plumage

Winter plumage

A musical, but sad, rising whistle is often the first clue that a flock of golden plovers is about. Searching the sky should then reveal this fast-flying species, looking almost like small white crosses from below. They wheel around in a tight flock, then, on banking, the dark, golden-brown upperparts show as they almost funnel down and seem to disappear on landing. When on the ground the flock slowly spreads over the chosen grass field, each bird showing the typical plover run-pause-bob feeding action. Watch one and you will see it sometimes cocks its head sideways, apparently listening for prey and sometimes clearly watching a spot for movement. It is estimated that about 250,000 spend the winter in Britain. These not only include Britain's breeding birds but also some from Iceland and others from Scandinavia. About 22,500 pairs breed in Britain, mainly on moorland, where their complex aerial display and almost melancholic song seem to suit the open landscapes. The few breeding on Dartmoor are the most southerly birds of their species in the world. Breeding golden plovers often favour bare areas or newly burnt ground with only limited regrowth.

■ *A medium-sized bird, standing upright. Always with golden spotted upperparts, prominent dark eye and short dark bill. Fairly wary.*
■ *In winter, it has a golden spotted breast and a white belly. In summer, the belly is black.*
■ *Northern race is very black below with white streak on side. Southern birds are less well marked in summer.*

Dotterel
CHARADRIUS MORINELLUS

As the winter snows melt on the mountain tops of northern Britain, so these spectacular little plovers appear. They will have spent the winter on poor agricultural land around the lower slopes of the Atlas mountains in northern Africa, and in late April and early May they move north, stopping for a day or two at a number of traditional sites, many in eastern England, before reaching the breeding grounds. At least 150 pairs nest in Britain, but they can be extremely elusive. Although brightly coloured, their patterns provide excellent disruptive camouflage against broken backgrounds. Dotterels are among the few waders where the female is more intensely coloured than the male. Her crown is dark brown, not streaked, and the stripes over the eyes (which meet on the back of the head) and breastband are sharply white. Females tend to take the lead in display and very rarely incubate the eggs or look after the young. The sex roles are, therefore, almost entirely reversed. By the time autumn migrants appear in late August the adults have already almost lost their breeding plumage. Dotterels are usually extremely tame, allowing an approach to within a few yards.

LENGTH: 20–22CM **WEIGHT:** 90–110G
WHERE TO LOOK: MOUNTAINTOPS IN
NORTHERN BRITAIN; MIGRANTS MAINLY IN
EASTERN ENGLAND **NEST:** USUALLY UNLINED
SCRAPE **EGGS:** 3, BUFF, HEAVILY SPOTTED
FOOD: MAINLY BEETLES AND FLIES
VOICE: A TRILL OR *KWIP-KWIP*

■ *In summer, white strip over eye, chestnut and black belly, pale line across the breast. Breastline clear in winter and on juveniles.*
■ *Sandy-buff and brown above. No white on wing or rump in flight. Often tame.*

Adult female

Adult male

Grey Plover
PLUVIALIS SQUATAROLA

LENGTH: 27–30CM **WEIGHT:** 200–250G **WHERE TO LOOK:** NEARLY ALL ARE ON ESTUARIES, MAINLY IN THE SOUTHERN HALF OF BRITAIN. DOES NOT BREED IN BRITAIN **FOOD:** SUMMER – INSECTS; WINTER – MARINE WORMS, SHELLFISH **VOICE:** A FLAT *TLEE-OO-EE*. WISTFUL BUT FAR-CARRYING

Winter plumage

Grey plovers in summer plumage are stunning in the contrast between their black underparts and silvery-white and grey upperparts. There can be few birds as striking as these, which appear during April/May and July/August. Most seek out large muddy estuaries in southern and eastern England. They are of a similar size to redshanks, but stand out on the mud flats because of their pale grey plumage and hunched, dejected stance, combined with a rather slow feeding action. Sight is the sense that is used when feeding. They watch for tiny movements on the surface, then lunge to catch the worms or molluscs before they retreat into the mud. Because they feed on items at the surface, bad weather (low temperature, high wind, rain) may affect their feeding rate significantly.

Typically, grey plovers spend the winter in warm climates, but during recent years the numbers wintering in Britain have doubled to 21,000. The Wash, Chichester Harbour and the area around Foulness in Essex have over 2,000 birds each. Very few are noted inland, even during migration. All the grey plovers seen in Britain come from breeding grounds on the tundra of northern Siberia.

▨ *Long-winged in flight and shows a clear white wingbar and square white rump. Characteristic black mark on the 'armpit' contrasts with white underwing from below.*
▨ *Winter birds are pale below, greyish and pale spotted above. The large dark eye is prominent. Juveniles have pale yellow spots on back.*
▨ *When disturbed, normally flies away silently.*

Stone-curlew
BURHINUS OEDICNEMUS

Secretive and inconspicuous, the stone-curlew is one of Britain's least familiar birds. Ideally, it requires large, open spaces where grass is kept very short by grazing, and where bare ground can be found. Such conditions are now only found in East Anglia's Breckland (where two-thirds of the 120–150 pairs of British stone-curlews breed) and to a lesser extent the upland chalk of southern England. It will also live on agricultural land that has areas of bare earth, but if it does it needs the active help of the farmer in not ploughing up its nest or eggs. It is inactive for much of the day, sitting or standing quietly by patches of taller vegetation. As dusk approaches so it comes to life, searching grass, open soil or dung piles for earthworms, burying beetles and other invertebrates. Even small mice and nesting birds are taken. Activity is intense through the night, and it is then that the extremely varied calls can be heard. These are a mixture of wailing and slurred curlew-like calls interspersed by oystercatcher-like piping. The large eye is adapted to its nocturnal habits.

▨ *When sitting, the buff and brown upperparts are well camouflaged. Note white streaking on the face.*
▨ *Most peculiar appearance with staring yellow and black eye and striking yellow bill. White and dark on wing.*

LENGTH: 40–44CM **WEIGHT:** 400–500G **WHERE TO LOOK:** RARE SUMMER MIGRANT TO SANDY HEATHS IN THE BRECKLAND AND CHALK IN SOUTH ENGLAND **NEST:** SIMPLE SCRAPE **EGGS:** 2, PALE, BLOTCHED **FOOD:** MAINLY EARTHWORMS, BEETLES **VOICE:** WAILING *CUR-LEE*; WHISTLES

Lapwing
VANELLUS VANELLUS

LENGTH: 28–31CM WEIGHT: 150–300G WHERE TO LOOK: FOUND IN MANY AREAS IN WINTER, MAINLY ON GRASSLAND, SOME ON PLOUGHED FIELDS. ON COASTS IN SEVERE WEATHER. IN SUMMER ON WET MEADOWS, MOORLAND AND SPRING CULTIVATED LAND NEST: SCRAPE ON DRY LAND, LITTLE LINING EGGS: 3–5, PALE BROWN, BLOTCHED DARK; MARCH–JUNE FOOD: WIDE RANGE OF ADULT AND LARVAL INVERTEBRATES, MANY WORMS, SOME PLANT MATERIAL. MANY FOOD ITEMS EATEN WOULD HARM CROPS VOICE: A RISING, TWO-NOTE, THIN, SLIGHTLY HARSH *WEE-IP* OR *PEE-WIT*

Spring display flight of the male

The English names for the lapwing show how well known it is. Lapwing itself describes the flapping, broad-winged flight; green plover the correct plumage colour, white peewit is an excellent description of its call note. In winter it can be found throughout Britain, shunning only the cold mountains and uplands. No accurate figures exist for the numbers present in winter, but there are certainly more than a million. These include not only British breeding birds, but birds from Scandinavia and western Europe, east to western Russia. The lapwing is almost always found in flocks, and flocks often number several thousands. In very severe weather, when the food it takes from the surface is almost impossible to find, huge daytime movements take place, with birds seeking milder grounds. In exceptionally harsh conditions birds can be seen feeding on road verges in towns or even in gardens. Many may die at such times. Territories are taken up during late February and March in southern England, but into April further north. It is then that the spectacular display flight can be seen. The birds engage in twisting and tumbling flying, the rounded wings looking almost moth-like.

Britain's breeding population has been estimated at 181,000 pairs. However, numbers have slumped in recent years as agricultural intensification has changed the landscape.

■ The flight silhouette is characteristic; the broad, rounded wings and shortish, blunt tail give it an appearance unlike that of any other British bird. The outer half of the wing bows down slightly.

■ Flies with distinctive, jerky, almost intermittent flaps. This is enhanced by the wings being sharply kinked at the 'wrist'.

■ In summer, adult males are easy to identify by the all-black chin, throat and breast. The long black crest is longer than in females.

■ The white-naped chicks feed close to the adults, who stand guard.

■ Adult females in summer have some white speckling on the chin and throat. Crests are shorter than males' and wings glossed blue-green, not dark blue.

■ Winter adults have a white chin and throat; breastband is black.

■ A fairly large, rounded wader with a distinct wispy crest. No other British bird has this plumage feature.

Adult male

Adult female

Juvenile

Knot
CALIDRIS CANUTUS

LENGTH: 23–25CM **WEIGHT:** 110–170G
WHERE TO LOOK: LARGE, MOSTLY SANDY
ESTUARIES; ROCKY COASTS. DOES NOT BREED
IN UK **FOOD:** SUMMER – INSECTS; WINTER –
MAINLY SMALL MOLLUSCS **VOICE:** A QUIET
KNUTT OR DOUBLE *KNUUP-KNUUP*

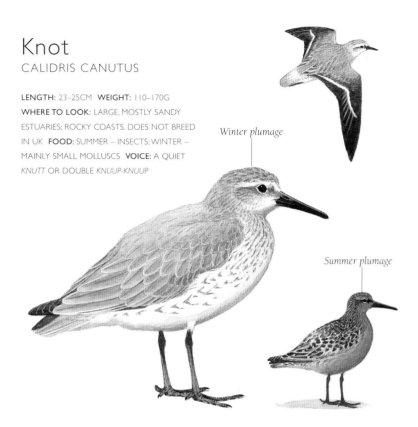

Winter plumage

Summer plumage

When seen singly, the knot's bulky size and mainly grey colour make it distinctive, but it is a very gregarious wader more often found in flocks of many thousands. Although 250,000 spend the winter in Britain, few occur away from areas with larger, sandier estuaries such as Morecambe Bay and the Wash, or the rocky coasts of north and east Scotland. They form extremely tight flocks, which carpet the ground, giving rise to the descriptive name of 'a pack' of knots. As the tightly packed flocks turn in their complex aerial manoeuvres, the colour changes as first the upper, then the lower parts of the birds come into view. Knots are among Britain's most spectacular migrants. Most come from north-east Canada and Greenland; others, which breed in Siberia, are only seen in May and autumn *en route* from and to Africa. A very restricted range of food is taken, consisting entirely of small cockles and, especially, Baltic tellins, which are obtained from probing. Tiny mussels help the birds put on weight before migration, for which fat is the essential fuel.

▨ *Look for the pale grey rump and indistinct wingbars in flight. Flocks of knot usually look very dense.*
▨ *A bulky, smallish wader with short greenish legs and straight bill. Looks low-slung.*
▨ *In winter, very grey with paler underparts: pale face. Legs more greyish.*
▨ *Transformed in summer to brick red below and blacker above.*

Sanderling
CALIDRIS ALBA

Frenzied activity is the sanderling's hallmark as it dashes up and down the beach picking up small shrimps exposed by each wave. So fast do the legs move that the birds look almost as though they are mechanically driven. The 14,000 that spend the winter in Britain are highly localised, many beaches being apparently unsuitable. The Western Isles are favoured. The pale winter dress is very obvious, even where the bird mixes with other waders at roost. Sanderlings breed on tundra near the Arctic Ocean and can be found wintering on beaches all around the world as far as the extreme southern tips of Africa and South America. Those coming to Britain breed mainly in northeast Canada, Greenland and Siberia. Summer plumaged birds are often mistaken for other waders, but the large white wingbar is always distinctive and the belly is always spotlessly white.

LENGTH: 20–21CM **WEIGHT:** 50–60G **WHERE TO LOOK:** SANDY BEACHES AND OUTER PART OF ESTUARIES **NEST:** ONLY ON THE TUNDRA OF THE HIGH ARCTIC. DOES NOT BREED IN UK **FOOD:** SUMMER – MAINLY INSECTS, WINTER – TINY SHRIMPS **VOICE:** A QUIET, POSITIVE *TWICK*

Winter plumage

▨ *Large white wingbar prominent, dark line down centre of rump. Flicks low along shoreline. In summer reddish back and breast.*
▨ *Usually very active in front of waves in small groups.*
▨ *Strikingly pale in winter; pearly grey above, white below with dark shoulder patch; black legs.*

Dunlin
CALIDRIS ALPINA

Variability in size and plumage makes this the most likely species to be confused with other small waders. As it is the most numerous wader on the coast, (approximately 430,000 spend the winter in Britain) it is usually best to assume a small wader is a dunlin unless you can prove to the contrary. Muddier estuaries are favoured, although groups can be found on sandy shores and rocky coasts. Small ragworms and the snails called *Hydrobia* are perhaps its favoured food. When worms are extracted they are often taken to the nearest water and washed before being eaten. Severe weather places much stress on small waders, and at those times dunlins crowd along the tideline where food is most easily found.

Those wintering in Britain breed in Siberia and northern Scandinavia, but others from Iceland and Greenland pass through to spend the winter in southern Europe and north-west Africa. There they are joined by the 9,000 pairs, which breed in northern Britain. Males have a beautiful song, a descending reedy trill, which seems to blend into the wild moorland and marshes. Dunlin are often associated on their breeding grounds with golden plovers, the two species sometimes nesting within a short distance of one another. This relationship has led to the dunlin's nickname of 'plover's page'.

Summer plumage

LENGTH: 16–22CM; WEIGHT: 40–60G WHERE TO LOOK: WIDESPREAD ON MUDDY ESTUARIES, LAKE SHORES NEST: IN DEEP VEGETATION NEAR NORTHERN WETLANDS EGGS: 4, BUFF, VARIABLY MARKED FOOD: INVERTEBRATES VOICE: A SLURRED, SLIGHTLY HARSH *TREEEP*

Juvenile

Winter plumage

- In flight looks quite brown but with distinct, fairly narrow white wingbar. Black line running through pale rump and grey tail.
- Dunlins come in many sizes; those from the East are long-billed, but birds from Greenland have much shorter, straighter bills.
- In spring, the back of the neck of the male is grey, but in female it has a strong reddish tinge.
- No other small wader has a black belly in summer plumage. Has chestnut markings above which wear to become darker.
- The dunlin's delightful song is evocative of its moorland breeding habitat.
- When feeding, they keep their heads down and probe into the mud very rapidly. They run quickly between feeding sites; often quarrelsome.
- Dull in winter, with grey-brown upperparts, white underparts and breast suffused grey, forming a breastband at a distance. Then more easily confused with other small, much scarcer waders.
- Juvenile has dark spots and streaks on belly; neat lines of pale fringed feathers on back. Breast and head suffused buff.

Little Stint
CALIDRIS MINUTA

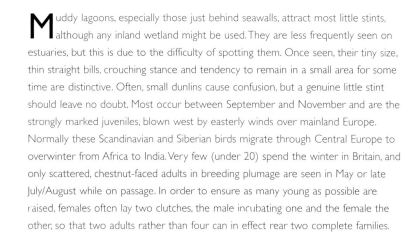

LENGTH: 12-14CM **WEIGHT:** 20-30G **WHERE TO LOOK:** EXPOSED
MUD INLAND, SOME ON ESTUARIES. MOSTLY SEEN IN AUTUMN.
DOES NOT BREED IN UK **FOOD:** SMALL INVERTEBRATES, MAINLY
INSECTS **VOICE:** A QUIET BUT CLEAR *TIP-TIP* OR *STIT-STIT*

Muddy lagoons, especially those just behind seawalls, attract most little stints, although any inland wetland might be used. They are less frequently seen on estuaries, but this is due to the difficulty of spotting them. Once seen, their tiny size, thin straight bills, crouching stance and tendency to remain in a small area for some time are distinctive. Often, small dunlins cause confusion, but a genuine little stint should leave no doubt. Most occur between September and November and are the strongly marked juveniles, blown west by easterly winds over mainland Europe. Normally these Scandinavian and Siberian birds migrate through Central Europe to overwinter from Africa to India. Very few (under 20) spend the winter in Britain, and only scattered, chestnut-faced adults in breeding plumage are seen in May or late July/August while on passage. In order to ensure as many young as possible are raised, females often lay two clutches, the male incubating one and the female the other, so that two adults rather than four can in effect rear two complete families.

- *Most often seen in autumn are the juveniles. Prominent white 'V' on back, reddish fringes to brown upperparts and cap; white flanks.*
- *A tiny wader, much smaller than the dunlin and with a diminutive straight bill and black legs. Feeds with very rapid pecks from the mud surface. Often tame.*
- *In flight looks small; narrow white wingbar and dark line over white rump and grey tail.*

Curlew Sandpiper
CALIDRIS FERRUGINEA

When feeding, curlew sandpipers often wade out into quite deep water and probe vertically, submerging their heads. Others probe for worms on mud flats. Females have longer bills than males, enabling them to probe more deeply. The neatly-patterned juveniles are seen from late August to October and greatly outnumber the adults. In exceptional years, with strong persistent easterly winds after a good breeding season, up to 3,500 have been seen in Britain, but 500–1,000 is more usual. These breed in central northern Siberia and over-winter throughout Africa; others fly to New Zealand for the winter, often in large numbers.

The curlew sandpiper is not very vocal, but sometimes can be picked out in a flying flock of small waders by its soft call. Often feeds with dunlins, but wades further out into deeper water up to its belly. In flight, its white rump is obvious during banking or landing. As its name suggests, the bill is relatively long and downcurved, recalling that of a curlew.

- *Flying birds show a prominent square white rump and a short-tailed, long-winged shape. A clear white wingbar.*
- *Like tall, long-legged dunlin with longer, downturned bill. On juveniles, note pale stripe over eye. Scaly back and pink-buff breast.*

LENGTH: 18–23CM **WEIGHT:** 55–70G **WHERE
TO LOOK:** MAINLY COASTAL LAGOONS AND
MUDDY ESTUARIES; SOME INLAND. MOST IN
AUTUMN. DOES NOT BREED IN UK. **FOOD:**
WIDE RANGE OF INVERTEBRATES, ESPECIALLY
WORMS **VOICE:** A GENTLE RIPPLING *CHIRRUP*

Purple Sandpiper
CALIDRIS MARTIMA

LENGTH: 20–22CM **WEIGHT:** 55–80G **WHERE TO LOOK:** ROCKY COASTS ESPECIALLY IN THE NORTH-EAS; OFTEN ON PIERS AND HARBOURS **NEST:** ON GROUND IN MOORLAND **EGGS:** 3–4, BUFF, BLOTCHED BROWN **FOOD:** SMALL MARINE INVERTEBRATES **VOICE:** LOW, SINGLE OR DOUBLE *WHIT*

Superb camouflage helps the purple sandpiper to merge perfectly into a background of dark, wet, seaweed-covered rocks. This habitat is preferred, but in many areas artificial structures such as groynes, piers or outer harbour walls hold small flocks. In total about 16,000 spend the winter in Britain, with the great majority on the flat rocky coasts of Shetland, Orkney, eastern Scotland and north-east England. Britain's birds come from breeding areas in Norway and, probably, Greenland. Most arrive in October and November. There have been up to three pairs breeding in Scotland since 1979, making a welcome addition to the list of breeding birds. Relying on their camouflage, they allow a very close approach. They are so tame that their behaviour can be studied in detail as they peck among the seaweed, taking many small periwinkles and a range of other invertebrates. Early in the winter juveniles can be identified by buff edges to the upperwing feathers. Females have noticeably longer bills than males, and there may be tiny differences in the way they feed.

■ *Dark in flight; neat white wingbar and sides of rump stand out. Tends to fly low over the water.*
■ *Chunky and neckless; slate-brown with pale chin, eye-ring and belly. Bill drooping.*
■ *Most often found in small flocks, feeding inconspicuously near the tide line. Very easy to overlook.*
■ *Pale, yellowish legs characteristic.*

Turnstone
ARENARIA INTERPRES

Although most abundant on the rocky coasts favoured by purple sandpipers, turnstones are also frequently seen on mussel beds, rocky outcrops or even shingle beaches where drifts of seaweed occur. They are very scarce inland, even when migrating. The birds seen in Britain are from two distinct areas – Scandinavia and Greenland/Canada. Those from Scandinavia pass through in autumn and spring on their way to and from wintering grounds in central and southern Africa, while the Canada/Greenland birds mostly spend the winter in Europe. About 45,000 of these remain in Britain. Turnstones are aptly named, for with their strong bills and necks they move stones, lifting up patches of seaweed or digging furiously in sand; the invertebrates there dash for cover, but are rapidly caught. In addition, many small periwinkles are eaten and limpets prised off rocks. Turnstone camouflage is excellent and thus feeding birds are confident and can be very approachable. In breeding plumage, males have much more white on the head than females. Occasionally pairs may breed in Scotland, but turnstones have not colonised Britain.

Summer plumage

Winter plumage

LENGTH: 21–25CM **WEIGHT:** 80–150G **WHERE TO LOOK:** ROCKY COASTS, OUTER PARTS OF ESTUARIES: RARELY INLAND. **NEST:** MOSTLY ON ARCTIC TUNDRA, MOORLAND **EGGS:** 4, GREEN, STREAKED BROWN **FOOD:** WIDE RANGE OF COASTAL INVERTEBRATES **VOICE:** CLEAR RATTLED *TRIK-TUK-TUK-TUK*

■ *Short chisel-shaped bill and orange legs. In summer, strikingly white-headed and chestnut-backed.*
■ *Sturdy and thickset; in winter, head dark, back brown and black.*

Snipe
GALLINAGO GALLINAGO

As the drainage of lowland grassland and its conversion to intensive agriculture has taken place, so the lowland populations of snipe have decreased substantially in Britain and elsewhere in Western Europe. Even so, taking into account the upland breeders, there are probably about 30,000 pairs remaining in Britain. In winter many more flood into the country, especially from Scandinavia and Iceland. Winter totals are not known, but must be much higher. Snipe love flooded grassland where worms have been forced to the surface, and where the ground is soft and there is plenty of vegetation to provide camouflage. In general they rely for protection on being hidden, but fly up if approached too closely. Sometimes they feed out on open mud beside reservoirs. In very cold winters most of their feeding grounds become unsuitable and then they can turn up in gardens, on roadsides and other unlikely places. Many die or become so weak that they can be caught by cats or hit by cars. A flock of snipe is given the collective name of a 'wisp', perhaps due to its rapid twisting and turning before the birds drop down again.

When feeding out in the open, snipe often look rather dark. Seen in good light, however, the plumage is an amazing mixture of brown, buff, black and white. Even among low vegetation, this affords the snipe exceptional camouflage.

■ *The long bill, almost twice the length of the strongly striped and mottled back, is a very distinctive feature.*

■ *Pale belly; the brown bill is darker at its tip; the legs are yellow or greyish-green.*

■ *On warm summer evenings the males dive in aerial displays; the outer tail feathers are spread and they vibrate to give a characteristic tremulous or drumming sound.*

■ *Appear to feed in small groups or singly, but camouflage is so effective they are difficult to see.*

■ *Feeding birds remain in the same spot, probing a small area rapidly. The bill is held vertically and inserted to its base. When disturbed the birds remain quite motionless, but alert.*

■ *Displaying birds often choose to stand on posts or lumps of soil and utter the distinctive* chipa-chipa *call note. Agitated adults with young will stand on posts, calling in alarm if danger is near. When flying up, parallel buff lines on the back are often noticeable. Thin white line along rear of wing; some white on the tail.*

■ *When flying high overhead looks rather jerky, with fast, flickering wing-beats. Wings are sharply pointed triangles; short tail; long bill held slightly angled down.*

LENGTH: 25–27CM **WEIGHT:** 90–150G **WHERE TO LOOK:** AROUND EDGES OF FRESHWATER AREAS WHERE MUD MEETS VEGETATION; MARSHES, WET FIELDS **NEST:** IN TUSSOCK OF GRASS OR RUSH IN WET MEADOWS, LINED WITH GRASS **EGGS:** 4, OLIVE, BLOTCHED BROWN **FOOD:** MOSTLY WORMS; INSECT LARVAE, OTHER INVERTEBRATES **VOICE:** HARSH *SCAAP* WHEN STARTLED

Woodcock
SCOLOPAX RUSTICOLA

Relying on camouflage, remaining still until almost trodden on, this bird is rarely seen unless driven into the open by severe weather, but it is worth a look at dusk at the edge of a wood on a fine spring evening. Then you may see its distinctive roding flights, and hear its strange calls. If put up, the large size, broad wings, rusty colour and noisy wing-beats make identification easy as the bird flies fast through the trees; the long bill and dark crown bars are distinctive if seen.

Up to 40,000 pairs breed, in both coniferous and broadleaved woods, and many more come to Britain from Western Europe in November and December.

If you are lucky enough to watch a bird feeding, in a boggy glade or in damp leaf litter, it has a peculiar to-and-fro rocking action with the head kept remarkably still. The woodcock has a most extraordinary and endearing habit – the adult flies with small young held between its legs when danger threatens. Several trips are needed to move a whole family to safety.

■ *Large, dark brown; long bill.*

LENGTH: 33–35CM **WEIGHT:** 290–320G **WHERE TO LOOK:** PUT UP FROM GROUND IN WOODS, BUT EASIEST IN SPRING DISPLAY FLIGHT OVER TREES. **NEST:** ON GROUND **EGGS:** 3–5, BLOTCHED BROWN **FOOD:** WORMS, INSECTS, GRUBS **VOICE:** SHARP *PITZ* OR *TSWIK* ALTERNATING WITH DEEP CROAK

Adult male

Jack Snipe
LYMNOCRYPTES MINIMUS

Although widely distributed, this small snipe is scarce and very difficult to see. It may be picked out when feeding among snipe or in vegetation by its remarkable up-and-down rhythmical bounding action, which is quite unlike any other species. Why it does this is not known. Otherwise it is only flushed from wet marshland when almost trodden on. Occasionally one may be seen flattened against the ground just in front of the advancing boot! If a good view is obtained, look for the dark centre to the crown and the dark, purple-tinged back. Birds arrive in Britain in late autumn from their Scandinavian breeding grounds and return during early spring. Considering how weak its flight appears to be when flushed, it is remarkable that it undertakes quite substantial migrations each year. Perhaps one summer a pair will remain to breed in Britain.

■ *Bill is short, just longer than the striped head. No white in tail.*
■ *A small snipe: when flushed it shows prominent, pale buff lines in the very dark, glossy back.*
■ *Flushes from underfoot and drops back into cover very quickly.*
■ *Relies on keeping very still and its almost perfect camouflage.*

LENGTH: 17–19CM **WEIGHT:** 40–70G **WHERE TO LOOK:** IN MARSHY AREAS WHEN SMALL WET, OPEN PATCHES ARE FOUND AMONG VEGETATION. DOES NOT BREED IN BRITAIN. **FOOD:** MOSTLY INVERTEBRATES, MANY WORMS. **VOICE:** NORMALLY SILENT IN BRITAIN, BUT SOMETIMES A WEAK *GAH* WHEN FLUSHED.

Black-tailed Godwit
LIMOSA LIMOSA

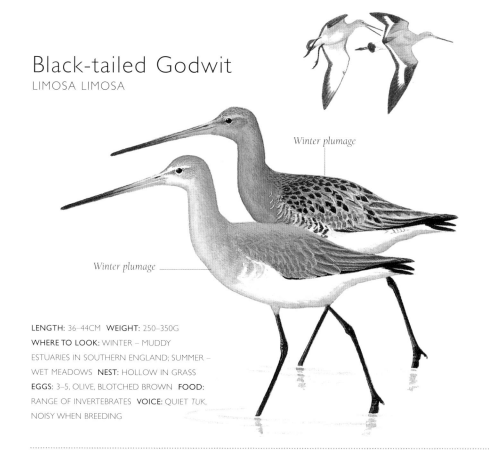

Winter plumage

Winter plumage

LENGTH: 36–44CM **WEIGHT:** 250–350G
WHERE TO LOOK: WINTER – MUDDY
ESTUARIES IN SOUTHERN ENGLAND; SUMMER –
WET MEADOWS **NEST:** HOLLOW IN GRASS
EGGS: 3–5, OLIVE, BLOTCHED BROWN **FOOD:**
RANGE OF INVERTEBRATES **VOICE:** QUIET *TUK*,
NOISY WHEN BREEDING

The outer third of the bill of the black-tailed godwit is packed with sensory cells, enabling it to follow underground movements of its prey. In any flock, some birds will be resting their bills on the surface while others will probe deeply. Another characteristic feeding action is seen in shallow lagoons, where the head is thrown back quickly to swallow items caught under the surface. Only 30–40 pairs breed in Britain, nearly all on wet meadow nature reserves such as the Ouse Washes in Cambridgeshire. When breeding, they have a complex aerial display and are very vocal with loud, nasal, slightly harsh *grutto-grutto* and *wicka-wicka* calls. Recolonisation of Britain took place in 1952, but despite optimism its hold is still precarious. Winter numbers have increased greatly over the last 50 years, but have remained at about 4,800 since 1970. The wintering birds breed in Iceland and form a distinct race. Birds breeding in Scotland also belong to this race, but those in eastern England are from the European continental race; these migrate to Africa for the winter.

■ *Neck and breast red in summer; flanks barred, belly white.*
■ *Winter birds have an even, brown-grey wash to the back and breast; stripe over eye distinct.*
■ *In flight, a solid black band at the end of the white tail is distinctive.*

Bar-tailed Godwit
LIMOSA LAPPONICA

There tends to be a clear separation in habitats used by the two godwit species. The bar-tailed is found in sandier areas, while the black-tailed will be inland or on muddier sections. The largest bar-tailed flocks are on major estuaries such as The Wash or Morecambe Bay, where they gather on sand flats rich in lugworms. They scan the surface looking for worms coming up to make their distinctive coiled casts, and then they probe deeply to catch them before they withdraw out of reach. Flocks are often at the tide edge, where lugworm activity is greatest. One of the spectacular sights of migration is of bar-tailed godwits sweeping east along the coast of south-east England during late April. The dark, brick-red males with their relatively short bills can be picked out from the long-billed females, which have only a tinge of red on their underparts. These birds have come from wintering grounds in West Africa and are on their way to breeding areas in arctic Scandinavia and Siberia. British wintering birds breed there as well and arrive in Britain in October and November. When coming in to roost they often plummet down, twisting and turning as they drop to the sand in an action called 'whiffling'.

LENGTH: 37–41CM **WEIGHT:** 200–350G
WHERE TO LOOK: LARGE SANDY AREAS,
MAINLY ON ESTUARIES. DOES NOT BREED IN
UK **FOOD:** MANY COASTAL INVERTEBRATES,
MAINLY LUGWORMS **VOICE:** A LOW
BARKING *KIRRUC-KIRRUC*

Male's summer plumage

Winter plumage

■ *Summer plumage is distinctive. In winter, upperparts are streaked grey and brown; breast is grey or buff and finely streaked. Stripe over the eye indistinct. Looks chunky.*
■ *Flying birds show white 'V' up back and pale tail; no white wingbar.*

Curlew
NUMENIUS ARQUATA

The curlew's bubbling song, given mainly during the hanging display flight, seems to express the nature of the lonely, open spaces where it breeds. Most of Britain's 35,000 pairs nest in the north and west, where some are under pressure from modern agricultural methods. Many of the birds that breed in Britain move to Ireland and France for the winter, while British estuaries are filled with 91,000 birds, which breed mainly in Scandinavia. These immigrants start arriving very early in the season; it is not unusual for the first birds to be back by August. When feeding, they take a wide range of invertebrates: inland, earthworms are favoured, but on mussel beds and rocky coasts it is not unusual to see them eating small crabs. They break off the legs before swallowing them. High-tide roosts are formed on salt marshes or on fields, but as the species is very wary, they are easily disturbed.

LENGTH: 50–60CM **WEIGHT:** 700–1,000G **WHERE TO LOOK:** ESTUARIES AND COASTAL MEADOWS IN WINTER. SUMMER – MOORS, FARMLAND EDGE **NEST:** GRASSY, HOLLOW **EGGS:** 3–5, SPOTTED **FOOD:** WIDE RANGE OF INVERTEBRATES **VOICE:** MELODIC *CUR-LEE*; BUBBLING SONG

■ *Very long, gently down-turned bill is unmistakable. A very large brown and buff streaked wader. Bland face pattern with no eye stripe.*
■ *In flight, large white 'V' on back. Leisurely flight action.*

Whimbrel
NUMENIUS PHAEOPUS

LENGTH: 40–46CM **WEIGHT:** 350–450G **WHERE TO LOOK:** ON MIGRATION WET MEADOWS, SALT MARSHES **NEST:** PARTLY LINED HOLLOW **EGGS:** 3–4, OLIVE, BLOTCHED **FOOD:** MOSTLY INVERTEBRATES; BERRIES IN SUMMER **VOICE:** MAINLY A RIPPLING *BIBIBIBIBIBIBI*

The motto for the whimbrel could be 'Heard before seen' – its characteristic rippling note carries a long way and is given frequently. One of its colloquial names is the 'seven whistler', as the single note is often given about seven times. Just to create some confusion, it also gives a *cur-lee* reminiscent of a curlew's call. A very small breeding population of about 400 pairs is found in northernmost Scotland; there the bubbling display song, recalling the curlew, can be heard. However, over most of Britain it is a relatively scarce migrant. Small flocks, rarely more than 50, may be encountered on the edges or seen flying along the coast. The speed of the wing-beats is closer to that of a godwit than of the slower curlew. April and early May is when spring migration is at its peak. Some birds stop on coastal grassland at night. One spectacular flock of over 1,000 birds builds up on Stert Island, in Bridgwater Bay, Somerset. These are on the way from sub-Saharan Africa to breed in Iceland; Scandinavian breeders pass through eastern Britain. They are not familiar birds to most birdwatchers, but at the right time on suitable coasts are not particularly rare.

■ *Like a dark curlew but smaller, with a shorter, more sharply down-turned bill. Head pattern distinctive, with prominent pale stripe over eye between two dark stripes. Narrow crown stripe.*
■ *Flying birds usually give distinctive rippling calls.*
■ *White 'V' on back clear in flight. Beats wings faster than a curlew.*
■ *General colour a dark oily brown, lightly spotted above. Seen in small parties.*

Redshank
TRINGA TOTANUS

Adult

Juvenile

LENGTH: 27–29CM **WEIGHT:** 100–160G **WHERE TO LOOK:** WINTER – MUDDY AND SANDY COASTS; SUMMER – WET MEADOWS, MARSHES **NEST:** LINED CUP IN TUSSOCK, WELL HIDDEN **EGGS:** 3–5, VARIABLE COLOUR, SPOTTED; APRIL–MAY **FOOD:** CREATURES FROM MUD **VOICE:** LOUD *TEU-HU-HU*

The title 'Sentinel of the Marshes' is most apt for this widespread, wary and noisy wader as it flies off yelling a warning to other birds. On the face of it, this is an adaptable species, being found on all types of coasts and on inland marshes in winter. However, though 75,000 still winter in Britain, the numbers have been dropping. Many that have bred in Britain remain for the winter (although often their young move down to southern Europe) and are joined by birds that breed in Iceland.

Most of the time redshanks feed on small shrimps, snails and worms found in the surface, but they will take a very wide variety of food. A rhythmical, even-paced walk with steady pecks is the typical and instinctive feeding action. By April, most of the British birds are back on their breeding territories. About 32,000 pairs breed in Britain, the favoured habitats being estuarine salt marshes, wet meadows and rough pastures. Drainage of inland wetlands poses problems for inland breeders.

The song, given in a hanging flight, on quivering wings, echoes beautifully over the marshes – but noisy alarm calls have a hysterical ring to them as redshanks dive at potential predators.

▨ *Bright-red legs characteristic. Bold dark spots in summer.*
▨ *Brownish-grey wash to upperparts; little sign of pale stripe over eye.*
▨ *In flight, striking white rear edge to dark wings, distinctive white 'V' on the back..*
Calls loudly.

Spotted Redshank
TRINGA ERYTHROPUS

This slim, active wader has many techniques for capturing its prey. At times it resembles a redshank, steadily walking and pecking at surface items; its gait is jerkier yet it seems to peck more delicately. At other times it forms lively parties, and group members seem to chase food items in almost exact unison. The bird usually wades in fairly deep water, but often swims, almost up-ending like a dabbling duck. Only about 1,000 can be found in Britain during the main migration period – July to September – and about 100 stay for the winter, nearly all in Wales and in the southern half of England. Despite its scarcity, migrants can be found on many estuaries and inland; they are usually first noted by the distinctive, clear *chu-it* call. Stunning in velvety black summer plumage, they are worth seeking in late June on the east coast.

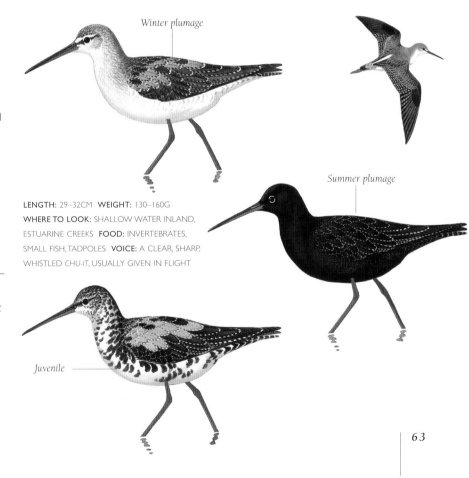

Winter plumage

Summer plumage

Juvenile

LENGTH: 29–32CM **WEIGHT:** 130–160G **WHERE TO LOOK:** SHALLOW WATER INLAND, ESTUARINE CREEKS **FOOD:** INVERTEBRATES, SMALL FISH, TADPOLES **VOICE:** A CLEAR, SHARP, WHISTLED *CHU-IT*, USUALLY GIVEN IN FLIGHT

▨ *Taller and more slender than the redshank, longer legs and a much longer, thinner tipped bill. Feeds with a jerkier action. Red legs darker than redshank's in summer; scarlet in winter.*
▨ *In flight, shows a long white oval up the back; no wingbar, long thin shape.*
▨ *Winter birds are white below, mid-grey above, with pale stripe over eye.*

Greenshank
TRINGA NEBULARIA

The loud, clear trisyllabic call draws attention to the greenshank, for these notes penetrate through other wader calls. In flight it gives the impression of being rather thick-set compared with similar species. Perhaps as many as 1,500 pairs breed in Britain, but they are restricted to northern Scotland, and choose some of the most beautiful, yet wildest, countryside. In winter up to 400 remain here, almost all on the western coasts, with at least as many again in Ireland. They are scattered in small muddy estuaries or on sea-lochs. For most of the time birds feed with a fairly steady, elegant walk, pecking at the surface, but at times they chase small fish in shallow water, running erratically with the bill held slightly open. The largest numbers are found in autumn, when Scandinavian migrants pass through to Africa. In winter, greenshank are mostly solitary, although they may form loose and temporary association with others of their kind.

LENGTH: 30–34CM WEIGHT: 170–200G
WHERE TO LOOK: PEAT BOGS, LAKES
ESTUARIES NEST: HOLLOW ON GROUND
EGGS: 3–4, OLIVE, SPOTTED DARK;
MAY–JUNE FOOD: WORMS, FISH VOICE: A
RINGING *TU-TU-TU*

- *Very dark wings and contrasting white blaze up the back. Noisy.*
- *Solid, upcurved bill; longish green legs distinctive.*
- *Summer birds with dark spotting on breast; heavily streaked head.*
- *Very white in winter and pale grey upperparts. Active feeder.*

Ruff
PHILOMACHUS PUGNAX

Juvenile

Male's summer plumage

Adult female

LENGTH: 26–32CM WEIGHT: 75–200G WHERE
TO LOOK: EDGES OF LAKES, SHALLOW,
FLOODED GRASSLAND; IN SUMMER – WET
MEADOWS NEST: IN GRASS TUSSOCK EGGS:
3–4, GREY-GREEN, BOLDLY SPOTTED; MAY–JUNE
FOOD: SMALL INVERTEBRATES

Britain is on the western edge of the breeding range of the ruff, and fewer than ten pairs breed in Britain each year, mainly on wet meadows in East Anglia. The males' communal dancing display (called lekking) is a complex ritual carried out on traditional leks (display grounds). Females watch and then choose with which male to mate. They then depart and bring up the young alone. The ruff is unusual not only in its display, but also in appearance. In many ways (size, shape, feeding action) it resembles a redshank, but it is actually more closely related to the dunlin. In the autumn, migrants from Scandinavia and Russia pass through Britain, some staying for the winter. About 1,500 remain, most on the Ouse Washes, and at Pagham Harbour, in Sussex. However, several million winter south of the Sahara in Africa. Interestingly, most wintering in Britain are males, but in Africa most are the smaller females.

- *An unusually shaped bird. Long legs but shortish, slightly down-curved bill. Head seems too small for the longish neck. Usually has pot-bellied, hump-backed shape.*
- *In summer, males are extraordinary, with huge variably coloured ruffs and head tufts. Main colours are white, chestnut-brown and purplish-black. Legs of adults are reddish. Ritualised display at lek.*
- *Juveniles have strongly washed, deep-buff underparts; the upperparts look neatly scaled with pale feathers. Bland face and greenish legs.*
- *Males are very much larger than females; the sexes can be told apart easily when in mixed flocks.*

Common Sandpiper
ACTITIS HYPOLEUCOS

LENGTH: 19–21CM **WEIGHT:** 40–60G **WHERE TO LOOK:**
SUMMER – UPLAND RIVERS, LAKESIDES; PASSAGE – WATER EDGE
ANYWHERE **NEST:** HIDDEN IN HOLLOW NEAR WATER **EGGS:**
3–5, BUFF, DARK SPOTS; MAY–JUNE **FOOD:** INVERTEBRATES
VOICE: NOISY; A THIN, PIPING, PENETRATING *TSE-WE-WEE*

The rhythmical, bobbing walk makes the common sandpiper one of the most distinctive small waders. It feeds along the edge of lakes, rivers, even sea-lochs and rocky shores. Food is usually pecked from the surface of the mud, but sometimes the bird can be watched stalking insects with its head held horizontally and slowly extended before giving a sudden snap to catch the prey. The bird is nearly always found singly or in very small groups. Many are seen on migration, especially in autumn, but only about 50 spend the winter in Britain, mainly in south-western Britain; most migrate to sub-Saharan Africa. Breeding birds are found in upland areas of Wales, northern England and Scotland, and about 18,500 pairs breed in Britain. The flickering, down-curved wings, combined with the penetrating whistled call, given almost continuously in flight, are distinctive.

▓ *A horizontal wader with a long tail and short, straight bill. Walks with strong bobbing action.*
▓ *Slight stripe over eye, and glossy green-brown above in summer.*
▓ *In flight, dark with white wingbar; flies on strongly bowed, stiff wings.*

Red-necked Phalarope
PHALAROPUS LOBATUS

Sadly, the beautifully marked red-necked phalarope is now very rare in Britain, with only 30 pairs breeding, all in the far north of Scotland where they seek out well-vegetated lochans. A few appear at other times, mainly in eastern England after north-east winds in autumn. Huge flocks gather in winter in the Arabian Sea, and it is probably there that the British breeding birds go. It is an unusually late migrant in spring, with few arriving before June; most return from late July onwards. Most sex roles are reversed; it is the male who incubates the eggs and looks after the chicks, so he is less brightly marked and better camouflaged than the female. Juveniles and summer-plumaged birds have characteristic golden lines down the back, but in winter plumage that are very like grey phalaropes. Subtle points such as bill shape, body size, flight action and call need to be assessed. The bird is very approachable.

▓ *Breeding adult has red and grey neck, and white chin. Female is brighter than the male.*
▓ *Very thin, black bill; small size. Autumn young (left) show thin, golden edges on the dark back feathers.*

Grey Phalarope
PHALAROPUS FULICARIUS

Grey phalaropes are very similar to red-necks in juvenile and winter plumages. Note the stocky appearance and thicker, shorter bill, often a little yellow at the base.

Summer plumage

LENGTH: 18–19CM; **WEIGHT:** 30–40G **WHERE TO LOOK:** A VERY FEW BREED ON POOLS IN NORTHERN SCOTLAND; COASTAL POOLS IN AUTUMN. **NEST:** IN GRASS BY WATER. **EGGS:** 3–4, BUFF, BLOTCHED BROWN; JUNE. **FOOD:** INVERTEBRATES. **VOICE:** FAIRLY LOW-PITCHED *TWIT.*

Green Sandpiper
TRINGA OCHROPUS

LENGTH: 21-24CM **WEIGHT:** 60-100G **WHERE TO LOOK:** BY EDGES OF INLAND WATERS, IN WINTER SOME ON ESTUARY CREEKS. DOES NOT BREED IN BRITAIN **FOOD:** MOSTLY INSECTS, OTHER INVERTEBRATES **VOICE:** A RAPID HIGH-WHISTLED *TUWIT-WIT-WIT*

A dark wader with white underparts, seen walking steadily in shallow water inland, is most likely to be a green sandpiper, for they are widely distributed across Britain during late summer and autumn. Nowhere do flocks of more than 30 appear, but in autumn the total number in Britain may be as high as 2,000. When feeding, they walk steadily, pecking at surface items, but with an occasional bob; if agitated they will bob vigorously before dashing away, calling very positively. In flight, the black lining to the wings is an instant identification feature; the flight itself is very snipe-like with sharp flicks of the wings. Green sandpipers are often picked up by their calls when flying high overhead.

Between 200 and 300 remain for the winter, most having departed for Africa. In Britain, they seek freshwater springs, chalk streams, or where rivers enter inner estuaries; all places where water rarely freezes. They have only bred twice in Britain. When breeding they seek old nests in trees, the young having to leap to the ground. They migrate back very early, and by late June many autumn passage birds are already in Britain; they seek the rich mud of sewage farms or reservoirs.

▓ *Relatively bulky for a smallish wader; always very dark above and white below. Small, white stripe in front of the white eye-ring. Legs dull; often bobs.*

▓ *Mid-brown above; square white rump. Feet extend past tail.*

▓ *In summer, stripe over eye distinctly white. Bird rather greyish, with large white and brown speckles. Bars usually distinct on flanks.*

▓ *Juveniles are warm brown above with bright buff spots and buff wash to finely-streaked breast.*

Wood Sandpiper
TRINGA GLAREOLA

LENGTH: 19–21CM **WEIGHT:** 55–80G **WHERE TO LOOK:** EDGES
OF LAKES AND POOLS, FLOODS **NEST:** ON GROUND AMONG
SPARSE TREES, SOMETIMES IN OLD NESTS IN TREES **EGGS:** 4,
BUFFISH, BOLDLY SPOTTED: MAY–JUNE **FOOD:** INVERTEBRATES
VOICE: HIGH, THIN *CHIFF-IFF-IFF*

This is one of the species to seek out in the eastern counties of Britain, for it is very scarce on the west coast. Small numbers are seen in August and September, with most appearing on the east winds that have blown them across from Scandinavian breeding grounds. Although resembling a green sandpiper, redshank or ruff, the yellowish legs, pale stripe over the eye and the slim, neat shape help to separate it.

Normally, wood sandpipers eat small invertebrates, but just occasionally are galvanised into action by tiny fish. Most of the time they wade in shallow water, especially where low vegetation is emerging, and walk steadily, pecking from the surface. They are quite wary and fly away rapidly, climbing quickly with peevish calls. Nearly all spend the winter in Africa, south of the Sahara. In spring, few are seen on passage and fewer than ten pairs remain to breed in Scotland. Here they give the melodic whistled song, delivered in a wing-quivering display flight, which is interspersed by glides on down-curved wings. Like many other waders nesting in wet, open woodland, they frequently perch in trees but are remarkably elusive.

Relatively slim and delicate for a medium-sized sandpiper; bill straight and rather short; legs longish, especially above the knee. Bobs less than its relatives.
Mid-brown above: square white rump. Feet extend past tail.
In summer, the stripe over the eye is distinctly white. Bird rather greyish, with large white and brown speckles. Bars usually distinct on flanks.
Juveniles are warm brown above with bright buff spots and a buff wash to finely streaked breast.

Great Skua
STERCORARIUS SKUA

Raised wing pose

LENGTH: 53–58CM **WEIGHT:** 1,300–2,000G
WHERE TO LOOK: AT SEA AND ON COASTAL
MOORS IN FAR NORTH **NEST:** ON GROUND
EGGS: 2, BLOTCHED DARK BROWN **FOOD:**
MAINLY FISH STOLEN FROM OTHER BIRDS; ALSO
BIRDS AND EGGS **VOICE:** RATHER QUIET CALLS
IN COLONY; SILENT AT SEA

Often called 'bonxies', the traditional Shetlanders' name, great skuas are not easy to see in the south, though they are relatively familiar in northern coastal waters and from eastern headlands in autumn. Shetland had 10 pairs in 1774, but that number had actually declined by the 1860s. However, with protection they survived, and birds spread to Orkney in 1915, the Outer Hebrides in 1945 and a few to mainland Scotland from 1949. There are now over 5,400 pairs in Shetland alone. Great skuas chase seabirds and terrify them into disgorging food, which they then eat. They also kill many birds in summer and are especially fond of immature kittiwakes, which often breed close to the skuas themselves. They are bold enough to bring down a gannet, and aggressive enough to dive at humans (and sheep), with repeated headlong rushes that sometimes end with a severe clout from the bonxie's feet – so they are not popular with crofters! After breeding, they leave for the mid-Atlantic and South American and West African coasts. Three-year-olds disperse most, spending summer far to the north; by five years old they are more attached to the colony and travel less widely in winter.

- *A heavy, gull-like bird; broad wings with big flashes of white visible at a great distance; may look more or less tawny or paler around neck.*
- *Raised wing pose used to display and aggressive encounters.*
- *Chases many seabirds; can kill gulls and auks.*
- *Stout, hooded, dark bill; triangular, capped head.*

Arctic Skua
STERCORARIUS PARASITICUS

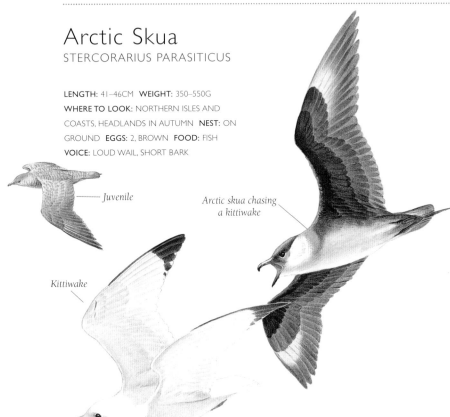

Juvenile

Kittiwake

Arctic skua chasing a kittiwake

LENGTH: 41–46CM **WEIGHT:** 350–550G
WHERE TO LOOK: NORTHERN ISLES AND
COASTS, HEADLANDS IN AUTUMN **NEST:** ON
GROUND **EGGS:** 2, BROWN **FOOD:** FISH
VOICE: LOUD WAIL, SHORT BARK

Lazily drifting over the sea, well offshore, the dark shape of the arctic skua suddenly raises its tempo, accelerating in pursuit of a tern, which it then harries relentlessly, following each desperate twist, until the tern drops a fish. Few birds have the exciting aura about them that this skua has, and few have such elegance of form. Arctics are far more widespread in northern parts of the world than great skuas, but only about 2,500 pairs breed in Britain, 1,600 of these in Shetland. In winter they go as far as South Africa. Arctic skuas chase terns, kittiwakes and puffins, whereas great skuas chase mostly guillemots and gannets. Nearly half their attacks on terns end in success, whereas a far smaller proportion of chases after larger birds yield food, so most skuas prefer to follow the terns in autumn. This takes them into the North Sea rather than south along the Atlantic coasts, where terns are fewer. They kill fewer birds than great skuas, but human intruders at the nest are equally likely to be attacked in fast, elegant, swooping dives at the head, though contact is rarely made.

- *Pale adult has a dark cap, white belly and often a slight breast band, dark phase uniform brown. All show wing flashes and tail spike. Immature birds are warm brown with paler bars, buffish wing patches and short tail projection.*
- *Chases and parasitizes other seabirds such as this kittiwake, forcing them to regurgitate food.*
- *In calm weather it has a direct flight, easy and relaxed; in wind glides and tilts it resembles the shearwater; at colonies great heights are often reached.*

Black-headed Gull
LARUS RIDIBUNDUS

LENGTH: 34–37CM WEIGHT: 200–300G
WHERE TO LOOK: ALMOST ANYWHERE NEST:
ON ISLAND OR BY POOL, FROM COAST TO
UPLAND MOORS EGGS: 2–3, BLOTCHED,
BROWN OR BLUE FOOD: WORMS, GRUBS, FISH,
SCRAPS VOICE: LONG SQUEALING CALLS;
SHORT, REPEATED YAPPING NOTES

Whether flying from a nest in a marsh to protest noisily at intrusion, following a plough to snap up worms, stealing bits of sandwich at the seaside or dipping into the fountain in Trafalgar Square, the black-headed gull is almost everywhere. A long drive in winter shows that it is one of the few birds so obvious in the landscape that it cannot be missed – gleaming white flocks in fields or thousands of them scrambling for food at rubbish tips catch the eye a mile away. Many breed inland, though the largest colonies are on coastal marshes and they are common on beaches all year round. Consequently, while many live on worms from the fields, others have a diet of fish scraps from harbours, all kinds of edible refuse from tips, and whatever awful food they get from sewage outflows. Britain's breeding population is much higher than a century ago, perhaps up to 300,000 pairs, but in winter there may be three million of them – two-thirds from mainland Europe (especially the Baltic countries) and well over a million of the overall number living inland.

■ *Adults in winter have a dark spot behind the eye; bright red bill tipped black and bright red legs; unlike any other commonly seen gull.*

■ *Breeding adult has a dark brown hood and dark red legs and bill; white primaries tipped black.*

■ *Below the wings is a dark patch before a translucent stripe near the tip. Young birds have much more brown in the wing, with a dark trailing edge, but still have the blaze of white on the outer primaries and coverts that is so characteristic of black-headed gulls.*

■ *If you see a flock of gulls following a plough, the chances are they will be black-headed gulls. The species is an opportunistic and adaptable feeder.*

Little Gull
LARUS MINUTUS

Tiny gull; buoyant flight. Adult has jet-black head in summer; grey and white in winter. Upperwing grey with white border (some show small black marks at tip); underwing black with white rim.

Mediterranean Gull
LARUS MELANOCEPHALUS

Adult has pearly upperwing and eye-catching, white underwing; jet black hood, white eyelids, red bill in summer; ghostly pale, dusky mask, dark bill in winter.

Summer plumage

Winter plumage

Juvenile

Herring Gull
LARUS ARGENTATUS

LENGTH: 52–55CM **WEIGHT:** 750–1,200G **WHERE TO LOOK:**
CLIFFS, ALL KINDS OF COASTS, RESERVOIRS, TIPS, FARMLAND IN
WINTER **NEST:** ON GROUND, CLIFF LEDGE OR BUILDING **EGGS:**
3, SPOTTED BROWN **FOOD:** FISH, OFFAL, REFUSE, EGGS **VOICE:**
LOUD SQUEALING, WAILING AND LAUGHING NOTES; DEEP *KYOW-
YOW-YOW*, SHORT BARKS. YOUNG BIRDS HAVE THIN WHINE

The herring gull is so common and approachable that it is worth using as a standard against which to compare others. The plumage sequences can be worked out easily and, once the pearly grey begins to appear on the back, it is not hard to identify. Because young gulls are brown and get progressively paler as they mature, it is possible to work out their age much more easily than with most birds, the changing patterns being obvious at a glance. Larger, darker birds arrive in Britain in winter from northern Scandinavia (Britain's breeding birds are the smallest and palest in Europe) and on some southern coasts, dark-backed, white-headed, and yellow-legged birds from the Mediterranean can be found. These may even be of a different species, but the relationships of these large gulls are notoriously difficult to work out clearly. Winter flocks resting on fields or roosting on reservoirs are often wary and require care and patience for close views; quite unlike those that dive for scraps at your feet at any summer seaside resort, or wait in line on railings at fish quays, ready to pounce and fight for fish heads, guts or spilled herrings.

◼ *In its first year it is largely pale brown with dark tail and wing-tips.*
◼ *In its second year it begins to get pale grey back, whiter head and body, and a paler bill; in its third year it is more like adult.*
◼ *Adults are clean grey and white in summer with sharply defined black wing-tips spotted white; pink legs, unlike lesser black-back's.*
◼ *In winter, adults streaked with grey-brown on head and breast; darker-backed birds are frequent.*

First year   *Second year*   *Adult*

Iceland Gull
LARUS GLAUCOIDES

Adult very pale with
wing-tips all white. Young
birds pale, creamy fawn,
with wing-tips and tail palest.

Glaucous Gull
LARUS HYPERBOREUS

Adult looks like a large herring gull
with white patch at back. In its first
year it is neatly barred brown and
cream, wing-tips palest.

In its second year it is paler still and often fading to almost creamy white. Bill pale pink with sharp black tip in first year, not blended like Iceland Gull's; later losing black and gaining yellow. Flight relatively ponderous.

Great Black-backed Gull
LARUS MARINUS

LENGTH; 62–65CM WEIGHT: 1,500–2,000G WHERE TO LOOK: ROCKY COASTS, BEACHES IN WINTER, REFUSE TIPS AND NEARBY FIELDS, RESERVOIRS, HARBOURS NEST: PAD OF GREASES, IN HOLLOW ON CLIFFTOP EGGS: 3, BLOTCHY FOOD: OFFAL FISH, BIRDS, EGGS, DEAD ANIMALS AND RUBBISH VOICE: DEEPER VERSION OF HERRING GULL'S WAILS AND SQUEALS AND DEER BARKING *OWK, UK-UK-UK*

Characteristic of a windswept clifftop, under blue summer skies and surrounded by sea pink and campion, the great black-backed gull is one of Britain's most impressive birds, in a land of predominantly small species. It does not, however, meet with universal approval, especially as it may eat a puffin or be seen feeding on a dead sheep. Even in winter a marauding great black-back will swoop at flocks of teal and coots, and it is quite capable of swallowing a big rat or a rabbit whole!

A flock of gulls resting in a field – which they do for hours at a stretch even in the shortest days of winter – may look a motley bunch, but when a great black-back flies down it simply dwarfs the rest, like a great bomber among lightweight fighters. On water, it is clearly the battleship of the fleet! About 25,000 pairs breed in Britain. In the north of Scotland, flocks of hundreds bathe in coastal freshwater lochs and fly off to feed around passing trawlers. In winter it is very widespread, with over half of the European population on the shores of Britain, especially on the east coast.

▨ *This species is the biggest gull of all and the blackest on back; legs pale pink.*
▨ *In winter, adults stand out due to their size, white head and black back; young have a long black bill, a pale head and chequered upperparts.*
▨ *Male gulls are larger (with bill and head bigger) than females, but the plumages of both are alike.*
▨ *Larger size, leg colour and black (not dark grey) back and upperwing are the best distinguishing features from lesser black-backed gull.*

Lesser Black-backed Gull
LARUS FUSCUS

As a breeding bird, the lesser black-backed gull is best known on Welsh islands, northern moors and thickly-vegetated areas above cliffs; it is less of a cliff-ledge breeder than the herring gull and is more likely to be surrounded by bluebells and campion as it sits on its eggs. Many leave Britain in winter, though now thousands do stay to feed at Midland tips and to roost on large reservoirs. On most coasts it is simply a passage migrant. The summer adult, with soft slate-grey back, and legs and beak of vivid yellow, is a most handsome bird and an elegant addition to the summer coastal scene. Juvenile birds are very dark and black-billed; in the winter they have all-dark flight feathers, unlike young herring gulls, and by the following autumn they are dark grey on the back like their parents, though still brown-winged and with black tail bands. In winter, adults have grey-brown heads and much duller yellow legs. A few birds from the southern Baltic may be seen in autumn, recognisable by their long wings, blacker backs and unstreaked white heads.

LENGTH: 50–52CM WEIGHT: 600–1,000G WHERE TO LOOK: ISLANDS LAKES AND RESERVOIRS, COASTS, TIPS NEST: ON GROUND, ON ISLANDS AND MOORS, COLONIAL EGGS: 3, BLOTCHED BROWN FOOD: FISH, OFFAL, WORMS, EGGS, SEABIRDS VOICE: DEEPER, MORE THROATY CALLS THAN HERRING BULL, ABRUPT *OW-OW-OW, KYOWW*, LONGER WAILING NOTES AND SQUEALS

▨ *Slim and low slung; legs yellow; red ring round eye; spot on bill. Shows white patches during autumn moult.*
▨ *Slightly longer-winged than the herring gull. The best clue from beneath is darker primaries. Dark grey blends into blacker wing-tips above, with small white spots.*

Kittiwake
LARUS TRIDACTYLA

LENGTH: 38–40CM **WEIGHT:** 350–425G
WHERE TO LOOK: AT SEA; IN SUMMER ON
CLIFFS, BEACHES; IN WINTER, HARBOURS **NEST:**
ON SHEER CLIFF **EGGS:** 2, SPOTTED **FOOD:**
FISH, OFFAL FROM TRAWLERS – NOT A TIDELINE
SCAVENGER **VOICE:** QUIET MEW AND
RINGING *KITTI-WAY-AKE*

At any great seabird colony, the most numerous species is likely to be the kittiwake. Vast ranks of gleaming white birds on ridiculously tiny, precarious nests, and hundreds more wheeling over the sea, create an eye-catching spectacle and a great volume of noise, all the birds calling their name (or perhaps it's 'sorry I'm late') in yodelling, nasal tones. It seems unlikely that a kittiwake will be misidentified, even when it goes to bathe or find nesting material at a nearby lake. But, from time to time, kittiwakes are seen inland, usually adults in early spring, or immature birds in autumn or winter after gales, and they frequently pass headlands a long way offshore. The bounding, banking flight (if there is a good wind), the mid-grey back fading out towards the wing-tips, and protruding head and neck (looking brilliant white in summer) then make an adult identifiable a mile away – even if you cannot see the black legs and wing-tips that would confirm it. Real birds of the sea, kittiwakes – unlike many gulls – do not scrounge at refuse tips or feed on beaches.

■ *Black legs, yellow bill and 'dipped-in-ink' tips of wings identify adult; dark eyes and round shape give head a gentle expression.*
■ *Colonies found on sheer cliffs with nests on tiny ledges, often thousands of pairs; constant noise and activity make kittiwakes unmistakable.*

Common Gull
LARUS CANUS

Looking like a small, gentler version of the herring gull, the common gull is far less widespread as a nesting bird and only found over most of England and Wales outside the breeding season. It is not at all common in some inland areas, though often abundant on the coast and in some eastern counties, frequenting pastures and sports fields where flocks spread out in search of worms. They are now seen more often in towns and on housing estates in winter. The greenish legs and bill, with no red spot, confirm that an adult is no herring gull, though in practice even at long range the slim shape, dark eye and darker back give it a quite distinctive look. Young birds have neat and attractive bands of brown, pale-edged wing coverts, and at first a scaly brown back, but this turns grey by the autumn; by the following spring the grey is often darker than the sun-bleached wings, which can be almost cream-coloured with pale, brown tips (on a young Mediterranean gull the back is always very pale). In winter, the head and upper breast of adults are heavily soiled with grey-brown streaks.

LENGTH: 40–42CM **WEIGHT:** 350–450G
WHERE TO LOOK: LAKES, COASTS, FARMLAND,
RUBBISH TIPS **NEST:** ON GROUND NEAR
COAST OR ON MOOR **EGGS:** 3, BLOTCHED
OLIVE-BROWN **FOOD:** INSECTS, WORMS, FISH,
SCRAPS **VOICE:** HIGH, SQUEALING CALLS
SHRILLER THAN LARGER GULLS

■ *Wing-tips have large black and white patches, more black than herring gull beneath; fluent flight.*
■ *Smaller than herring gull, back a shade darker with bolder white patches; greenish bill and long wings.*

Sandwich Tern
STERNA SANDVICENSIS

LENGTH: 36–38CM WEIGHT: 210–250G WHERE TO LOOK: ALL COASTS; DUNES, COASTAL LAGOONS NEST: ON GROUND, SCRAPE IN SAND; IN LARGE COLONIES EGGS: 1–2, MOTTLED FOOD: SMALL FISH, SUCH AS SAND EELS VOICE: RASPING *KIERR-INK* OR *KIRRICK* IS DISTINCTIVE; SHORT *KIK*

The Sandwich tern is the largest of the terns found regularly in Britain, and when flying over the sea or standing on a beach is noticeably the palest. Its whiteness is the best identification feature, along with the yellow-tipped black bill. The rhythm of the quick, double, or nearly triple call in late March or early April is also an instant pointer that the first Sandwich terns are back after their long winter in West Africa. Most birds reared the previous summer will spend their first year of life in the winter quarters, sometimes as far as South Africa (even on the east coast). In 1962 nearly 6,000 pairs bred in Britain and Ireland, then the highest 20th-century figure, but since then numbers have increased and are now stable at around 15,000 pairs. They are greatly helped by protection of their colonies on coastal dunes and lagoons, though they have a tendency to shift site for no very obvious reason after several years. Like all terns, they seem highly-strung, unpredictable birds, quick to take alarm and easily disturbed by insensitive intruders.

- In direct flight, bill held level and wing-beats regular and strong; when fishing, looks down with bill pointing at water.
- Tail deeply forked, but streamers short. Wing-tips streaked with black, increasingly by autumn as paler grey gradually wears away.
- Large, angular, long-winged and short-tailed; very pale; purer white beneath than common or Arctic terns.
- Long, black bill with yellow tip unlike any other tern's; legs black; crested black cap.

Little Tern
STERNA ALBIFRONS

LENGTH: 25CM WEIGHT: 50–60G WHERE TO LOOK: SANDY AND PEBBLY COASTS, SHALLOW COASTAL LAGOONS NEST: ON GROUND, SAND OR SHINGLE EGGS: 2–3, BUFF WITH DARK SPOTS FOOD: SMALL FISH VOICE: FAST, CHATTERING *KIRRIKIKI*, HIGH, QUICK *KIK-KIK*, *KYIK*

The little tern was once Britain's rarest breeding sea-bird, and its position is still near the foot of the table, but with recent special protection measures its numbers have increased again to over 2,000 pairs. Because they like to nest on stretches of fine beach and shingle ridges, they are always subject to human disturbance in summer – people tend to like exactly the same beaches on a hot weekend – and many of their colonies have only succeeded after being roped off and dotted with polite 'Keep Out' notices. In general, people have responded well, but the other problem – unusually high tides sweeping away eggs and chicks – is not so easy to guard against. Some colonies have even become the target of kestrels, and few chicks have been reared. Little terns arrive in Britain in April and leave by September, going south to spend the winter in the rich fishing grounds along the West African coasts. There they join others from most European coasts and also inland breeders from parts of France, Spain, Italy and eastern Europe. As with other terns, the one-year-olds remain all year round in their southern quarters, enjoying the sun and surf.

- Yellow bill with very small black tip unlike any other tern's. Bill may show signs of black winter colour in autumn.
- Very pale except for strip of black along front of outer wing and black cap. Short yellow legs unique.
- Often dives into breaking waves right at edge of beach; likes shelving shingle beaches for fishing and nesting, but also breeds on sandier spots.

Common Tern
STERNA HIRUNDO

LENGTH: 32–33CM **WEIGHT:** 100–140G
WHERE TO LOOK: COASTS, LAKES **NEST:** ON
GROUND, OFTEN ON ISLAND **EGGS:** 3,
MOTTLED BUFFISH OR OLIVE **FOOD:** SMALL
FISH AND INSECTS FROM WATER SURFACE
VOICE: SHORT, SHARP *KIT, KIKIK*; HIGH, GRATING,
EMPHATIC *KEEY-YAH*

Arriving in April and leaving by October, the common tern is as much a harbinger of spring as the swallow. It is very widespread, but tends to be more southerly than the closely similar arctic tern, and is much more often seen inland, although arctic terns do move through Britain on migration in April and May and large numbers sometimes appear briefly at reservoirs. It is always as well to check a tern's identity carefully, but good views are needed to see the details of bill colour and wing translucency; the pattern of the upper wing is more useful. Young birds are sometimes easier to separate than adults. Common terns often swoop for insects when inland, but usually they catch fish, hovering before a headlong dive. Their dives are more hesitant than the plunges of arctic and Sandwich terns. A tern colony has an air of belligerence and hectic activity about it; intruders are spotted from afar and greeted with noisy swoops from the brave, offended birds. They mix elegance with pugnacity. They are easily disturbed and colonies should be left well alone, though those on offshore islands can often be watched from the shore with no risk of harm being done.

Colonies along the north Norfolk coast are among the largest and strongest in Britain. Visitors to Blakeney Point, for example, can see hundreds of birds, some nesting alongside little terns and black-headed gulls.

■ *Slender, with a black cap and forked tail; more buoyant and slower flight than gulls; slim, pointed bill.*
■ *By late autumn, the adults show a dark patch on front of wing, a white forehead and black bill.*
■ *Bill orange-red with black tip; rarely darker or without black.*
■ *Young bird is much shorter-tailed and blunter-winged than adult, and is much browner in appearance.*
■ *Juvenile bird has a pale orange bill with black tip; grey line near back of wing, so palest part is the centre.*
■ *Wing-tips more streaked than on arctic tern, especially in autumn.*
■ *Inner primaries paler than outer ones, with central dark streak or wedge often obvious – useful as this is not seen on arctic tern.*

Adult

Juvenile

Arctic Tern
STERNA PARADISAEA

LENGTH: 32–35CM **WEIGHT:** 80–110G **WHERE TO LOOK:** COASTS, ROCKY ISLANDS. ON MIGRATION IN SPRING MAY VISIT INLAND LAKES **NEST:** ON GROUND, ON ROCKS OR SHINGLY BEACH **EGGS:** 2, SPOTTED AND MOTTLED BROWN AND BLACK **FOOD:** SMALL FISH, ESPECIALLY SAND EELS **VOICE:** NASAL, GRATING *PEE-AIRR*, *KIK*, RISING *KEE KEE*, *KEEYAH*. COLONIES VERY NOISY

Few birds exceed the elegance of the arctic tern – yet few exceed its vehemence in defence of its eggs and chicks. For many people a memorable experience is a visit to the Farne Islands, where the terns are almost tame enough to be touched; yet, should someone venture too close to the colony, they are quite ready to dive down and draw blood with that dagger-like bill. A few pairs are scattered among nesting common terns on southern coasts, but most are in the innumerable small colonies, and a few very large ones, around the Scottish and Irish coasts, especially in Orkney and Shetland. For several years in the 1980s the largest Shetland colony failed to rear chicks due to a lack of sand eels of a suitable size to feed to them. Orkney colonies suffered a similar fate, but eventually had a good year to make up the losses. Arctic terns nest as far north as any bird, but move so far south that a few get caught up in the strong westerlies of the South Atlantic and end up in Australia. They undertake one of the most enormous migrations of any bird.

▪ *Summer adult has blood-red bill, a little shorter than common tern's and with no black tip; head smaller and more rounded, on short, thick neck. Wings longer and tapering to more pointed tip.*

▪ *Calls similar to the common tern's, but arctic has a more whistling, upward inflection to some notes at colony.*

▪ *All arctic tern's flight feathers are pale and translucent from below (not just a central patch), and the dark trailing edge is thin and tapered.*

Roseate Tern
STERNA DOUGALLII

LENGTH: 33–38CM **WEIGHT:** 95–130G **WHERE TO LOOK:** RARE AWAY FROM COLONIES ON ROCKY ISLETS **NEST:** IN HOLLOW, CREVICE, OR UNDER VEGETATION ON GROUND **EGGS:** 1 OR 2, CREAM, BLOTCHED DARKER **FOOD:** SMALL FISH **VOICE:** DISTINCT RASPING *AAKH* AND WHISTLED *CHIV-Y*, *CHEWIT*

The beautiful roseate tern is now very rare and the causes of its continued decline are not fully understood – which means that efforts to protect it are not always successful. Some – probably far too many – are killed in winter in Ghana, where small boys catch them in snares and with baited hooks on fishing lines. At the colonies in Britain they are killed by peregrines, foxes and rats. In Ireland some colonies have been deserted, for no clear reason. Yet there may be some other, unknown cause for a long-term decline in many parts of the wide range of this tern. It is a lovely bird, especially in spring, with extremely long tail streamers and a pink flush on the otherwise very white underparts. The very pale back and whiteness of its breast help to distinguish individuals in mixed tern flock. Bill colour (though with nearly as much bright red as a common tern's in late summer), flight action, wing pattern and other subtle differences also help to confirm the identity of an adult. Juveniles are coarsely marked and have dark foreheads, black bills and black legs.

▪ *Bill black in spring, dark red at base in summer, then half red.*

▪ *Long bill, round head and long tail give recognisable profile.*

▪ *Shape similar to Sandwich tern, with long bill and black cap smoothed down over nape, rather chesty appearance – subtly different.*

▪ *Shorter, blunter wings than common or Arctic terns; flight action quicker and stiffer, with fast hover almost like little tern. Wing-tip has blackish marks on top, but a white edge (no black) beneath – unlike common or Arctic terns.*

Guillemot
URIA AALGE

LENGTH: 38–41CM **WEIGHT:** 750–1,000G **WHERE TO LOOK:**
CLIFFS AND SEA AT BREEDING COLONIES (MARCH TO JULY);
OTHERWISE OUT TO SEA **NEST:** ON CLIFF LEDGES, LESS OFTEN
AMONG BOULDERS **EGGS:** 1, EXTREMELY VARIABLE COLOURS
FOOD: MAINLY FISH **VOICE:** PROLONGED WHIRRING *AAARGH*

White 'spectacles'

Guillemots usually nest on narrow, densely packed ledges in colonies sometimes numbering tens of thousands of birds. The ledges are often so densely occupied that birds may be in physical contact with several neighbours, thereby defending the smallest-known nest area territory of any bird.

The guillemot's egg is perfectly designed for the bird's precarious nest site. It is pointed at one end, rounded at the other and rather flat-sided. If it rolls, it tends to do so in a circle, thereby avoiding the danger of rolling off the cliff.

The colonies are all action, the birds noisy and aggressive, stabbing at neighbours with their dagger-like bills. This appears vicious, but they seldom seem to be injured. In contrast, paired birds commonly preen their partner's head and neck feathers most delicately (this is called allopreening). Like razorbills, guillemots are strong, but not agile, fliers and are superbly adapted for life in the sea. Underwater they are strong swimmers, propelled by feet and wings, and capable of diving to depths of over 50 metres. Like razorbills, the largest colonies are in northern Britain, particularly in Scotland. The numbers of birds have increased at many northern and eastern colonies, but the western colonies have shown little change. In the smaller colonies in the south, the declines recorded earlier this century appear to have halted. The breeding population of Britain and Ireland exceeds 700,000 birds, but guillemots are always vunerable to oil spills.

▨ *At colonies — sometimes numbering hundreds of noisy, squabbling and sparring birds — it breeds on tightly packed ledges.*

▨ *In summer, adults in southern Britain have warm, chocolate-brown upperparts, gradually becoming darker in colour further north, and almost black in Scotland.*

▨ *In winter, chin, throat and sides of neck are white. Note the dark line running back from the eye.*

▨ *Birds with white 'spectacles' are known as 'bridled' guillemots. Their frequency increases from south to north, but the reason is unclear.*

▨ *On land, the guillemot may appear rather awkward. In the water, however, it is streamlined and an excellent swimmer.*

▨ *Egg shape may have evolved to prevent it rolling off ledges, or perhaps as a consequence of the size and shape of the adult's body.*

Black Guillemot
CEPPHUS GRYLLE

LENGTH: 30–32CM **WEIGHT:** 340–45G
WHERE TO LOOK: ON CLIFFS, BOULDER-STREWN SHORES OR ON SEA **NEST:** IN A CREVICE OR AMONG BOULDERS, OCCASIONALLY UNDER DRIFTWOOD **EGGS:** 2, WHITE **FOOD:** MAINLY FISH **VOICE:** VARIETY OF HIGH-PITCHED WHISTLES

The black guillemot, or tystie, as it is also known, is the most sedentary of Britain's auks, and the only one with white wing patches. It is widespread along the rocky shores of north and west Scotland and Ireland. In Wales it breeds only in Anglesey, and in England only at St Bees Head, Cumbria.

Tysties are usually seen singly or in small groups, but they do not nest together in large numbers like the other auks. They dive for food, usually submerging for up to a minute, and prefer the shallower, inshore waters. The white patch on the wings makes it possible to follow diving birds under water if watched from a clifftop using binoculars. Butterfish and sand eels are the most frequently taken foods.

Only one fish at a time is brought to the chicks, and this is usually carried crosswise in the bill. Occasionally, a parent bringing food may be robbed by another parent from a neighbouring nest. Tysties are vulnerable to oil spillages near the shore and their eggs and young may be eaten by introduced mink, but are otherwise fairly free to enjoy their seaside existence.

■ *In summer, plumage resembles a striking black, pigeon-sized auk, with white wing patches and red feet. Flies fast and low over water,*
■ *In winter, appears pale grey, but retains the white wing patches.*
■ *The vermilion gape is only likely to be seen during threat or courtship displays.*
■ *At close range, the adult's bright red feet are even visible through the water when the bird is swimming or diving.*

Razorbill
ALCA TORDA

LENGTH: 37–39CM **WEIGHT:** 590–730G
WHERE TO LOOK: CLIFFS AND SEA AT BREEDING COLONIES (APRIL TO JULY); OTHERWISE OUT TO SEA **NEST:** IN CREVICE, ON LEDGE, OR AMONG BOULDERS **EGGS:** 1, BOLDLY BLOTCHED **FOOD:** MAINLY FISH **VOICE:** A DEEP, GROWLING *GURRRRR* AT COLONIES

Razorbills nest on cliffs and among boulders, usually in colonies with other seabirds, especially guillemots and kittiwakes. Although seldom as numerous as guillemots, some colonies number several thousand birds. The larger colonies are in northern England, Scotland and Ireland. Some colonies in Wales and southern England are now much smaller than early in the 20th century. At the colonies, birds are noisy and often quarrelsome, disputing territories with intruders or neighbours. They are rather ungainly on land, and though swift and strong fliers they lack manoeuvrability in the air. Landing usually requires several attempts, using tail and feet to aid control. They are at their most adept in the sea, where they dive for food, swimming under water using feet and half-open wings. Outside the breeding season, birds disperse widely at sea, some travelling to the Bay of Biscay and even as far as the Mediterranean. Around 100,000 pairs of razorbills probably breed in Britain and Ireland – about 20 per cent of the world population. Overall, numbers appear to have changed little recently, although birds are often killed by oil pollution and by being trapped in fishing nets.

■ *The square-ended, jet-black bill has two black and one white vertical ridges, and a white line joins the bill and eye.*
■ *Between August and March the chin, throat and sides of the neck become white, and the markings along and across the bill fade into dull grey.*
■ *In summer, the razorbill's velvet black head, wings and back contrast with silky white below. Best distinguished from guillemot by the bill shape and pattern.*

Puffin

FRATERCULA ARCTICA

Chick, under three weeks

Four weeks

Six weeks

Six months

Adult, winter

Adult, summer

Standing on a grassy slope outside its burrow, the puffin is unmistakable. It is Britain's most colourful seabird, comical to watch and naturally inquisitive. The main colonies are in northern Scotland, the largest on St Kilda, west of the Outer Hebrides. In the 19th century, St Kilda may have held over one million pairs, but now there are probably about one-fifth that number. Numbers also declined earlier in the 20th century at other colonies, especially in southern England and Wales. The decline now appears to have halted, and some northern colonies may be increasing. The decline was probably caused by climatic change influencing sea temperature, which affected the distribution of fish rather than by pesticides or oil pollution. About 700,000 puffins now breed in Britain and Ireland. Most nest in burrows, many of which are regularly occupied from year to year. The birds may excavate the burrows themselves, or use those of Manx shearwaters or rabbits, with whom they sometimes share a common entrance. Early in the breeding season thousands of birds may be present on one day and almost none on the next. July is the best month to watch them. By mid-August they have left the colony, not to return to land until the following March.

■ *The triangular red, yellow and blue bill, white face, curious eye markings, black head, back and wings, white undersides and bright red feet make puffins quite unmistakable. Amusing to watch, they walk with a waddle, display, fight each other, and cock their heads to one side to watch you watching them.*

■ *The large, powerful bill is slightly hooked to help hold slippery prey. The feet are strong and used for swimming, for extra control when flying and for excavating burrows.*

■ *In flight, the large head and bill give a rounded profile to the front. The underside of the wing is darker than other auks.*

■ *Usually stands upright on land. Moves by shuffling or waddling, but may run, flapping its wings.*

■ *Adults may suddenly take flight, circling the colony in wheeling flocks of thousands of birds.*

■ *As evening approaches, puffins gather at their burrow entrances.*

LENGTH: 26–29CM **WEIGHT:** 310–490G **WHERE TO LOOK:** AT COLONIES ON GRASSY SLOPES, OR CLIFFS, OR ON THE SEA FROM MARCH TO AUGUST. ATTENDANCE CAN BE ERRATIC, ESPECIALLY EARLY IN THE SEASON. BIRDS MOST NUMEROUS IN EARLY EVENINGS IN JULY **NEST:** IN A BURROW 1–2 METRES LONG, LESS OFTEN IN CREVICES ON CLIFFS **EGGS:** I **FOOD:** MAINLY FISH, BUT ALSO CRUSTACEANS **VOICE:** A LOW NASAL *KAA–ARR–ARR* AT THE COLONIES, SILENT ELSEWHERE

Woodpigeon
COLUMBA PALUMBUS

Shot in thousands, woodpigeons are reluctant to allow people too close. Yet when unmolested, in a town park or public grounds, they quickly become approachable. Only then does the full beauty and size of this pigeon become apparent. The dash and agility shown in a sudden, noisy escape flight through a shrubbery should hardly fail to impress – but pigeons are pigeons, and usually ignored!

Town woodpigeons start to nest in February, with a peak in April and May. Rural birds start later, peaking from July to September. This is due to the different availability of food.

These pigeons have been thoroughly studied. They are very agile in trees, but feed mainly on the ground. Flocks have subordinate birds in front, with slower pecking rates than the dominant pigeons. Their feeding rate increases to a peak just before they fly to roost, but most feed is taken in the afternoon. In the autumn, only 5–10 per cent of the daylight is spent feeding; but in winter, 95 per cent is spent feeding on pastures, and a little less in richer habitats.

- *Large, heavy, deep-chested pigeon with long, broad tail. Bigger-bodied and smaller-headed than falcons and sparrowhawks.*
- *Looks grey at a distance, but close views reveal browner back, pink breast, attractive eye and bill colour, and a smooth appearance.*
- *When it takes to the wing in fright, the woodpigeon's wings may make a loud clattering sound.*
- *Crescents of white on wing and the adult's neck patch are unique. The tail has a pale central band with a dark tip.*
- *Underwing soft grey; head well forward on thin neck.*

LENGTH: 40–42CM **WEIGHT:** 480–550G **WHERE TO LOOK:** FARMLAND WITH TREES, WOODS, PARKS **NEST:** THIN PLATFORM OF STICKS IN TREE **EGGS:** 1–2, WHITE **FOOD:** LEAVES, SEEDS, BERRIES, BUDS, GRAIN **VOICE:** *COO COOO COO, COO-COO,* IN SERIES, LAST WITH AN EXTRA *OO* AT END

Rock Dove/Feral Pigeon
COLUMBA LIVIA

LENGTH: 31–34CM **WEIGHT:** 250–350G
WHERE TO LOOK: CLIFFS, FIELDS, TOWNS,
QUARRIES **NEST:** ON LEDGE IN CAVE, ON
BUILDING **EGGS:** 2, WHITE **FOOD:** CEREALS,
SEEDS, BUDS, TAKEN FROM GROUND **VOICE:**
MOANING *OORH* OR *OH-OO-OOR*, LONGER
CROONING IN DISPLAY

The rock dove is the ancestor of all tame and town pigeons. Escaped racing and dovecot pigeons long ago established themselves back in the wild, living off people's scraps in the cities or finding more natural places in quarries, or even on the sea cliffs where wild rock doves live. They provide colour and life in many a railway station or city street, but leave rather a mess, so they get no thanks in return. But the gleaming red eye of a pigeon is always worth a look! On the cliffs, they have interbred with the wild birds until many populations have become so tainted with domestic stock that few 'wild' birds remain. This is a pity, as rock doves are immaculate birds, more beautiful than many more highly praised species and living a dramatic life in magnificent coastal cliff surroundings. Feral pigeons are treated as if they are not birds at all – no bird book does them justice – yet they are at least as much 'British birds' as pheasants and little owls. The wild rock dove is widespread, occurring in a variety of forms from Britain's seaboard to Alpine peaks and African desert cliffs.

The true rock dove has a blue body, greyer back, black wingbars and a white rump. The underwing is white, unlike the stock dove.

■ Rock doves are swift, powerful fliers with the most pointed, swept-back wings of any large pigeon.

■ Domestic birds gone wild (feral) often look very similar, reverting to this type on cliffs, but racers and town birds are all sorts of colours.

Stock Dove
COLUMBA OENAS

LENGTH: 32–34CM **WEIGHT:** 290–330G
WHERE TO LOOK: FIELDS, WOODS, OPEN
SPACES NEAR GRAVEL PITS. **NEST:** HOLE IN
TREE, LEDGE OF CLIFF OR BUILDING. **EGGS:** 2,
WHITE. **FOOD:** SEEDS, LEAVES, BUDS, FLOWERS.
VOICE: DEEP SERIES OF *OOO–UH* OR *ORR–WUMP*
CALLS, SECOND NOTE ABRUPT

The stock dove is best known as a bird of farmland and parkland with old trees, which give it nest sites in cavities and holes where branches have been wrenched away in gales. But it is also at home wherever a cliff ledge or cavity provides room to lay its glossy eggs, so long as this is within easy flying distance of suitable feeding grounds. Consequently, it can be seen, rather unexpectedly, high up on moorland crags or even on sea cliffs. The stock dove often visits open pools, such as new gravel pits, to drink at the water's edge. It is less likely to become tame or to live in a park than the woodpigeon.

Often overlooked, stock doves become easy to spot with practice – in flight they look like neat, rounded pigeons without the speed and dash of a racing pigeon, but far less ponderous, shorter-tailed and rounded-headed than the bigger, more numerous woodpigeon. On the ground, they are likely to be seen in pairs rather than huge flocks (though occasionally up to a hundred or two may gather together), and in good light, they look a lovely shade of slightly purplish blue. The call is also a give-away, especially from the depths of a big tree or from an overgrown quarry face. It has a loud, almost booming quality about it, with a rhythmic pattern quite unlike the lazy crooning of the woodpigeon.

■ On the ground it looks a darker, bluer bird than the woodpigeon, with a shorter tail, rounder body and a neater shape.

■ Flight is fast; quicker action than woodpigeon.

■ Upperside shows pale centre and blackish edges to wings; no white, but two small bars near body.

Collared Dove
STREPTOPELIA DECAOCTO

LENGTH: 31–33CM **WEIGHT:** 150–220G
WHERE TO LOOK: SUBURBS WITH
CONIFERS, PARKS, FARMS **NEST:** IN
TREE, NEAR TRUNK **EGGS:** 2, WHITE
FOOD: GRAIN, SEEDS, FRUITS **VOICE:**
KU-KOO-KUK, ABRUPT AT END; NASAL
KWURR OR *GHEE-GHEEE* IN ALARM AND
IN GLIDING DISPLAY

The collared dove arrived in Britain in the 1950s. Its spread across Europe, from ancestral dry, hot habitats in India, to a cooler, damper environment closely connected with people and split grain has been well documented. By 1964 about 3,000 pairs were breeding in Britain; by 1972 there were between 30,000 and 40,000 pairs, but the increase was beginning to ease off. The north-westward spread took the bird to the Faroes and Iceland, but the cause of the phenomenal expansion has not been fully explained. Collared doves are gregarious and good feeding sites attract flocks even in the breeding season. Town centres and open country where other pigeons are common are usually avoided, but gardens, shrubberies, allotments and farms are eagerly sought, and these doves often come to bird tables. Unless persecuted, they become very approachable, but the monotonous *ku-koo-kuk* calls can be tiresome just after dawn in mid-summer, and are also the chief cause of over-optimistic reports of early cuckoos! The breeding season is very prolonged and there may be three, sometimes even six broods of two young each reared by a single pair each year.

■ *Pale grey-fawn with pink breast and thin, black half-ring on neck.*
■ *Head paler and wing-tips darker than basic colour; tail rather long, with white corners on top and black base with broad white tip below.*
■ *Small, slim dove with long, broad wings and long tail held closed in normal flight. Flight active, with quick, rhythmic wing-beats; wings quite bowed or arched.*

Turtle Dove
STREPTOPELIA TURTUR

LENGTH: 26–28CM **WEIGHT:** 130–180G
WHERE TO LOOK: WOODLAND EDGE,
LOWLAND FARMLAND HEDGES **NEST:** IN
HEDGE OR TREE **EGGS:** 1–2, WHITE **FOOD:**
WEED SEEDS, BUDS, LEAVES, CEREALS **VOICE:**
PURRING SONG *COORRR-COORRR*, RATHER DEEP,
LAZY

As the pleasant cawing of rooks epitomises spring in wooded parkland and the bubbling of the curlew is the essence of early summer in the hills, so the long, rolling, deep song of the turtle dove means high summer in the country lanes of southern England. The main problem for the turtle dove, other than cool, wet summers that reduce the breeding success, is that the tall, ancient hedges which it loves so well are often grubbed out, so that there is less room for it than ever before. It needs big hawthorns, unkempt elders and small trees in farmland or on the edge of a broken, sunny wood if it is to survive in the face of agricultural change. Though happy to forage in the quiet lanes of a village, it is unlikely to nest close to human habitation and is far less of a garden bird than the collared dove. In the winter it makes for the Sahel, south of the Sahara, where the droughts of recent years, compounded by loss of forest and scrub may also affect its numbers. However, in some African areas large concentrations still occur. Sadly, huge numbers are illegally killed in southern Europe each spring.

■ *Often seen in flocks in late spring, migrating along coasts; then in feeding parties in late summer on arable land.*
■ *Note blue on wing.*
■ *Upperside neatly patterned with light orange-brown and black; head pink.*
■ *Pattern recalls kestrel, but flight and shape quite different.*
■ *Agile dove, quick to fly off if disturbed, quieter than pigeon, but some clatter of wings; has no flight call, unlike the collared dove.*

Cuckoo
CUCULUS CANORUS

LENGTH: 33CM WEIGHT: 105–130G **WHERE TO LOOK:** WOODS,
DUNES, FARMLAND, MOORLAND, REED BEDS **NEST:** NONE OF ITS
OWN; PARASITIC ON OTHER BIRDS **EGGS:** 15–25 LAID, ONE PER
FOSTER-NEST. COLOUR VARIES WITH HOST SPECIES **FOOD:**
MOSTLY CATERPILLARS AND OTHER INSECTS **VOICE:** MALE HAS
FAMILIAR *CU-COO*, FEMALE HAS A RICH, LIQUID BUBBLING CALL

Adult

Chick

Juvenile

Cuckoos, wandering voices of the summer, are brood parasites, laying their eggs in the nest of other species, which raise their young for them. When the young cuckoos hatch they push out any other eggs or young they find in the nest, becoming the sole occupant. Cuckoos usually choose the nests of the host species that brought them up, and their eggs will usually closely resemble the eggs of that species. Young cuckoos bear a close resemblance to sparrowhawks and even have the same white nape patch; this may be a disguise which helps to protect them from enemies. Cuckoos are more often heard than seen and most views are of a slim grey bird flying away and directly into a tree or bush. Male and females are virtually alike, but the female can occur in a rare chestnut brown or 'hepatic' colour form. Cuckoos feed on hairy caterpillars that are poisonous to other birds. Their stomachs are protected from the irritating hairs of the caterpillars by a protective lining which can be shed and renewed.

Cuckoos start calling soon after their arrival in late April. They continue for another six weeks or so before becoming silent. By July, adult birds are beginning to contemplate the return trip to their wintering grounds.

■ *Cuckoos are slender, with pointed wings, a long tail and a low, direct flight with shallow wing-beats. They are often confused with hawks.*
■ *Adult males are grey above and white with dark barring below. When perched, they tend to hold their tail above their wingtips.*
■ *Juvenile cuckoos are dark grey-brown or rufous above, with dark barring and a white nape patch.*
■ *The male keeps its bill closed, waves its tail from side to side and sways when calling.*
■ *The male's familiar call and the less well-known bubbling chuckle of the female are often all that indicates their presence.*
■ *The young cuckoo will eject other eggs or young from the nest.*

Barn Owl
TYTO ALBA

The barn owl is one of the most widely distributed birds in the world. Those in Britain are at the extreme north-west edge of the range in Europe, and Scottish barn owls are probably the most northerly in the world. Sadly, in many areas the barn owl is now very scarce, or has gone altogether. This decline is known to have been going on for over 50 years, but it has clearly accelerated in the last 25 years or so. It is not known whether any long-term factor such as climate is involved, nor is it easy to be totally clear about other, more short-term causes. But it seems highly likely that the enormous changes in agriculture, especially in arable farming, during the last 20–30 years are at the root of the matter. The loss of prey-rich field edges and corners, rough pastures and similar areas has been critical; this habitat loss has been exacerbated by pesticides and also by the loss of nest sites as hedgerow trees disappear and farm buildings are pulled down, modernised or converted. Persecution has probably been minimal: barn owls have long been welcomed as neighbours on farmland. More research into barn owl habitat needs, and co-operative work with farmers, may provide some answers and some remedies.

LENGTH: 33–37CM **WEIGHT:** 250–350G **WHERE TO LOOK:** MAINLY FARMLAND, FIELD EDGES, ROUGH GRASSLAND **NEST:** HOLE IN TREE, SOMETIMES IN QUARRIES, OR IN RUINS, BARNS OR OTHER OUTBUILDINGS **EGGS:** 4–7, WHITE **FOOD:** MAINLY RODENTS. **VOICE:** SNORES, SHRIEKS.

■ *Seen well, a barn owl is unmistakable. Note large, round-topped head with characteristic heart-shaped face and dark eyes, very long legs (looks 'knock-kneed' when seen from front). Always looks extremely pale and flashes ghostly white in car headlights – but beware deceptively pale look of all owls in headlights at night. Very rare snowy owl is much bigger and bulkier; male all white, female and young barred; yellow eyes.*

■ *Owls have relatively long, muscular legs; in most species (all those in Britain) these are feathered to the base of the toes – the reason for this is not fully understood.*

■ *The toes are powerful and equipped with long, sharp talons. The outer toe is reversible, giving a better grip on prey.*

■ *The barn owl's extraordinarily well-developed sense of hearing may be more important in hunting than vision: prey located by ear can be caught in total darkness.*

■ *The call of the barn owl is popularly described as a blood-curdling shriek, but is not familiar to many people. A variety of snores and hisses come from the nest site.*

■ *No nest as such: bird lays on floor, ledge, beam in building etc.*

■ *Nesting barn owls require freedom from disturbance: nest visits are illegal without a licence.*

■ *Prey may be carried in bill as owl flies up, but is usually quickly transferred to one foot while carried to nest; then passed to bill again on arrival.*

■ *Eggs are laid at intervals of 2–3 days, but incubation begins with first egg laid: this results in a staggered hatch – first owlet in family eight days older than eighth.*

Tawny Owl
STRIX ALUCO

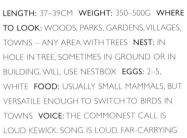

LENGTH: 37–39CM **WEIGHT:** 350–500G **WHERE TO LOOK:** WOODS, PARKS, GARDENS, VILLAGES, TOWNS – ANY AREA WITH TREES **NEST:** IN HOLE IN TREE, SOMETIMES IN GROUND OR IN BUILDING. WILL USE NESTBOX **EGGS:** 2–5, WHITE **FOOD:** USUALLY SMALL MAMMALS, BUT VERSATILE ENOUGH TO SWITCH TO BIRDS IN TOWNS **VOICE:** THE COMMONEST CALL IS LOUD *KEWICK*. SONG IS LOUD, FAR-CARRYING MUSICAL *HOOOO…HOO-HOO HUHOOO*

Adaptability can be the key to a species' success; this is certainly the case with the tawny owl. Originally purely a woodland bird, it has moved out into many man-modified habitats in the lowlands and, despite being absent from Ireland, is easily the commonest and most widespread of Britain's owls. It even lives in parks and large gardens in the hearts of cities. Woodland tawny owls feed mainly on wood mice and bank voles, but elsewhere they adapt readily to whatever small mammal species are available; in towns and cities they prey on small birds.

Tawny owls are thoroughly nocturnal and are thus seldom seen in daylight, unless found at a roost, where their presence may be revealed by the mobbing behaviour of small birds. After dark, they can often be found on the regular perches on their nightly 'beat', but are usually hard to see in treetops and other thick cover.

They are more often heard than seen: the commonest call is a loud *kewick*. The tremulous, far-carrying song is almost too well known to require description. The word 'hooting' scarcely does it justice, however. Occasionally an owl will hoot in the middle of the day, but the full performance is reserved until after dark.

■ *Plumage variable, but 'tawny' is a misnomer. May be more chestnut than shown, or much greyer. Note the big, rounded head, black eyes and stocky appearance.*
■ *Superb camouflage helps to hide the tawny owl at its (often regular) roosting place. Its presence may be given away, however, by gathering of small birds mobbing owl and alarm-calling continuously.*

Little Owl
ATHENE NOCTUA

LENGTH: 21–23CM **WEIGHT:** 150–200G **WHERE TO LOOK:** FARMLAND, FIELD EDGES, SEMI-OPEN HABITAT WITH SCATTERED TREES, QUARRIES, WASTE GROUND, ETC **NEST:** HOLE IN TREE, BANK, CLIFF, OR GROUND. MAY USE NESTBOX **EGGS:** 2–5, WHITE **FOOD:** SMALL MAMMALS AND BIRDS, BUT ALSO MANY INSECTS AND OTHER INVERTEBRATES, INCLUDING EARTHWORMS **VOICE:** SONG IS REPEATED, PLAINTIVE *KIU*. CALL IS LOUD, RINGING *WERRO*

Over much of central and southern England, the little owl is much the most likely owl to be seen by the average birdwatcher. Although it does much of its hunting after dark, it is often abroad well before dusk, especially in summer. This is not a native British bird, but owes its presence in Britain to a series of introductions during the latter half of the 19th century. Its spread has been limited by bouts of persecution, by occasional severe winters and by the use of agricultural pesticides. It may also have lost some ground in areas where intensive arable farming has caused widespread changes in habitat and, especially perhaps, the loss of old hedgerow trees. While it is a common and widespread bird in other parts of Europe, its distribution in Britain is much more confined to the lowlands and – a direct reflection of the high proportion of insects and other invertebrates in its diet – is clearly also related to climatic conditions, especially winter temperatures. The loud, clear calls of this owl are not familiar to most people, yet give one of the best means of locating a pair in spring. They have a distinctive, clear quality and carry far, yet even experienced birdwatchers are often left puzzled by the sound.

■ *Small size, rather broad and flat-topped head readily distinguish the little owl. Usually looks squat and dumpy – yellow eyes very obvious. Habit of using conspicuous daytime perches a good identification point.*
■ *Dumpy in flight, with its blunt head and rounded wings. Quick wing-beats, and characteristic heavy, bounding flight action.*

Long-eared Owl
ASIO OTUS

Very often the first clue to the presence of this elusive bird is the 'squeaky gate' call of the young waiting to be fed. Breeding long-eared owls easily escape detection – the song period is short, and the low cooing song quiet. Even the male's aerial display flying and wing-clapping can pass unnoticed. The birdwatcher's task is made no easier by the bird's strongly nocturnal habits and the fact that it chooses to nest in dense cover, generally preferring plantations and copses, but also using larger woods, shelterbelts and thick, tall scrub or bushes. Winter roosts, often in traditional sites, usually provide the best chance of seeing these owls, although birds feeding young may appear well before dark (and after dawn): hunting takes place over open areas, not in thick cover. The ear-tufts can be raised or lowered and the facial discs opened or closed, according to mood; alarmed birds often assume a characteristically slim, upright posture. In a tangled willow thicket or hawthorn scrub they blend in amazingly well; even in a green pine they are surprisingly hard to spot.

■ *Facial discs are mobile, giving different expressions: open with ear-tufts erect when alarmed, shut and tufts down when relaxed. Orange eyes are often concealed by partly closed eyelids. Superb camouflage in tree foliage.*

■ *In flight, long-winged, but darker on underparts than short-eared owl.*

Ear-tufts raised

Owlet in threat posture

LENGTH: 35–37CM **WEIGHT:** 220–300G
WHERE TO LOOK: PLANTATIONS, WOODS, COPSES, ETC **NEST:** OLD NEST OF MAGPIE, CROW; IN SOME AREAS IN COVER ON GROUND **EGGS:** 3–5, WHITE **FOOD:** MAINLY VOLES, ALSO OTHER SMALL MAMMALS AND BIRDS **VOICE:** SONG IS LOW, QUIET COOING

Short-eared Owl
ASIO FLAMMEUS

LENGTH: 37–39CM **WEIGHT:** 280–350G
WHERE TO LOOK: OPEN MOORLAND, ROUGH PASTURES, MARSHES, COASTS **NEST:** NONE MADE **EGGS:** 4–8 (OR MORE), WHITE **FOOD:** PRINCIPALLY VOLES **VOICE:** LEAST VOCAL OF OWLS, BUT RASPING AND BARKING CALLS, DEEP *BOO-BOO-BOO*

Adult

Owlet

Unlike the long-eared owl, this bird is not too difficult to see. It is often abroad in full daylight and can be very conspicuous as it hunts over the open moors, heaths, rough grasslands and young plantations where it breeds, or the coastal marshes where it is often found in winter. The principal prey of the short-eared owl is, in most areas, the short-tailed vole. It is the abundance or otherwise of this small mammal which governs both the numbers and breeding of the owl; in years when voles are plentiful, short-eared owls will lay several numbers of eggs and rear large families. Similarly, the amount of prey available in winter quarters dictates how many owls will be in an area, or whether, as often happens, they will be absent altogether. The classic relationship between the predator and its prey is strikingly illustrated by this species. It shows too how the effects can be very marked with such a specialised predator: they are much less obvious with a more versatile bird like the tawny owl. In late winter and spring the short-eared owl may fly high up in display, calling with hollow, booming notes and clapping its wings rapidly beneath its body.

■ *Pale underwing very like long-eared owl, but upperwing looks more barred and underparts whiter. Ear-tufts very small; seldom seen except on wary or alarmed bird.*

■ *In flight, typically looks pale and long-winged, moving buoyantly; perches on posts or level ground.*

■ *Yellow eyes surprisingly obvious, even on flying bird.*

■ *Always nests on ground in thick cover. Like other owls, male hunts for family and female remains at nest with young.*

Nightjar
CAPRIMULGUS EUROPAEUS

LENGTH: 27CM WEIGHT: 75–100G WHERE TO LOOK:
HEATHLAND, FELLED WOODLAND, NEW PLANTATIONS,
MOORLAND AND DUNES WITH BRACKEN AND SCRUB NEST:
ON BARE GROUND EGGS: 2, MOTTLED GREY FOOD: FLYING
INSECTS, MAINLY MOTHS AND BEETLES VOICE: SONG IS A LOUD
CHURRING TRILL WHICH RISES AND FALLS, GIVEN BY PERCHED
MALE. BOTH SEXES ALSO HAVE A DEEP *KOOICK* FLIGHT CALL

Secret and mysterious birds of bushy heaths and rough gorsy commons, nightjars are never easy to observe. Unless it is a clear, calm, warm evening there is no guarantee that they will be seen or heard, but late twilight on a midsummer evening is the best time to seek them. You may have to be content with hearing the sustained churring song, but with luck a pair will hunt for moths against the dim light of the sky, or come twisting and swirling around a birdwatcher's head as they would an isolated bush. During the day they sit along a log or on a patch of bare ground, almost impossible to find. They arrive in Britain in May and leave for Africa in August and September, when several may migrate together. The British population is small and declining due to habitat loss and disturbance (sometimes by birdwatchers), pesticides and climatic change – a combination which is difficult to resist.

Nightjars rest on the ground. Their amazing plumage renders them almost invisible as they sit motionless and with eyes shut among fallen twigs and leaves. Not until they are almost trodden on will they actually fly.

■ *Nightjars are best seen at dusk when they begin to call. They fly silently after insects with many sudden twists and glides.*
■ *Males have conspicuous white spots near the wing-tips and on the outer tips of the tail. Females and young lack these.*
■ *The churring song is loud and vibrant at close range, far less high and metallic than song of grasshopper warbler.*
■ *Wings clapped loudly in display flight; also glide with wings raised and tail spread.*
■ *Superb camouflage when resting or nesting on ground.*

Adult male

Adult female

Swift
APUS APUS

LENGTH: 16–17CM **WEIGHT:** 35–50G **WHERE TO LOOK:** IN THE
SUMMER SKY, ANYWHERE **NEST:** HOLE IN LEAVES, THATCH,
TOWERS, RARELY IN CLIFFS; SHALLOW CUP OF FEATHERS AND
SALIVA **EGGS:** 2–3, WHITE **FOOD:** INSECTS, SPIDERS **VOICE:**
LOUD, SHRILL SCREAM

The swift is a very remarkable bird: it is the only insectivorous bird whose young hatch at staggered intervals, thus ensuring that at least the oldest survives. Moreover, both eggs and young can survive long periods of chilling if the weather prevents the adults from feeding close by. Adults, too, are able to enter a state of torpor, and remarkable clusters of birds clinging to walls like swarms of bees have, very occasionally, been recorded.

On leaving the nest for the first and only time, a young swift heads south to Africa immediately, without its parents, and may remain on the wing non-stop for two or three years! Swifts not only feed, bathe and 'sleep' aloft, but even on occasions mate on the wing. Only when nesting do they roost 'normally'. They may fly well over a million miles in their life of maybe ten years or more.

They probably eat more animals than any other British bird. Analysis of 12 food-balls intended for the young revealed more than 300 species of insects and spiders. One bird may catch 10,000 individual insects in a day. Although it does fly fast, a feeding swift takes insects in slow, steady glides.

Swifts prefer to nest in roofs of older houses where they have easy access to the rafters. They are semi-colonial, with often several pairs nesting in one roof and many more in nearby suitable houses. They are usually faithful to the same site year after year.

▨ *Adults are dark sooty brown, appearing black, with a pale chin. Young show more white on the throat and forehead, which is visible in flight.*
▨ *Although the bill is small, the gape is enormous to help catch its insect food.*
▨ *Exceptionally long primary feathers and short inner wings create the familiar crescent shape, ideal for rapid sustained flight.*
▨ *Parties of screaming swifts chase low over roofs on fine evenings. Non-breeding swifts may undertake journeys of 300 kilometres or more to avoid heavy rain.*
▨ *The shallow-forked tail, usually closed, is used for greater control.*
▨ *Every swift seems to carry more than its fair share of parasites, including the large, green, flightless louse-fly.*

Kingfisher
ALCEDO ATTHIS

LENGTH: 16–17CM (OF WHICH BILL 4CM) **WEIGHT:** 35–40G
WHERE TO LOOK: UNPOLLUTED, STILL OR SLOW-FLOWING
WATERS OVER MUCH OF BRITAIN AND IRELAND, THOUGH RARE
IN SCOTLAND; SEDENTARY, SOME MOVING TO ESTUARIES,
SHELTERED COASTS IN WINTER **NEST:** NARROW TUNNEL
60–90CM LONG, EXCAVATED IN BANK, USUALLY OVER WATER
EGGS: 6–7, WHITE, RATHER ROUND, LAID IN SHALLOW
DEPRESSION ON BARE EARTH, IN CHAMBER AT END OF TUNNEL
FOOD: SMALL FISH **VOICE:** LOUD, SHRILL *CHEE* OFTEN
REPEATED; AGGRESSIVE *SHRIT-IT-IT*; ESPECIALLY VOCAL IN SPRING
AND AUTUMN WHEN ESTABLISHING BREEDING AND
WINTERING TERRITORY

On seeing their first kingfisher, most people are surprised how small it is. It is Britain's most exotic-looking bird and indeed is the widest ranging representative of a mainly tropical family of some 90 species. Often, all that is seen of this shy bird, first located by call, is a streak of brilliant electric blue flashing low and fast over the water surface. In ancient Greece, a dead kingfisher was hung up as a protection against lightning!

Each young bird needs between 12 and 18 fish daily; youngsters are fed in rotation, the hungriest bird taking position at the front of the nest chamber. For such a beautiful bird, the nesting habits are distinctly insalubrious, the chamber becoming fouled with fish bones and scales – regurgitated as pellets and then trodden into the earth. The young excrete towards the light, so the tunnel also becomes filthy, and often shows a tell-tale white trickle below the entrance: on leaving the nest, the adults usually plunge-bathe to clean their plumage.

Kingfishers are highly territorial: they will even chase their own young away within three or four days of leaving the nest, starting a second brood almost immediately. Many young starve or drown in the first week, before they have learnt to fish.

■ *Male and female share the same combination of iridescent blues, orange-red and white, with bright-red feet. The male's bill is all black, whereas the female has a red base to the lower mandible. Young are duller with dark feet.*

■ *Perched motionless among vegetation, it can be surprisingly difficult to see, the strong colour contrast breaking up the bird's outline. When fishing, often bobs head nervously.*

■ *Where small fish abound, adults are successful four dives out of five. They can handle fish up to 8cm long – half their own body length.*

■ *Having dived and caught a fish, the kingfisher struggles free of the water with strong wing-beats, returning to the same perch to beat its prey before swallowing it head-first. The dive is over in a trice.*

Adult male

Adult female

Green Woodpecker
PICUS VIRIDIS

LENGTH: 30–33CM **WEIGHT:** 190G **WHERE TO LOOK:**
DECIDUOUS WOODS, PARKLAND, HEATHS AND COMMONS
NEST: DEEP CAVITY EXCAVATED IN TRUNK OR LARGE LIMB
OF MATURE TREE. UNLINED **EGGS:** 4–7, GLOSSY WHITE, LAID ON
WOOD CHIPPINGS **FOOD:** MAINLY ANTS AND THEIR PUPA
VOICE: LOUD, LAUGHING *YAFFLE*

The green woodpecker is more often heard than seen; its loud almost laughing yaffle call carries a great distance, yet the bird itself is often shy and elusive. Britain's largest woodpecker, it is about the size of a jackdaw, and when seen is unmistakable, with green plumage, striking red crown and yellow rump. In flight the pointed shape of the head and tail and the short bursts of flapping interspersed with long swooping glides are characteristic. At rest it can be difficult to locate, often perching motionless for many minutes, occasionally giving an alarm call.

Old pasture and heaths are favoured feeding areas, for it is here that the bird finds the ants that are its staple diet. It uses its stout beak and long tongue to extract ants and pupae from galleries deep within the nest. The tongue can be extended up to 10cm and is used to explore the galleries, while the sticky tip is used to catch the prey. At most times of the year the birds are seen singly, but the young accompany their parents for a few weeks after fledging in July and such family parties can often be located by the loud begging calls of the young. Although they sometimes occur in well-wooded gardens, green woodpeckers are extremely shy birds and at the slightest hint of disturbance they fly off, calling loudly in alarm with shouted, rapid notes, more screeching than the pleasant yaffle.

■ *In both the male and female the crown and central nape are deep crimson mottled with grey.*
■ *Moustachial stripe of male has red a central streak..*

Wryneck
JYNX TORQUILLA

The wryneck is a close relative of the woodpeckers. Like the green woodpecker, it feeds almost exclusively on ants and uses its long mobile tongue to scoop them up. Unlike the woodpecker, it is seen mainly on the ground, does not often climb up vertical limbs and only rarely excavates dead wood. For a nest site it uses any available cavity, including artificial boxes. Another difference from Britain's true woodpeckers is that it is migratory, spending the winter in sub-Saharan Africa. At a distance it looks like a rather dull, long songbird, but close views reveal complex brown and lilac patterning on the back with two lilac and one blackish band running down from the nape. The undersides are barred and spotted and the tail has complex transverse patterning – all reminiscent of a small nightjar. In England the breeding population has declined to extinction in recent decades and now the only birds seen are occasional migrants in spring and autumn. These birds often appear in the most unlikely places, including suburban gardens, feeding on ants. A small number of wrynecks now breed in Scotland; these are thought to be an offshoot of the large Scandinavian population.

■ *On the ground it hops clumsily and collects food with a darting tongue. It often remains motionless for long periods, collecting ants that pass by.*
■ *The mottled brown back and barred tail are distinctive.*

LENGTH: 15–16CM **WEIGHT:** 32G **WHERE TO LOOK:** A RARE
BREEDING BIRD IN SEMI-NATURAL PINE FORESTS IN SCOTLAND;
IN ENGLAND AND WALES ONLY SEEN ON PASSAGE IN SPRING
AND AUTUMN **NEST:** ANY CAVITY, INCLUDING NESTBOX,
UNLINED **EGGS:** 7–10, WHITE **FOOD:** ANTS AND OTHER INSECTS
VOICE: WEAK *QUEE…QUEE…QUEE*, SIMILAR TO LESSER SPOTTED
WOODPECKER

Great Spotted Woodpecker
DENDROCOPUS MAJOR

LENGTH: 22–23CM WEIGHT: 80G WHERE TO LOOK:
CONIFEROUS AND DECIDUOUS WOODLAND, HEDGEROW TREES
AND GARDENS NEST: CAVITY EXCAVATED IN DEAD OR
DECAYING TREE, UNLINED EGGS: 3–7, WHITE FOOD: INSECTS,
SEEDS VOICE: LOUD *TCHIK* AND RATTLING *TRILL*

Adult female

Adult male

A distinctive black, white and red bird, the great spotted is Britain's most widespread woodpecker. It is about the size of a blackbird and can be encountered almost anywhere where there are trees. In the breeding season it prefers mature broadleaved woodland, but at other times may wander widely and be found in isolated trees and copses. The first indication of its presence is often a loud repeated *tchik* call. After searching, the bird can usually be found high in a tree or glimpsed as it flies off. Its territorial drumming is the most evocative early morning woodland sound in spring, and is often punctuated by aerial chases through the canopy with two or three birds chattering loudly. Most of its food is obtained by pecking at dead and decaying wood to extract insects and larvae – crevices and decayed spots are attacked with rapid blows of the beak. In spring, the young are fed on caterpillars. A new nest cavity is usually excavated each year and this can take the birds one or two weeks, depending on the hardness of the chosen tree. Dead birch stumps and oaks are preferred.

■ *The woodpecker's bill is used to peck at decaying wood to obtain food and to excavate the nest cavity.*
■ *Adults and immature birds of both sexes have bright red under-tail coverts. The male is readily distinguished from the female by the brilliant red patch on his nape.*
■ *In flight, the large white wing flashes, white-barred primaries and brilliant red under-tail coverts are obvious.*

Lesser Spotted Woodpecker
DENDROCOPUS MINOR

This small woodpecker is only the size of a house sparrow. It spends much of its time high in the tree canopy feeding among the smallest branches; with a rapid sewing-machine-like action of its beak it searches out its insect food. In winter it often joins mixed feeding flocks of tits. For a few weeks in early spring its pee...pee...pee...pee... calls, conspicuous butterfly-like display flights and weak drumming betray its breeding areas. The drumming is much softer than that of the great spotted woodpecker, and each burst lasts for well over a second. Both male and female drum, usually from high in the crown of a tree. The nest cavity is excavated by both birds and can be between one and 25 metres above the ground, often placed on the underside of a dead limb. The entrance hole is only 3cm in diameter, distinguishing the nest from those of other woodpecker species. The nest is usually very inconspicuous and difficult to find.

■ *Distinguished from great spotted woodpecker by its small size, barred black and white wing pattern without any large white flashes, and lack of red vent.*
■ *Male has distinct red crown which is absent in female.*
■ *Usually feeds high in woodland trees, but will also feed close to the ground in hedgerows and scrub.*
■ *When feeding, flutters more like a perching bird than a woodpecker.*

Adult male

Adult female

LENGTH: 13–14CM WEIGHT: 20G WHERE TO LOOK:
DECIDUOUS WOODLAND, PARKS, ORCHARDS AND GARDENS
NEST: CAVITY EXCAVATED IN DECAYING WOOD, UNLINED
EGGS: 3–8, WHITE FOOD: INSECTS VOICE: SLOW, NASAL
PEE...PEE....PEE....PEE; WEAK *CHICK*

Skylark
ALAUDA ARVENSIS

LENGTH: 18CM **WEIGHT:** 33–45G **WHERE TO LOOK:** OPEN FIELDS, MOORS, DUNES AND SALT MARSHES **NEST:** ON GROUND IN GRASS TUSSOCKS WITH FINE GRASS/HAIR LINING **EGGS:** 3–5, WHITE WITH HEAVY BROWN MARKINGS **FOOD:** INSECTS, SEEDS AND WORMS **VOICE:** LOUD, CLEAR, VERY RAPID WARBLING IN FLIGHT. CALL A LIQUID *CHIRRUP*

These familiar birds of the open countryside are often visible only as small specks in the sky as they hang in the air, singing non-stop. They are numerous throughout the country in the breeding season, but in winter many leave the bleaker upland areas for more hospitable lowland fields. Large numbers of skylarks from northern Europe arrive in Britain in October and November to spend the winter. During very severe winters Britain's skylarks may move south to warmer parts of mainland Europe. Skylarks give their glorious song all year round, but tend to go quiet in August and September when they moult. They have probably benefited more than any other bird from the advent of arable farming and the deforestation of the countryside, which has provided the open cultivated areas that the species prefers. They rarely even feed close to a tall hedge.

■ *In flight, the white trailing wing edge, white outer tail feathers and loud chirruping call help to identify them.*

■ *The aerial song is a familiar sound, with the bird often too high to be seen. The song flight can last for anything up to five minutes. Skylarks also sing from perches.*

■ *The crest is not always easily seen, but can be raised when the bird is excited or alarmed.*

Woodlark
LULLULA ARBOREA

Woodlarks are very patchily distributed in southern and eastern England with, until recently, a few in Wales. They are often difficult to find, feeding inconspicuously on the ground, but they perch on the tops of trees and bushes. They sing beautifully through most of the year, especially from March to June, and often at night. The song flight is different from a skylark's, with the male circling at a constant height with a more fluttering action. In flight, the short tail, undulating flight and call – *tit-looeet* – help to distinguish them from skylarks. They are particularly fond of forestry plantations where trees have been felled or recently planted. Their numbers have been declining both in Britain and in mainland Europe. It is thought that habitat loss combined with climatic change may have caused this. It is very sad that their lovely song is now so rarely heard.

■ *Woodlark has a small crest and clear buff-white stripe over the eyes which meet at the back of the head.*

■ *Black and white mark at bend of wing is visible when perched.*

■ *In flight shows very short tail with brown sides, and broader, more rounded wings than skylark's.*

■ *Compared to skylark, flight is weak and fluttering. When flushed, the bird flies low over the ground.*

LENGTH: 15CM **WEIGHT:** 24–36 **WHERE TO LOOK:** HEATHLAND WITH SCRUB, PLANTATIONS **NEST:** FINE GRASS LINING IN SHELTERED HOLLOW **EGGS:** 3–4, PALE BROWN-SPECKLED **FOOD:** INSECTS AND SEEDS **VOICE:** MELODIOUS DESCENDING SONG PHRASES; *TLOO-EE, TITLOOEET* CALLS

Swallow
HIRUNDO RUSTICA

LENGTH: 18–20CM WEIGHT: 18–19G WHERE
TO LOOK: OPEN COUNTRY NEST: OF MUD
AND DRY GRASS ON A LEDGE IN AN
OUTBUILDING EGGS: 4–5, WHITE, DARK-
SPECKLED FOOD: INSECTS TAKEN ON THE
WING VOICE: *TSWIT-TSWIT*; ALARM *TSWEE*;
PROLONGED SONG OF CALLS AND A
ROLLING TRILL

Female

Male

B ritain's swallows winter in Africa, as far south as the cape, returning between
March and May to take up territories around buildings, but in less urban areas
than house martins. The male sings from a wire or on the wing, and soon the pair will
be dashing through a door, a broken window, even the observation slit in a birdwatching hide to build their mud-saucer nest. A chimney-stack or old mine-shaft may
also be used: one nest in Cornwall was 17 metres below ground. A nest may be
occupied several years in succession by the same birds – a tribute to amazing
navigation skills. Food-balls of small insects and individual larger ones are brought to
the young. When they have fledged, the young sit in a prominent spot, often on a
branch, and wait to be fed; they must soon learn to feed themselves and to drink and
bathe on the wing. A classic autumn sight is that of swallows gathering on wires; at
the same time reed-bed roosts may hold thousands of birds. Swallows melt away
south in September and October, with stragglers hanging on until November. Soon
after their arrival in spring and also in late summer, swallows and other hirundines
often feed over water.

Nest

■ *Swallows are glossy blue-black above; below they vary from nearly white to orange-pink,
with a blue band across the breast. The throat and forehead are a rich, deep red. The dark
tail has oval white spots.*
■ *With tail feathers splayed, white dots are revealed.*
■ *Their long tails give them great manoeuvrability near ground or water, and around
obstacles such as grazing animals.*
■ *Females have shorter tail streamers then males. The young are duller, with more orange
foreheads and throats.*
■ *Swallows will sometimes take food while they are perched, but they are predominantly
aerial feeders.*
■ *Flies and sometimes butterflies are important sources of food.*

House Martin
DELICHON URBICA

LENGTH: 12.5CM **WEIGHT:**
18G **WHERE TO LOOK:**
AROUND HOUSES, OVER
OPEN AREAS AND WETLANDS
NEST: OF MUD PELLETS AND
A LITTLE DRY GRASS, UNDER
EAVES, OCCASIONALLY ON
BRIDGES AND CLIFFS; OFTEN
COLONIAL **EGGS:** 4–5, WHITE
FOOD: INSECTS TAKEN IN
FLIGHT **VOICE:** *CHRRRP*,
ALARM A SHRILL *TREEP*

Before people built houses, house martins nested on cliffs. A few still do so, but most now build under eaves (or other sites such as street-lamp shades) in villages, towns and city suburbs. Some have even nested on sea-ferries (including a cross-Channel vessel), the adults feeding the young between voyages and raising them successfully! Nesting may be delayed by drought, as mud is the main building material. The adults gather this in their bills and apply it with trembling movements of their chins. The bird is social and some sites have dozens of nests: why some houses are chosen and others not is still not clear. Old nests may be repaired and re-used and artificial nests may encourage birds to colonise. Fledglings of earlier broods often help feed the latest young. Unlike the swallow and sand martin, which make up the trio collectively called the hirundines, this bird rarely roosts in reed beds; it may use trees mainly, or sleep on the wing, but this, and precisely where it spends the winter in Africa, is still mysterious.

House martins are among the first migrants to arrive in this country in spring. Pairs feed over gravel pits and lakes but soon move to likely nesting sites. Here they gather on wires and collect mud from puddle margins. Over a period of several days, the mud is used to construct their sound and solid cup-shaped nests. Their presence on a house is considered by most people as a sign of favour.

Adults are blue-black above with a white rump and underparts; and white feathering on their short legs. Young are browner above and below.

Sand Martin
RIPARIA RIPARIA

LENGTH: 12CM **WEIGHT:** 13–14G **WHERE TO
LOOK:** FRESHWATER WETLANDS, ESPECIALLY
NEAR MINERAL WORKINGS **NEST:** IN
COLONIES, IN A TUNNEL, IN A BANK OR CLIFF,
OCCASIONALLY IN MAN-MADE HOLES, EG PIPES
EGGS: 4–5, WHITE **FOOD:** INSECTS TAKEN IN
FLIGHT **VOICE:** A DRY, HARD *CHRRP*; ALARM
SHARPER; SONG A SERIES OF CALL NOTES

The sand martin is often the first summer migrant to arrive in the spring, beating the swallow by several days. Catastrophic declines in sand martin numbers have followed the long drought in the southern Sahara, where the birds spend winter. Some long-established colonies are empty, and those still active are at a low ebb; it remains to be seen whether the species can make a come-back.

Sand martins are the smallest of Britain's hirundines and rather delicate-looking, yet in excavating their burrows in sand or soil, they may dig in 2 metres or more and move stones four times heavier than themselves. Living in colonies has several advantages, notably 'safety in numbers' and more eyes to spot predators. The bird has a special alarm call to warn of birds of prey; nevertheless many are taken. Migrants roost in reed-beds, often with swallows.

Sand martins feed primarily on insects that are caught mainly on the wing. During periods of prolonged bad weather, they sometimes have great difficulty in feeding. During such weather, and also in late summer prior to migration, many hundreds will gather over suitable lakes and gravel pits to feed. They dip low over the water, feasting on midges and mosquitoes in particular. Nesting in somewhat inaccessible cliffside colonies, sand martins are relatively immune to attacks from ground predators. They are however, frequently subject to predation by hobbies whose speed and agility enable them to catch the martins on the wing.

Plain brown above, off-white below with a brown band across the breast. Tail only slightly forked.

Rock Pipit
ANTHUS PETROSUS

LENGTH: 16CM **WEIGHT:** 21–30G **WHERE TO LOOK:** ROCKY COASTS AND SALT MARSHES **NEST:** IN ROCK CREVICE. GRASS CUP, LINED WITH HAIR **EGGS:** 4–5, WHITE WITH GREY/BROWN SPOTS **FOOD:** SEEDS, MARINE ANIMALS AND INSECTS **VOICE:** LOUD MUSICAL SONG. CALL – STRONG *FEEST*

Almost exclusively coastal, rock pipits search for food among rocks, seaweed and shore vegetation. They always make their nests close to the shore, in sheltered gullies and coves. Breeding usually begins in April and two broods are not uncommon; in some areas they are a host species for cuckoos. Lack of suitable rocky coastline from North Humberside to Kent means that they are absent from that whole stretch of coast.

They are difficult to spot among the rocks, and their presence is often first noticed as they fly up, calling as they go. In winter they may eat more than 15,000 small molluscs and larvae each day. They are usually solitary and territorial, but may form flocks in winter and can be quite approachable. Rock pipits are resident and most do not move from their home territories, although in winter birds are found on coasts where they do not breed and in March and October, especially, a few turn up by reservoirs inland. Birds of the Scandinavian race migrate south and appear regularly on the east and south coasts of England. In spring they can be distinguished from Britain's rock pipits by their browner upperparts and whiter belly.

■ *A heavy-bodied pipit with dark olive upperparts and buff underparts, and poorly defined breast streaks. Dark legs and grey outer tail feathers.*
■ *Habitually perches on rocks. Often seen in small parties feeding on the shoreline.*

Water Pipit
ANTHUS SPINOLETTA

In spring, the water pipit is a very attractive bird, with a brown, almost unstreaked back, greyish head and unstreaked under parts which have a warm, pinkish flush. The white tail sides are not easy to see, but the bold, pale stripe over the eye and wingbars stand out. Water pipits breed in the mountainous regions of Europe; they leave the upland pastures between August and November, moving down to lowland regions, often dispersing some distance. The nearest breeding birds to Britain are probably in the Alps. No more than 100 are recorded in Britain each winter, usually between October and April. They like watercress beds, coastal fresh water, inland marshes and rivers. Most are seen in southern and eastern England. They are metres before settling again. After a while they will be found back at their preferred feeding place. Until recently, water pipits were regarded as a race of the rock pipit, but the two have been split into separate species along with the American water pipit, or buff-bellied pipit, a rare accidental visitor to Britain.

LENGTH: 17CM **WEIGHT:** 21–36G **WHERE TO LOOK:** LAKES, WATERCRESS BEDS IN WINTER AND SPRING. DOES NOT BREED IN BRITAIN **FOOD:** INSECTS AND SEEDS **VOICE:** SONG SIMILAR TO MEADOW PIPIT. CALLS ARE A SHARP *DZIT* AND A SHORT *DRRT*

■ *Bold stripe over eye, white outer tail, dark legs, white throat all year.*
■ *In winter, bigger, browner and plainer above than rock pipit; white wingbars and belly.*
■ *In summer, breast is pinkish and unstreaked. Head is grey.*

Meadow Pipit
ANTHUS PRAENSIS

LENGTH: 14CM **WEIGHT:** 16–25G **WHERE TO LOOK:** MOORS, MEADOWS AND DUNES **NEST:** ON GROUND IN TUSSOCK OF GRASS WITH FINE LINING **EGGS:** 4–5, WHITE WITH GREY/BROWN SPOTS **FOOD:** INSECTS AND SEEDS **VOICE:** ACCELERATING SONG WITH TRILL. CALL HIGH *TSEEP* REPEATED.

Meadow pipits are classic 'little brown birds'. Often only seen as they fly away from rough grass, the best clue to their identity is the thin, squeaky call, repeated persistently. They are often hard to see when on the ground, as they run between clumps of grass, occasionally pausing in the open. They are widely distributed throughout the country in the breeding season, but in winter leave the high ground for lowland areas, often feeding in urban parks and gardens and living secretively in weedy fields. Many of Britain's northern birds migrate south to southern and south-western England and Ireland and some will travel as far south as Spain. Migrants from northern Europe arrive in Britain each autumn and may spend the winter. Meadow pipits are important hosts for the cuckoo, especially in Ireland. They make up a large part of the prey of species such as hen harrier, merlin and kestrel, too.

***

■ The upperparts can vary from grey to olive-buff. Underparts yellowish to pale grey; pale legs.
■ Display flight is like a tree pipit's, but starts from the ground; song is less musical.
■ Always prefers ground to trees.
■ The squeaky call and white outer tail are distinctive in flight.

Tree Pipit
ANTHUS TRIVIALIS

As their name suggests, tree pipits make more use of trees than other pipits, especially in the lovely display flight. They feed on the ground, but when disturbed they will fly up into a tree or bush. They are summer visitors, arriving from April to June and leaving for tropical Africa from late July to October. Males usually arrive first and take up territory, announcing their presence with spectacular song flights.

They fly upwards from a tree perch and begin to sing as they reach the top of their ascent, descending with wings open and tail spread. The birds need song posts for display, as well as clear ground to feed on, and so choose heathland, commons and pasture with scattered trees or woodland edges. Newly planted conifers are readily used, and recently felled areas with some trees still standing are favourite sites. Tree pipits have spread north in Scotland during the last 100 years, and now breed extensively in mature birch woods. They are still absent as breeding birds in Ireland and only occur there as rare migrants.

LENGTH: 15CM **WEIGHT:** 20–25G **WHERE TO LOOK:** PLANTATIONS, HEATHS, SCATTERED TREES AND SCRUB **NEST:** GRASS CUP WITH FINE LINING IN TUSSOCK OR BANK **EGGS:** 4–6, VARIABLE WITH DARK SPOTS **FOOD:** INSECTS AND SEEDS **VOICE:** LOUD SONG WITH TRILLS. CALL A HOARSE *TEEZ*

***

■ Solitary, perching on trees, but feeding on ground. Stronger bill, stouter build, bolder actions and different call from meadow pipit.
■ Breast lightly streaked and yellower than a meadow pipit's.
■ The song is given after an upward flight from a tree during a 'parachute' drop.

Yellow Wagtail
MOTACILLA FLAVA

LENGTH: 17CM **WEIGHT:** 16–22G **WHERE TO LOOK:** WATER MEADOWS, PASTURE, MOORS AND LAKESIDES **NEST:** ON GROUND IN GRASS. ROOTS AND GRASS LINED WITH HAIR **EGGS:** 5–6, BUFF WITH DARKER SPOTS **FOOD:** MAINLY INSECTS. **VOICE:** A LOUD *TSWEE-IP*; WARBLING SONG

Yellow wagtails are among the most colourful summer visitors, the males shining out from grassy meadows like buttercups. They arrive from March to May and leave in August and September. There are occasional reports of over-wintering birds, but care must be taken not to confuse them with grey wagtails. Yellow wagtails are a race of the blue-headed wagtail and breed only in England and Wales, except for a few pairs in Scotland and even fewer in Ireland. Blue-headed wagtails breed from Scandinavia eastwards into Asia, and are seen as rare passage migrants in Britain in spring by their blue-grey crowns and ear-coverts with a white stripe over the eye and white chin. Odd ones turn up now and then in spring wagtail flocks.

■ *Male mostly bright yellow, long, spindly legs, fast walk, wingbars; unlike any other yellow bird.*
■ *Female is paler yellow, with browner green upperparts.*
■ *Found in damp meadows and fields by water; often feeding on insects disturbed by cattle.*
■ *Long, white-edged black tail is a useful feature in flight.*

Grey Wagtail
MOTACILLA CINEREA

Grey wagtails live up to the family name more than the others as their longer tail accentuates the vertical wagging motion. They delight in the rush and tumble of upland streams and rivers, perching on boulders and flying out after passing insects. They also feed on the ground, running quickly and pumping their tail, up and down each time they stop. In winter they leave the upland areas and move to lower ground, frequenting lakes, reservoirs, farmyards and sewage farms. Some birds travel south, even as far as France and Spain. Britain's residents are joined by northern European birds, which arrive in Britain for the winter. Grey wagtails suffer badly in severe winters, in common with other birds that feed by fresh water that becomes frozen. Watercress beds then become favourite haunts of these delightful and attractive birds.

LENGTH: 18CM **WEIGHT:** 15–23G **WHERE TO LOOK:** FAST RIVERS AND STREAMS **NEST:** LEDGES, HOLES IN WALLS AND BANKS NEAR WATER. MOSS, GRASS AND LEAVES, HAIR LINING **EGGS:** 4–6, BUFF WITH GREY/BROWN MARKS **FOOD:** INSECTS **VOICE:** INFREQUENT WARBLE, CALL IS A HIGH *TZTZI*

■ *Often mistaken for yellow wagtail, but legs pink.*
■ *In winter, male and female are similar, with buff-white throat.*
■ *Grey crown, yellow underparts, yellow-green rump, long white-edged tail; very sharp call.*
■ *In summer, male has a black throat.*
■ *Often seen perched on rocks and overhanging trees near streams.*

Pied Wagtail
MOTACILLA ALBA

LENGTH: 18CM WEIGHT: 19–20G **WHERE TO LOOK:** FARMLAND, OPEN COUNTRY, OFTEN NEAR WATER **NEST:** HOLES IN WALLS, SHEDS, BANKS, IVY; GRASS AND MOSS LINED WITH FEATHERS AND HAIR **EGGS:** 5–6, PALE GREY WITH SPECKLES **FOOD:** INSECTS AND SEEDS **VOICE:** TWITTERING WARBLE; SHRILL *TCHISSICK, TCHUWEE*

The black-and-white plumage and constant tail-bobbing of the pied wagtail make it a distinctive bird, found commonly in open country, especially farmyards, parks and gardens. It can be seen in paddocks and fields, trotting along the ground and dashing after insects scared up by the horses or cattle.

In many parts of Britain the pied wagtail is a familiar bird of urban environments, favouring in particular school playing fields and even supermarket car parks. Small groups may be seen flying overhead towards dusk, making their way to a communal roost, where hundreds noisily gather on a tree before flying to a reed bed, bush or even a building ledge for the night.

Pied wagtails breed over the whole of Britain with the exception of the Shetland Islands. In winter, northern birds move south to spend the winter in central and southern England, although many go to France, Spain and even Morocco. Pied wagtails are a race (ie sub-species) of the white wagtail and only breed regularly in Britain and Ireland. White wagtails breed from Iceland to the Mediterranean and are seen in Britain on passage in spring and autumn, especially on the west and north coasts. There have been records of white wagtails breeding in England and of hybridisation between the two races.

Female

Male

▨ *Black and white plumage and a long bobbing tail make this an easily recognisable bird as it chases across short grass for insects.*

▨ *Females have a greyer back and a smaller bib than males.*

▨ *Highly territorial in spring, they will even attack their reflections in the wing mirrors and hubcaps of parked cars.*

▨ *Pied wagtails prefer short grass or tarmac, where they can run along the ground. They are agile and can dart rapidly or fly up to catch passing insect prey.*

▨ *In flight, note the long tail and distinctive call.*

Great Grey Shrike
LANIUS EXCUBITOR

Flight is deeply undulating, often low, with a sweep up to perch. Bold, white wing bars are obvious.

Red-backed Shrike
LANIUS COLLURIO

Colourful but increasingly rare. Coastal breeder, now most likely to be seen on migration. In flight 'too big for a warbler, too small for a thrush'.

Starling
STURNUS VULGARIS

Juvenile

Adult, winter plumage

LENGTH: 22CM **WEIGHT:** 75–90G **WHERE TO LOOK:** WIDESPREAD **NEST:** IN HOLE IN BUILDING OR TREE **EGGS:** 4–6, BLUE **FOOD:** SEEDS, FRUIT, CATERPILLARS, LEATHERJACKETS, ANTS **VOICE:** TRILLS, BUZZY AND SCREECHING CALLS; A GOOD MIMIC OF BIRDS AND OF OTHER SOUNDS

Though familiar in gardens, parks and even town centres, the starling's lifestyle still holds secrets little known even to the keenest observer of birds. As with so many species, research reveals fascinating facts. A male in spring, having built his rough nest, sings with puffed-out throat and drooped wings to attract a mate. Should a female come close he will sing in a frenzy of wing-waving, with his back hunched and tail fanned. If she stops nearby, he will sing from the nest itself to attract her in, and she will complete the lining. If there are several pairs of starlings in an area, by some unknown means they will synchronise their breeding and start laying eggs at the same time. Some females lay an egg in another's nest, and bright blue eggs can often be found on a lawn, mysteriously intact – removed from a nest by a starling, but whether by an intruding female is not known. Some males are polygamous, leaving one mate on the eggs, while going off with another, often younger, female. The male incubates the eggs for a small part of the day, leaving the rest of the day and all night to the female.

■ *In spring, the male is very glossy and colourful with blue base to beak (female has a pink patch on bill).*

■ *From December onwards the bill turns yellow and in spring, the legs change from dull brown to orange or reddish. Pale feather tips weaken and crumble away to reveal glossy colours beneath, most obvious in males.*

■ *Females often keep more orange-brown on wings than males in summer.*

Waxwing
BOMBYCILLA GARRULUS

Every winter, British birdwatchers hope for an invasion of these gorgeous birds. Such 'irruptions', caused by overcrowding and food shortages on their normal wintering grounds in northern Europe occur irregularly and may be becoming less frequent. Nevertheless, in most winters there are at least a few along the east coast of England and Scotland and, in some years, they are more numerous and get as far west as Wales and even Ireland. Waxwings are remarkable in many other ways: they turn up regularly in gardens and parks and allow a close approach. This will show their handsome plumage, including the secondary feathers with their extraordinary red blobs of 'sealing wax' at the tips, which give the bird its name. Very occasionally, the buttercup-yellow end of the tail will show these tips too. Waxwings feed acrobatically among the branches of berry-bearing shrubs and trees, sometimes gorging themselves to a state of total inactivity.

LENGTH: 18CM **WEIGHT:** 50–55G **WHERE TO LOOK:** ANYWHERE WITH BERRY-BEARING BUSHES OR TREES, FROM COUNTRY LANES TO CITY CENTRES **FOOD:** IN WINTER ALMOST ENTIRELY BERRIES, EG ROWAN, HAWTHORN, COTONEASTER, ROSE, VIBURNUM **VOICE:** A LONG, SILVERY TRILL

Juvenile

Adult male

Adult female

■ *Females tend to show less intense black bibs and less bright yellow and red markings on the wings and tail, but sexing is not easy.*

■ *Gregarious and tame, waxwings may feed in one bush for some days.*

■ *Pink-brown, with obvious crest, black mask and throat, grey rump, colourful wing and tail patterns.*

Jay
GARRULUS GLANDARIUS

LENGTH: 34CM **WEIGHT:** 140–190G **WHERE TO LOOK:**
DECIDUOUS AND CONIFER WOODS, WOODED FARMLAND,
PARKS, GARDENS **NEST:** WELL-HIDDEN, OF STICKS **EGGS:** 4–5,
PALE BLUISH, SPOTTED **FOOD:** ALMOST ANYTHING, ESPECIALLY
ACORNS **VOICE:** A HARSH *SKRAAAK*, QUIET MEWING

Jays are widespread in wooded counties of England and Wales, absent from the southern and northern counties of Scotland, but occur in a band from Argyll to the east coast. They were badly persecuted in the 19th century, but this is lessening and the bird is now increasing, spreading into suburbs, and into upland areas where coniferous woodland has been created.

Jays eat a wide variety of foods, but acorns are the most important and persecution is quite unjustified on the grounds of their eating habits. They are responsible for the large-scale dispersal of acorns in the autumn, probably involving several thousand acorns per bird. This helps to sustain the birds, and is also vital for future survival of oak woods.

Jays do not normally move far in Britain, although large movements occur on mainland Europe continent in autumn, and in most years some birds reach southern and eastern Britain. Huge movements of jays were recorded in southern Britain in autumn 1983, caused by the widespread failure of the acorn crop both in Britain and on mainland Europe. In rural gardens, jays will sometimes come to bird feeders and take nuts and fat. Despite this apparently bold behaviour, they are, nevertheless, always wary of humans.

▨ *The most colourful of the crows. The body is pinkish, browner above than below, with a white rump and black tail. The wing has a bright white panel and a patch of blue with black bars.*

Magpie
PICA PICA

LENGTH: 40–45CM **WEIGHT:** 200–250G
WHERE TO LOOK: FARMLAND, OPEN COUNTRY
WITH SCATTERED TREES OR BUSHES, ALSO
INCREASINGLY IN SUBURBAN AND URBAN
AREAS **NEST:** LARGE, DOMED, OF STICKS LINED
WITH EARTH AND FINE ROOTS **EGGS:** UP TO 8,
NORMALLY 5–6 **FOOD:** OMNIVOROUS **VOICE:**
A LOUD, RAPID *CHAK-CHAK-CHAK*

Unmistakable as this bird is, it is often the call that gives away the magpie's presence. Except for large parts of Scotland, magpies are common in Britain. They are found in many habitats, though their preference is for grassland with thick hedges or scattered trees. Recent years have seen an increase in numbers, especially in towns and suburbs with thick shrubberies, though in eastern England, where many hedgerows have been removed, magpie numbers have declined.

The magpie, beautiful and intelligent, is much persecuted, especially in game-rearing areas, and is not appreciated in gardens where it is accused of eating too many eggs and chicks of small birds (though it is far less of a nuisance than the domestic cat and eats far fewer birds than protected hawks and falcons). Magpies eat mostly invertebrates in summer, and seeds and berries in the winter. They do not move from their home territories and no birds from mainland Europe arrive in winter. One of the commonest ways of seeing a magpie these days is feeding on animal road casualties. This rich source of food undoubtedly helps magpies thrive.

▨ *Even at a distance, the black-and-white plumage and long, graduated tail are unmistakable – as is the distinctive 'machine gun' call.*
▨ *Sometimes comical on the ground. Walks with high-stepping gait and often hops or bounces sideways when excited or seeking food.*
▨ *The wing feathers have a purplish-blue iridescent sheen, and the tail is iridescent green, with a band of reddish-purple near the tip.*
▨ *Juveniles have very short tails and lack the brightness and gloss of adults' plumage.*

Chough
PYRRHOCORAX PYRRHOCORAX

Choughs are slightly larger than jackdaws, and the scarcest of Britain's crows. Although once common, they are now confined to the cliff coasts of Wales, the Isle of Man, some of the Inner Hebridean islands, and Ireland. A few pairs breed on inland cliffs in Wales.

Choughs are gregarious, even in the breeding season, often flying along the cliffs in small flocks. Their flight is superbly graceful, agile and buoyant, often with aerobatic swoops and dives. The noisy calls are distinctive and far reaching; though usually pronounced 'chuff', the English name may originally have been 'chow' in imitation of the call. They feed on the maritime heath and pasture above cliff tops. The loss of these areas to arable farming has contributed to the chough's recent decline. About 1,000 pairs breed in the British Isles, the majority found in western Ireland.

LENGTH: 40CM WEIGHT: 280–360G WHERE TO LOOK: SEA CLIFFS, VERY OCCASIONALLY INLAND AT ROCK FACES AND QUARRIES NEST: OF STICKS, LINED WITH WOOL OR FINE GRASS, ON A LEDGE OR CREVICE, OFTEN HIGH ON ROCK FACE FOOD: CHIEFLY INVERTEBRATES VOICE: *KWEE-OW; CHEE-A*

- *Adults have slim, down-curved red bills and red legs. Juveniles' bills are shorter and orange in colour.*
- *Plumage glossy and entirely black. Walks, runs and hops.*
- *May advertise its presence with noisy calls and wing flicking.*
- *In flight, wings are broad and the primary feathers on the wings well separated, giving a characteristic silhouette.*

Jackdaw
CORVUS MONEDULA

LENGTH: 33CM WEIGHT: 220–270G WHERE TO LOOK: TOWNS, CITIES, FARMLAND, PARKLAND, WOODLAND AND SEA CLIFFS NEST: PILE OF STICKS IN HOLES OR CREVICE IN TREES, BUILDINGS OR ROCKS EGGS: 4–6, BLUE-GREEN FOOD: VIRTUALLY ANYTHING VOICE: *KOW, CHUK-CHUK, JAK*

Jackdaws are widespread throughout the British Isles, except for parts of Scotland (although numbers have increased and the breeding range expanded in the 20th century), yet oddly rare in places. They nest in loose colonies, often using the same nest sites year after year. Almost any suitably large crevice or hole, which the birds fill with a tangle of sticks, might be used as a nest site. Less material is used at cliff sites, where the nest often occupies a rabbit burrow. Jackdaws usually eat vegetable matter, especially grain and seeds, and surface-dwelling invertebrates, but will take almost any food. They readily exploit temporary abundances of food, such as the large numbers of leaf-eating caterpillars in woodlands in May or June, or animal foodstuffs. In winter they commonly scavenge at domestic refuse tips. Some migration occurs in winter when British birds move west, sometimes to Ireland, and birds from mainland Europe arrive on the east and south coasts.

- *Quicker and more active on the ground than other crows. Flight also quicker, and primary wing feathers only slightly separated. Has pale eye.*
- *Plumage is entirely black except for the ash-grey sides of the neck, nape and back of the head.*
- *Gregarious at all seasons, often roosting and feeding communally with other crows, notably rooks.*
- *Noisy and sometimes aggressive, fluffs out feathers and spreads tail when defending nest site.*

Rook
CORVUS FRUGILEGUS

LENGTH: 46CM **WEIGHT:** 460–520G **WHERE TO LOOK:** FARMLAND, GRASSLANDS, PARKS AND WOODED SUBURBS **NEST:** COMMUNALLY IN ROOKERIES IN TREES, RE-USING STICK NEST FROM PREVIOUS YEAR **EGGS:** 2–7, USUALLY 4–5 **FOOD:** OMNIVOROUS **VOICE:** A DEEP CAW OR *KAAAH*

W hat would the countryside be without its lively, noisy, busybody rooks! The very essence of lowland farmland, but less common in the uplands, they are gregarious, quarrelsome birds, nesting in tree-top rookeries which sway precariously in the wind, with anything from a handful to several thousand nests. Life at a rookery is fascinating and easily observed, since nesting begins well before the leaves appear. In winter a rookery may become a traditional roost.

Travelling flocks of rooks, using set routes, may amalgamate into spectacular gatherings of several thousand birds. The amiable 'caws' are among the essential countryside sounds. Accused of damaging crops, rooks eat mainly worms and leatherjackets, though grain undoubtedly forms a large part of the diet when they can reach it. On balance, rooks seem to be beneficial and it would be a sad loss if the village rookery or the roaming flocks of big, black birds were to disappear from the rural scene. British rooks are resident, but numbers are boosted by birds from mainland Europe in winter.

Adult

Juvenile

■ *The face and chin of adults lack feathers and are pale grey. The base of the bill is also grey. Juveniles have feathered bills and face patches which do not become bare like the adults' until they are 9–12 months old.*

■ *The all-black plumage has a purplish gloss, and the long thigh feathers give the 'baggy trousers' appearance.*

■ *The iridescent sheen of the feathers gives a silvery effect when they are viewed against the sun.*

■ *Walks sedately, probing the soil and picking at invertebrates or seeds. Gregarious when feeding.*

■ *The communal roost, which may be at a rookery, attracts rooks from several other rookeries, as well as jackdaws and carrion crows.*

■ *Activity and noise reach a peak at the rookery in early spring. Birds quarrel over territories, make pursuit flights around the rookery, and display by bowing, tail fanning and wing drooping.*

Carrion and Hooded Crow
CORVUS CORONE

LENGTH: 47CM WEIGHT: 540–600G WHERE TO LOOK:
FARMLAND, OPEN WOODLAND, HEATHS, COASTS, TOWNS AND
PARKS NEST: USUALLY IN TREES, MADE OF STICKS AND EARTH,
LINED WITH WOOL OR HAIR EGGS: USUALLY 4, GREENISH,
SPOTTED FOOD: OMNIVOROUS VOICE: *KAAAW*

Carrion crow

Hooded crow

The all-back carrion crow is found throughout England, Wales and most of
Scotland. The grey-and-black hooded crow occurs in north-west Scotland, in
Ireland and the Isle of Man. They are distinct forms, or subspecies, of the European
crow. Although they have separate breeding ranges and different plumages, they are
regarded as the same species because they interbreed freely where their ranges
overlap and they produce fertile offspring (often called hybrids). The zone where
inter-breeding occurs is rather narrow, which indicates that the hybrids are less
successful breeders than either of the pure forms. Both forms are usually resident,
although there is some dispersal of young in autumn. Numbers of hooded crows are
boosted in winter by the arrival in northern and eastern Britain of birds from
Scandinavia. Crows will eat almost anything, and scavenge widely in winter, including
at refuse tips and on the shore. They are widely considered to be pests, eating
gamebird eggs, or causing damage to trapped sheep or young lambs. Although some
damage is caused, it is rarely as serious as often suggested – hoodies eat a lot from
tips and cattle troughs! People sometimes confuse carrion crows with rooks. A rule-
of-thumb way of distinguishing the two is to observe their social behaviour: rooks
are invariably seen in large groups, while crows are usually solitary or seen in pairs.

◼ *The hooded crow has a grey back, breast and underside, and is grey underneath the
front of the wing.*
◼ *The carrion crow is entirely black, with a blue and green gloss.*
◼ *The powerful dagger-like bill of both birds is capable of tearing flesh.*
◼ *Both hooded and carrion crows often mob birds of prey, and are usually successful in
driving them away.*
◼ *Where hooded and carrion crows interbreed, the young may have mixed black and
grey plumages.*

Raven

CORVUS CORAX

The spectacular raven is an inseparable part of the upland and coastal scene in western and northern Britain and much of Ireland. More widespread at the turn of the century, it has withdrawn westwards due to persecution. There has been a slight recovery since 1914 in places adjacent to ancient strongholds, partly due to a return to tree nesting by birds unable to find a suitable, unoccupied crag. More recently the range has contracted again, and large conifer plantations, which result in the removal of sheep, trigger a decline. In Ireland, where conifer planting is less concentrated and the food supply (largely dead sheep) consequently less affected, ravens may be on the increase. The British and Irish population is still less than 5,000 pairs. Most ravens are crag-nesters, ideally suited to the harsh and expansive upland environment or the windswept sea coast, but trees, quarry faces and old buildings are also used for nesting. Ravens with territories stay in them all year round, but young birds disperse and non-breeders form sizeable itinerant flocks. At a suitable windy crag they dive and roll in the upcurrents in an expression of sheer exuberance in their mastery of a difficult environment.

LENGTH: 64CM WEIGHT: 800–1,500G WHERE TO LOOK: SEA CLIFFS, WOODS AND CRAGS ON VALLEY SIDES, MOUNTAINS AND MOORS NEST: USUALLY ON ROCKY CRAGS AND LEDGES, LESS OFTEN IN TREES; LARGE AND BUILT OF SMALL BRANCHES AND STICKS, LINED IN LAYERS, FIRST WITH EARTH AND ROOTS, THEN PLANT MATERIAL, MAINLY MOSS, THEN WOOL, HAIR AND FINE GRASS EGGS: 3–7, (USUALLY 5) LAID IN MARCH FOOD: OMNIVOROUS, BUT SHEEP CARRION FORMS THE MAJORITY OF THE DIET VOICE: A DEEP CROAKING *PRRUK* OFTEN REPEATED. ALSO AN ALMOST BELL-LIKE *TOC* AND QUIET, RATTLING 'SONG'

▓ *The largest crow in Britain. Entirely black plumage with blue, purplish and greenish gloss, and black bare parts. Readily told from other crows by large size.*

▓ *The larger, heavier and more powerful bill helps distinguish the raven from the carrion crow. The feathers on the throat are rather shaggy, giving the bird a distinctive profile.*

▓ *Perches on rocks and boulders, also on the ground. Has a stately walk. Hops clumsily when hurried.*

▓ *In flight, note well-separated tips to primary wing feathers, large head, and long, wedge-shaped tail.*

▓ *Flight is direct, with deep, heavy wing-beats; rather slower than carrion crow. Glides, and frequently soars on thermals.*

▓ *The principal food is dead sheep, which may be abundant after hard winter weather. In the lambing season the placentae are eaten.*

▓ *Ravens eat small mammals, frogs, lizards, insects and even refuse.*

Throat feathers

Dipper
CINCLUS CINCLUS

LENGTH: 18CM **WEIGHT:** 60–65G **WHERE TO LOOK:** FAST-
FLOWING UPLAND STREAMS; LESS OFTEN LOWLAND RIVERS,
MILL-RACES, WEIRS **NEST:** UNDER BRIDGE, BANK OVERHANG,
TREE ROOTS, BEHIND A WATERFALL. DOMED **EGGS:** 4–6, WHITE
FOOD: AQUATIC INVERTEBRATES; SOME SMALL FISH, TADPOLES
VOICE: PIERCING, RASPED *ZIT* OR METALLIC *CHINK*; SONG A
LONG WARBLE OF LIQUID AND GRATING NOTES

'Black-bellied'
dipper

British dipper

Living chiefly in the north and west of Britain, dippers love fast, shallow water. A bird will stand on a rock in mid-stream, 'curtseying' every few seconds as if on springs, then slip smoothly beneath the surface and walk along the stream bed, or 'fly' under water – tricks that no other songbird can achieve: the plumage is soft and dense for good insulation in the water.

Dippers sometimes perch on trees or wires, and they even search house gutters for food at times! Usually solitary or in pairs, several birds may roost together in winter, in a sheltered spot such as under a bridge. In winter, too, some birds move to lowland rivers or even to the coast, and some reach the south-east – although a winter dipper there may well be in the 'black-bellied' race from Europe, which lacks the chestnut of British birds. A hazard for upland dippers could prove to be acid rain, which may reduce populations of their animal food.

■ *Brown head, slate-grey back, with dark 'scaly' markings only visible at close range.*
■ *Brilliant white chin. Throat and breast separated from dark belly and undertail by a chestnut band. White eyelid obvious when blinked.*
■ *Juveniles are greyer than adults, and more 'scaly' in appearance.*
■ *Dippers are unique among songbirds in feeding under water. Despite unwebbed feet, they swim very well.*
■ *They fly low and fast on shore with whirring wings, following the course of the stream or river.*

Wren
TROGLODYTES TROGLODYTES

LENGTH: 9.5CM **WEIGHT:** 10G **WHERE TO LOOK:** LOW COVER ANYWHERE FROM GARDENS TO REMOTE SEA CLIFFS, BUT ESPECIALLY IN WOODLANDS **NEST:** DOMED, USUALLY LOW IN TREE, IVY OR CREVICE **EGGS:** 5-6, WHITE, SPOTTED RED **FOOD:** INSECTS, SPIDERS **VOICE:** A HARD *CHITI*; DRY RATTLE. SONG IS STARTINGLY LOUD OUTBURST

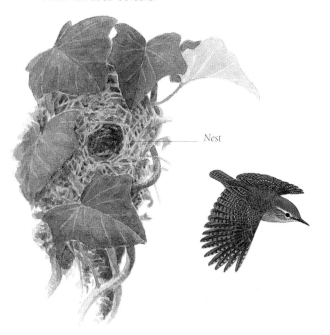

Nest

Most British and Irish wrens look the same as European ones, red-brown and buff, barred darker. However, there are four other subspecies on British islands – on St Kilda, on Fair Isle, in the Hebrides, and in the Shetlands. The first two races are greyer than mainland birds, the last two darker. One day they may form different species: at present, they all share the restless and excitable nature of the familiar woodland wren, and its explosive calls and song.

Few people would name the wren as the commonest British bird, and yet in many years it is exactly that, with perhaps 10 million pairs. Its ability to survive and breed from southern heathlands to northern sea-stacks is the reason for its success in these years. But hard winters are murderous for the species: sometimes seven out of ten are killed. Some wrens combat severe weather by moving to better feeding places. Some roost communally in natural or artificial holes, and at dusk over 60 have been watched going into a standard-size nestbox! Special roosting nests are occasionally built, or old breeding nests may be used. How the birds all learn of such roosts is a mystery. Their live-food diet is one reason for wrens' winter vulnerability, but they can be helped by sprinkling grated cheese under hedges and in other likely places.

▓ *Tiny; red-brown above with darker bars; buffish below. Short, cocked tail. Both sexes, and young birds, look alike.*

▓ *Normal flight is whirring, direct and low, the bird quickly diving back into cover again.*

▓ *Wrens often spend winter in odd places such as reed beds.*

▓ *Wrens thread invisibly through the undergrowth; then they pop up to sing or to scold the observer.*

▓ *A wren's nest is an intricate structure. Usually spherical in shape, it has a neat opening on one side.*

▓ *The male builds several nests and the female (or females when the male is polygamous) lines one with feathers. A second brood may be reared in the same nest.*

Dunnock
PRUNELLA MODULARIS

LENGTH: 14.5CM **WEIGHT:** 20–22G **WHERE TO LOOK:** GARDENS, WOODLAND, HEDGES, OPEN SPACES WITH BUSHES **NEST:** LOW IN HEDGES, BUSHES, OFTEN IN EVERGREENS **EGGS:** 4–5, TURQUOISE **FOOD:** INSECTS; MAINLY SEEDS IN WINTER **VOICE:** A PIERCING *PEEP*; SONG IS A HIGH, PLEASANT WARBLE, LIKE WREN'S, BUT WEAKER, MORE RAMBLING

The dunnock is the perfect example of the proverb 'Still waters run deep'. Sober in colouring and demeanour, it has a reputation among birdwatchers for being a bit boring, and yet it has an enormously interesting sex life! A male may have a single mate, two or even three; a female might have two or three males; and sometimes several males are associated with several females. The commonest arrangement is a simple pair, or a female with two males.

Because of these complications, it is a biological advantage to a male to ensure that he is the one to fertilize the eggs; to do this, before mating he uses his bill to stimulate the female to eject sperm from any previous mating. In a two-male/one-female relationship, one male tends to be subordinate and may be prevented from mating: if so, he will not help to feed the young, which may not even be of their own species – dunnocks are frequent victims of the cuckoo, the speckled eggs of which they are unable to distinguish from their own unmarked ones.

Dunnocks are widespread in Britain. They occur in a wide variety of habitats, from upland areas of moderate elevation down to windswept headlands around the coast. The one thing all these different locations have in common is good ground cover, be it bramble or bracken.

■ *Adult dunnocks are a rich brown above, streaked with black, slate grey on the head and underparts. They have a thin, buff wingbar.*

■ *Once commonly known as the hedge sparrow, the dunnock is sparrow-like in colouration, but with a quite different lifestyle.*

■ *Dunnocks have a distinctive gait, hopping slowly and deliberately, keeping the body close to the ground.*

■ *Dunnocks have the fine bill of an insect-eater, though they mostly eat small seeds in the winter.*

■ *Not usually sociable, but in winter loose feeding flocks of 100 or more birds may gather at food-rich sites.*

■ *They hunt for food under hedges, on lawns, along field borders and in root crops and weed patches.*

Sedge Warbler
ACROCEPHALUS SCHOENOBAENUS

LENGTH: 13CM **WEIGHT:** 10–13G **WHERE TO LOOK:** WATERSIDE
VEGETATION, CEREAL FIELDS, PLANTATIONS **NEST:** DEEP CUP OF
GRASS, SEDGE, LOW IN BRAMBLES, ETC **EGGS:** 5–6, PALE OLIVE,
AND WELL SPECKLED **FOOD:** INSECTS, LARVAE, APHIDS **VOICE:**
IMPATIENT CHATTER OF HARSH AND SWEET NOTES

Adult

Old country names for the sedge warbler include mock nightingale and Scotch nightingale, for this lively summer visitor sings night and day when it first arrives back in Britain. A mass overnight arrival can be very exciting, with singing birds occupying every riverside bush where the previous day there were none. Often a bird will suddenly emerge from the depths of the vegetation where it has been feeding low down, and burst into its exuberant song, full of mimicry, seldom repeating itself, suddenly halting, then tearing off again, and always sounding vaguely irritated. It may also fly up vertically and spiral down, with fluttering wings and spread tail, singing excitedly.

Normally weighing only about 10g, the sedge warbler feeds avidly on plum-reed aphids before migration and puts on large fat deposits which may be double its weight. This enables it to cross the Sahara in one hop from France or Spain, a distance of some 3,800km. The Sahel drought in West Africa has caused a decline in numbers since 1968, as returning birds use this zone for feeding prior to spring migration.

The sedge warbler is primarily an insect feeder. The waterside vegetation which forms its ideal habitat is a rich hunting ground for flies of numerous species, as well as mayflies and caddis flies; moth caterpillars are also important in the sedge warbler's diet.

Juvenile

▨ *Broad, creamy stripe over the eye, streaky back, and upstreaked tawny rump; tail spread and depressed.*
▨ *The yellower juveniles show a paler, streaked, central crown stripe.*
▨ *May perch horizontally, looking rather furtive.*
▨ *Inquisitive, often sidling up vertical stems to investigate an intruder or strange noise.*
▨ *At close range, the orange-red gape of the singing bird can be seen.*

Cetti's Warbler
CETTIA CETTI

Dark, thick-set, whiter beneath; dark bars under rounded tail. The song is given in incredibly loud bursts.

Grasshopper Warbler
LOCUSTELLA NAEVIA

Perhaps Britain's most mouse-like bird in its movements. Will drop into low vegetation when disturbed, and run and creep in preference to flying. The song is insect-like, or perhaps recalls a freewheeling bicycle.

Reed Warbler
ACROCEPHALUS SCIRPACEUS

LENGTH: 13CM **WEIGHT:** 10–15G **WHERE TO LOOK:** REED BEDS
ACROSS SOUTHERN BRITAIN **NEST:** DEEP CUP OF GRASSED
WOVEN AROUND REED STEMS, OVER SHALLOW WATER **EGGS:** 4,
GREENISH-WHITE, MOTTLED DARKER **FOOD:** VARIETY OF
INSECTS **VOICE:** LIKE SEDGE WARBLER, BUT MORE RELAXED,
EACH PHRASE REPEATED

On the edge of its range in Britain, the reed warbler has spread west and north to occupy most suitable red beds in England and Wales. Large numbers may nest in one reed bed, though the birds themselves are not social, and are highly aggressive to others of their kind. Along with the meadow pipit and the dunnock, this bird is the main host of the cuckoo in Britain. Studies have shown that the proportion of reed warbler nests parasitised has more than doubled in recent years, and 'reed warbler cuckoos' are significantly more successful in having their young reared to maturity than those using other hosts. Because of high cuckoo predation in reed bed colonies, nests outside reed beds are, paradoxically, more successful from the warblers' viewpoint.

For such small birds, reed warblers are long-lived. Ringing studies have revealed several 10 and 11-year old birds.

The song may recall that of the sedge warbler at first, and like that species includes mimicry, but it is much more repetitive, with a steadier rhythm. Unlike the neurotic sedge warbler, the reed warbler's song sounds rather 'laid-back', perhaps in keeping with drowsy summer days by the waterside.

Like its relative the sedge warbler, the reed warbler feeds mainly on insects. Both adults and larvae are taken, and the diet includes moth larvae, grasshoppers, caddis flies and aphids. The bird is an agile climber and can move through reeds and tangled vegetation with ease, using its fine bill to pluck an unsuspecting insect from leaf or stem.

■ *Seasonal and age variation in plumage colour, though always with warm red-brown hues, especially on the rump.*

■ *The neat, woven nest has living reed stems incorporated into its structure.*

■ *Though nesting in reed beds, they regularly forage in nearby bushes, especially willows. Often seen far from water on migration.*

■ *Very agile. Clings to vertical stems with both feet, or to adjacent stems, thereby doing the splits! Moves up and down in jerks, or hops and flits from plant to plant.*

Marsh Warbler
ACROCEPHALUS PALUSTRIS

Reed and marsh warblers
both have long bills and legs,
long undertail coverts and rounded
tails. Voice only reliable distinction,
that of the marsh warbler being
rich and mimetic.

Blackcap
SYLVIA ATRICAPILLA

LENGTH: 13–15CM WEIGHT: 14-20G WHERE
TO LOOK: WOODS, PARKS, GARDENS,
BIRDTABLES IN WINTER NESTS: COMPACT
GRASS CUP EGGS: 5, PALE, SPOTTED
BROWNISH FOOD: INSECTS, BERRIES, ALSO FAT
AND SCRAPS IN WINTER VOICE: BEAUTIFUL
LOUD, RICH, PURE WARBLING

Although (like other warblers) they are primarily summer visitors, increasing numbers of blackcaps now spend the winter in Britain. At this time they most often live in gardens, where they feed on bird table scraps, fat, bread and, not infrequently, even peck at hanging nut bags. British breeding birds migrate to the Mediterranean and North Africa; those seen in Britain during winter have come from Eastern Europe. The habit of over-wintering is not new, but it is growing, with perhaps 2,000 birds now, some regularly as far north as Aberdeen. Although smaller than many other garden birds, blackcaps are usually very aggressive, and may be the dominant bird present at the 'feeding station'. They often puff out their feathers to appear larger than they really are, and as an added protection against the cold.

The full song consists of short phrases, often with a terminal flourish of loud, clear notes, and is regarded by many as equal to the nightingale in quality. By contrast, the call is a *tac-tac*, harder than that of the garden warbler. However, the softer, more rambling sub-song is very garden-warbler-like and many people are happier identifying them by sight, not sound.

■ *Female unmistakable with bright, red-brown cap. Juvenile similar but more rusty-brown, less olive-brown above, yellower below, with orange-brown or dark brown cap.*
■ *In autumn, blackberries are regularly and greedily taken; in winter, ivy and holly berries.*
■ *Often sings from high in an oak tree in spring. In jerky flight from tree to tree, the longish tail shows no white, ruling out whitethroats.*

Garden Warbler
SYLVIA BORIN

The nondescript garden warbler more than makes up for its lack of looks with its beautiful song. It is always with a feeling of satisfaction that one catches sight of the songster to confirm the sound identification, for it can be tricky to separate the songs of garden warbler and blackcap. The former sings longer phrases with shorter intervals, and the song is quieter and mellower, more rapid and even, without the almost abrupt outburst of the blackcap.

The garden warbler arrives later than the blackcap. Competition between the two species is largely avoided by the garden warbler's preferences for feeding in lower vegetation. The male builds several 'cock's nests' of dried grass before the actual nest site is chosen.

In autumn, late migrants hang on well into October, and then turn to fruit and berries to supplement the basic insectivorous diet. Like many birds, the garden warbler is rather inappropriately named, rarely occurring in the average garden, and unfamiliar to most garden birdwatchers. Only small numbers breed in Ireland, and it is scarce in the north of Scotland.

LENGTH: 13–15 CM WEIGHT: 16–23G WHERE
TO LOOK: WOODS, SCRUB, OVERGROWN
HEDGEROWS NEST: LOOSE CUP OF DRY
GRASS, USUALLY LOW EGGS: 4–5, WHITE AND
BUFF, BLOTCHED DARKER. FOOD: INSECTS,
LARVAE, FRUIT VOICE: RICH, SUSTAINED, EVEN
WARBLING. CALL *CHECK-CHECK*

■ *When in full song, it has few rivals, and must rank in the British 'top ten' songsters.*
■ *Greyish-brown sides of nape and hind neck, and, in close view, narrow pale eye-ring.*
■ *In flight, note shortish square-ended tail without 'white outers', longish wings and rather plump appearance.*

Whitethroat
SYLVIA COMMUNIS

LENGTH: 13–15 CM **WEIGHT:** 12–18G **WHERE TO LOOK:** LOW HEDGEROWS, SCRUB, WOODLAND EDGE **NEST:** LOW CUP OF DRY GRASS, ROOTS **EGGS:** 4–5, BLUE/GREEN, SPOTTED GREY **FOOD:** INSECTS, BERRIES **VOICE:** VIGOROUS, SCRATCHY WARBLE. CALLS INCLUDE *WHET-WHET-WHET*

Adult male

Adult female

In the spring of 1969, birdwatchers were asking, 'Where have all the whitethroats gone?'. Until then, whitethroats had been among Britian's most abundant birds. Subsequent analysis showed that less than one bird in four had returned, and that the factor responsible was the disastrous drought in the arid thorn-scrub zone of the Sahel, south of the Sahara, which holds Britain's whitethroats in winter. The population has never recovered, though the rather tetchy song remains a characteristic summer sound. The old country name of 'nettlecreeper' reflects the bird's favourite nesting site.

The males return a fortnight before their mates to set up territory. They are restless birds, forever complaining, raising their crown feathers or fanning the rather long, prominently white-edged tail. The song may be given while on the move inside bushes, from an exposed perch or (especially where there are no trees or taller features in the territory) in a jerky, dancing, short song-flight, the bird bouncing as if on an invisible piece of elastic.

■ *In spring, the male is a very smart bird with grey head, white throat and beautiful, pinkish wash across his breast.*
■ *The female is rather duller, with a browner head. Note also the white eye-ring and pale eye.*
■ *Easily told in all plumages from lesser whitethroat by the rusty fringes to the flight feathers, pale legs, longer tail and large-headed, often rather unkempt, appearance.*

Lesser Whitethroat
SYLVIA CURRUCA

LENGTH: 14CM **WEIGHT:** 10–16G **WHERE TO LOOK:** TALL, THICK HEDGEROWS, SCRUB **NEST:** FLIMSIER THAN WHITETHROAT'S, HIGHER ABOVE GROUND **EGGS:** 4–6, CREAM, SPECKLED DARKER **FOOD:** INSECTS; FRUIT IN AUTUMN **VOICE:** UNMUSICAL, LOUD RATTLE. CALL HARD *TAC-TAC*

One of a small group of birds which migrates south-east to spend the winter in north-east Africa (mainly in the Sudan and Ethiopia), lesser whitethroats take different routes in spring and autumn. Ringing recoveries have shown that British birds pass through northern Italy *en route* to Egypt, where they follow the Nile, but when returning north they pass to the east of the Mediterranean, through Cyprus and Turkey.

Lesser whitethroats are rather retiring birds, but once their song has been learnt, it will reveal the species to be quite common over much of England. Care must be taken not to confuse the far-carrying, rattled song with that of the now rare cirl bunting. Birds often sing while on the move, almost always from within a thick hedge, or concealed in the canopy of a tree. At close range, a soft, inward whitethroat-like warble can be heard preceding the song proper, which is a simple, quick rattle sounding like *chakakakakake*.

In autumn, young birds may be seen in gardens, diligently searching bushes for insects, or taking berries. Their presence may be announced by a hard *tac* or, occasionally, a high-pitched squeak.

■ *Male and female similar. Not shy, but often stay well concealed.*
■ *Dark face and lower edge to ear-coverts.*
■ *In flight, shows less white on outer tail than whitethroat.*
■ *The song makes up for its lack of musicality by its carrying power.*

Dartford Warbler
SYLVIA UNDATA

LENGTH: 13CM WEIGHT: 9–12G WHERE TO
LOOK: RESIDENT ON SOUTHERN HEATHS
WITH GORSE AND HEATHER NEST: CUP OF
DEAD GRASSES, MOSS EGGS: 4, PALE, SPECKLED
GREY FOOD: INSECTS, IN WINTER MAINLY
SPIDERS VOICE: SCRATCHY WARBLE. CALL A
SOFT *TCHIRR*

Until recently Britain's only resident warbler, this entirely insectivorous bird is
badly hit by hard winters, and by fragmentation of its specialised heathland
habitat. It was first described in 1773 from Bexley Heath, near Dartford in Kent,
but has not occurred in that county for many years other than as a vagrant.
Nowadays it is confined mainly to Hampshire and Dorset, with outlying groups in
Surrey and Devon. Birds which occasionally appear elsewhere probably come from
the French population.

Often hard to find, because they skulk and (for a small bird) have large territories,
the males may sing from the tops of gorse bushes, or ascend in a song flight. At other
times the birds usually reveal their presence by a soft churring call, almost a buzz
which, once learnt, is very characteristic. A bird may appear briefly on top of a gorse
bush, tail cocked and flicked, and crown feathers raised, before diving abruptly out of
sight, leaving the observer excited but anxious for more.

The male builds a series of flimsy 'cock's nests', but the actual nest, often
decorated with spider cocoons, is built mainly by the female.

▥ *Identified by its distinctive silhouette and jerky action during flight, together with its
restricted habitat.*
▥ *Both sexes appear all dark at any distance. Male is dark chocolate-brown with slate-
grey head above, and dark wine colour below with white belly, the pale throat spots
invisible except at close range. His mate is paler, greyer; younger greyer still.*

Wood Warbler
PHYLLOSCOPUS SIBILATRIX

LENGTH: 12–13 CM WEIGHT: 7–12G WHERE
TO LOOK: OAK AND BEECH WOODS WITH
SPARSE GROUND COVER, LOCAL NEST: DOME
OF DEAD LEAVES; GRASS ON GROUND EGGS:
5–7, WHITE, SPECKLED REDDISH FOOD:
INSECTS VOICE: ACCELERATED SHIVERING
TRILL, OR REPEATED *PEW-PEW*

Largest of the green warblers, the wood warbler is peculiar in having two totally
different songs. Only the willow tit shares this characteristic. A beautiful, silvery
shivering trill, uttered with head thrown back and causing the whole bird to vibrate, is
the regular song, but interspersed less frequently in these phrases is a powerful,
rather melancholy repetition of the call note *pew*.

Though nesting on the ground, the wood warbler spends more time in trees than
the willow warbler or chiffchaff. The beautiful spiralling courtship display flight of the
male in and below the canopy attracts attention in the open woods with little
undergrowth that are its favoured habitat.

Wood warblers are seldom seen on spring passage, as they head straight for their
breeding grounds. In autumn, like the lesser whitethroat, they move south-east
through Italy to their equatorial wintering grounds in central and eastern Africa.

Unlike other leaf warblers, wood warblers do not give their nests a cosy feather
lining. The parents are kept busy feeding their young for a month after fledging, and
thus only have a single brood.

▥ *Clear yellow stripe above eye; yellow throat and upper breast sharply divided from
white lower down.*
▥ *Adults become duller and browner above as season progresses.*
▥ *Yellow fringes to tail and wing feathers, forming paler panel.*
▥ *Bright colours harmonise with fresh greens in late spring sun.*

Willow Warbler
PHYLLOSCOPUS TROCHILUS

LENGTH: 10.5–11.5CM **WEIGHT:** 6–10G **WHERE TO LOOK:**
WOODS OF ALL TYPES, SCRUB **NEST:** DOME OF GRASS, LINED
WITH FEATHERS, ON GROUND **EGGS:** 6–7, WHITE, SPECKLED
RED-BROWN **FOOD:** SMALL INSECTS, LARVAE **VOICE:** FALLING
CADENCE OF PURE NOTES. CALL SOFT *HOO-EET*

Juvenile

Adult

Gilbert White, of Selborne fame, was the first to distinguish the three species of 'willow wren' – willow warbler, chiffchaff and wood warbler – noticing that their songs were quite different.

For many birdwatchers the first real feeling of spring comes with the overnight arrival, in early April, of willow warblers – their effortless, beautiful cascade of sweet, liquid notes coming from still leafless trees and bushes. They are the commonest summer visitors, with some 3 million pairs in Britain and Ireland, their huge range stretching right across northern Eurasia. East Siberian breeding birds undertake a 10–11,000km journey twice a year to and from their winter quarters in East Africa – an astonishing journey for such tiny bundles of feathers. Their resilience is further evidenced by the record of a bird, alive and well, but completely transfixed by a thorn which must have pierced it some time previously, for dead skin surrounded the thorn.

Willow warblers are the only British birds to undergo two complete moults annually – once in summer, and again in West Africa in late winter; a remarkable fact considering the extra energy requirements needed to form a complete new set of feathers.

■ *Freshly arrived adult is brown-olive above, whitish buff below, with yellowish breast and stripe over eye. Legs usually pale. 'Brighter' plumage than chiffchaff.*
■ *Juvenile is bright primrose-yellow below. Often misidentified as icterine warbler.*

Chiffchaff
PHYLLOSCOPUS COLLYBITA

LENGTH: 11CM **WEIGHT:** 6–9G **WHERE TO
LOOK:** WOODS, SCRUB WITH TREES. IN WINTER,
OFTEN BY WATER **NEST:** GRASS DOME, JUST
ABOVE GROUND **EGGS:** 5–6, WHITE, LIGHTLY
MARKED DARKER **FOOD:** SMALL INSECTS
VOICE: REPEATED *CHIFF-CHAFF*. CALL EMPHATIC
HWEET

Like the cuckoo, the chiffchaff derives its name in many European languages from its rather monotonous, but unmistakable, song – *chiff chaff chaff chip chap chiff chep*. Many who recognise the song have little idea of the appearance of the singer, for this tiny bird, the first summer songbird to arrive back, in late March, usually sings from high in a tall tree. Most spend the winter around the Mediterranean, with small numbers braving the British winter, mainly in the south-west, and often at sewage farms. These residents may occasionally include the greyer Siberian-race birds, with their different, chick-like call. Bright autumn days may cause migrants to burst into unseasonal song.

The males play little part in the nesting cycle, leaving nest building, incubation and most of the feeding of the young to the female.

This short-haul migrant has shorter, more rounded wings than the long-winged, tropical-wintering willow warbler.

■ *Brownish-olive upperparts, dirty white underparts with yellow tinge on breast. Rounder-headed, dumpier than willow warbler, with clearer eye-ring.*
■ *Juvenile chiffchaff is browner above and yellower below than adult, less bright than young willow warbler.*
■ *In worn plumage in midsummer, becomes browner and whiter.*
■ *Though requiring more mature trees than willow warbler, it also feeds more regularly on the ground, especially on migration and in winter, hopping in an agile way, flicking its wings and tail frequently.*

Goldcrest
REGULUS REGULUS

LENGTH: 9CM **WEIGHT:** 5–7G **WHERE TO LOOK:** WOODLAND, PARKS, GARDENS WITH CONIFERS **NEST:** TINY SUSPENDED CUP OF MOSS, COBWEBS **EGGS:** 7–8, WHITE WITH FAINT SPOTS **FOOD:** TINY INSECTS **VOICE:** THIN, HIGH, RHYTHMICAL SONG, ENDING IN FLOURISH

Adult

Juvenile

A long with the similar but much rarer firecrest, this is Britain's smallest bird, weighing only as much as a 10p coin. It is sobering to spot a minute dot heading over the waves towards land on the east coast in late autumn, at last pitching into a bramble where lively actions and a thin, high call note reveal its identity. That such a tiny, entirely insectivorous bird not only survives the British winter, but chooses to migrate here from Scandinavia, is one of the nature's wonders. In Yorkshire, it was known as the 'woodcock pilot', arriving at the same time as that species, and in Norfolk it was even thought that they sometimes hitched a lift on the backs of short-eared owls!

Often joining tit flocks in winter, the restless and confiding goldcrest keeps in constant touch by means of its thin contact call. Along with the coal tit, it may be the dominant species in conifer plantations, both in summer and winter. Its ability to exploit these alien trees has resulted in a huge increase in numbers.

▨ Pugnacious birds; the crown stripe flares in anger, even at its own reflection. Juveniles lack the black and yellow crown markings.
▨ Large, beady black eye in bare face gives a rather 'surprised' expression. Yellowish feet.
▨ Lively actions: hovering or flycatching like a leaf warbler; flicking wings while carefully searching the tiniest twigs and pine needles.

Firecrest
REGULUS IGNICAPILLUS

LENGTH: 9CM **WEIGHT:** 5–7G **WHERE TO LOOK:** LESS RELIANT ON CONIFERS THAN GOLDCREST; WOODS, COASTAL SCRUB **NEST:** LIKE GOLDCREST. **EGGS:** 7–11, WHITE OR PINKISH, FAINTLY MARKED **FOOD:** TINY INSECTS **VOICE:** SONG – SIMPLE, REPEATED CRESCENDO OF ONE NOTE, WITHOUT END FLOURISH

I t is always a tremendous thrill to see this tiny gem, surely one of Britain's most beautiful birds. Formerly only a rare visitor on migration and in winter, mainly to the south and south-west coasts, breeding in Britain was not recorded until the early 1960s; since then, though breeding remains sporadic, numbers have slowly increased and small colonies are now scattered over a number of English and Welsh counties. These initial attempts at colonisation follow an increase in Western Europe this century. The song has similarities with that of the goldcrest, and it is likely that the bird is often overlooked. Evidence of the close relationship of these species is shown by reports of cross-breeding.

In Britain, at least, Norway spruce is usually present where firecrests nest, with some deciduous trees and often holly, too. Firecrests often feed closer to the ground than goldcrests. On migration they frequent bracken, bramble and sea buckthorn. The thin call is very similar to that of the goldcrest, but to the practised ear sounds harder and slightly lower-pitched, a repeated *zit*, the last note rising a little in pitch.

▨ Bright orange sheen on shoulder patches, greener above and whiter below than goldcrest. Males have richer, fiery orange central crown stripe, best seen in display.
▨ When displaying, males flash their brilliant crowns at a potential mate or intruder.
▨ Juveniles lack the striking head pattern, though may be identified by suggestion of adult markings.

Pied Flycatcher
FICEDULA HYPOLEUCA

LENGTH: 12.5CM **WEIGHT:** 13–14G **WHERE TO LOOK:** MATURE
DECIDUOUS WOODS. **NEST:** IN A HOLE, USUALLY IN A TREE;
NEST-BOXES **EGGS:** 5–9, UNMARKED PALE BLUE. **FOOD:** MAINLY
INSECTS **VOICE:** A SHARP *SQUICK* OR A SOFT *WHEET.* THE SONG
IS A SHORT, SWEET WARBLE

Autumn plumage

Spring plumage

This is a classic bird of wooded hillsides in the west and north of Britain. In spring, the male calls attention to himself with his repeated, musical song and his flashing plumage. The female is much more discreet, and she incubates the eggs alone.

The male is sometimes bigamous and may then hold territories up to 3.5km apart, perhaps in order to convince the second female that he is unattached! But if both the clutches hatch, he will only help feed the young of the first. Many broods are raised in nest boxes, and the provision of these has undoubtedly helped the bird to maintain or increase its numbers in some areas.

Feeding among leaves, on trunks and branches, and on the ground, pied flycatchers take a good deal of non-flying prey, particularly caterpillars, and occasionally even worms. Snails are also eaten, and the bird has been observed hammering a snail on a road to break open the shell, in the manner of a song thrush.

Once the young have fledged the family moves up into the canopy and becomes silent and difficult to find. In autumn they depart and, at the same time, the east coast of Britain may receive 'falls' of pied flycatchers on migration from mainland Europe.

■ *Although they do take prey in the air, pied flycatchers frequently pick food from leaves and branches, as well as the ground.*
■ *Some males in autumn retain the white forehead and black on the wings and tail. A spring moult restores the pied plumage.*
■ *Pied flycatchers do not sit bolt upright like spotted flycatchers: they appear more restless, flicking a wing, or wings, and waving their tails.*
■ *Smaller and stouter than the spotted flycatcher; juveniles are difficult to distinguish, but more white in tail of pied flycatcher.*
■ *The male in spring is most striking. Females, young birds and males in autumn are grey-brown above and white below, with obvious white patches in the wings and on the sides of the tail.*

Spotted Flycatcher
MUSCICAPA STRIATA

LENGTH: 14CM **WEIGHT:** 15–16G **WHERE TO LOOK:**
WOODLAND EDGES, CLEARINGS, PARKS AND GARDENS **NEST:** IN
NATURAL AND MAN-MADE CREVICES AND EDGES, CREEPERS, ETC
EGGS: 4–5, WHITE BLOTCHED RED **FOOD:** CHIEFLY INSECTS
VOICE: THIN, HIGH CALLS AND SONG

Juvenile

Adult

So great is its dependence on insects and because it needs to be quite sure of the supply of its food, the spotted flycatcher is among the last of the summer migrants to return to Britain from Africa.

One day in late May the spotted flycatcher will be back, sitting erect on a dead bough, or perhaps a post or a wire. It launches out in agile pursuit of some insect, catches it (sometimes with an audible snap of its bill) and perches again, often in the original place, with a flick on its wings. It pursues most flying insects, including butterflies, bees and wasps, and it strikes large and dangerous victims against its perch to subdue them. In colder, wet weather, it will hunt among branches for aphids and the like. The female will also eat snails and woodlice for the calcium she needs to form egg-shells. To avoid competing with each other, males and females may feed in different parts of their territory.

A favourite nest site is provided by a climbing plant against a wall or tree trunk, but spotted flycatchers will nest anywhere from an old nest to a corpse hanging on a gamekeeper's gibbet! Open-fronted nest boxes will often attract them.

■ *Adults are grey-brown above, with blackish, pale-edged wings; off-white, streaked with grey, below; noticeably pale. Similar plumage for male and female.*

■ *Characteristic broad-based, flattish beak, as other flycatchers; wings comparatively long, tail square at end; brownish spots over throat and breast.*

■ *Juvenile birds are truly 'spotted' on the breast and 'scaly' above, and may be confused with the juvenile pied warbler.*

■ *Preferred location is on the edge of woodland or in open clearings; they may also be seen in parks and spacious gardens, especially with mature trees and old walls to offer nesting sites.*

■ *The bird perches in a distinctive upright pose in a prominent place on a bare twig or fence post.*

■ *The bird flies out in pursuit of passing insects, often returning to its original perch. Flight may twist and turn with the chase; frequently low over the ground.*

Wheatear
OENANTHE OENANTHE

LENGTH: 14.5CM WEIGHT: 17–30G WHERE TO LOOK: OPEN
COUNTRY, PARTICULARLY UPLAND AREAS. NEST: IN HOLE,
GROUND OR WALL; GRASS, LINED WITH HAIR AND FEATHERS.
EGGS: 5–6, BLUE. FOOD: CHIEFLY INSECTS. VOICE: SONG
SCRATCHY, OFTEN IN FLIGHT. CALL A HARSH *CHACK*.

*Juvenile or
adult female*

*Male's winter
plumage*

Northern wheatear

*Male's summer
plumage*

Wheatears are typically birds of open country, from mountain tops to moorland, from heaths to sandy coastlands. They are ground-living birds with long legs and short tails. Highly active and very distinctive, when disturbed they fly away to display a gleaming white rump and base of the tail. A frequent perch is the top of a stone wall or exposed fence post, but as a substitute they will hover some distance above the ground, giving their harsh warning alarm note.

They have a wide distribution, from Greenland across Europe and Asia to Alaska. Throughout the range they are summer migrants, all individuals migrating south each winter to tropical Africa. Some of the migratory flights are particularly spectacular; a regular crossing being from Iceland to northern Spain, for example. They are among the earliest of the returning spring migrants, the first individuals reaching the south coast of England before mid-March. The sudden surprise of a flashing white rump announces the return of what, for the moment, seems the prettiest bird of spring.

■ *Breeding throughout the British Isles, from the south coast of England to the Shetland Isles, the wheatear demonstrates how a population can vary in plumage and size. The males of the southern birds are smaller and paler, being almost pure white on the underparts compared with the rich buff of birds further north. The northern birds are also bigger and heavier.*

■ *Spring males are clean, clear-cut, handsome birds.*

■ *Spring females are a uniform, rich buffish-brown.*

■ *The autumn male loses his striking markings.*

■ *Autumn females and juveniles are similar.*

■ *The long, black legs and upright stance are characteristic.*

■ *When flying away, all wheatears show the distinctive white rump and black 'T' shape on the tail.*

■ *The song is frequently delivered from a hovering flight.*

Stonechat
SAXICOLA TORQUATA

Adult male

Adult female

Juvenile

LENGTH: 12.5CM WEIGHT: 14–17G **WHERE TO LOOK:** OPEN COUNTRY WITH GORSE, AND NEAR COAST **NEST:** ON GROUND; GRASS, LINED WITH HAIR **EGGS:** 5–6, GREENISH, SPECKLED WITH RUST COLOUR **FOOD:** CHIEFLY INSECTS **VOICE:** SONG SERIES OF DOUBLE NOTES, CALL HARSH *TSAK*, *WHEE-TSAK-TSAK*

The number of stonechats in Britain is highly variable, a result of their susceptibility to cold winters, when local populations may be eliminated. Although some individuals are migrants (there are records of British ringed stonechats being found in the Mediterranean in winter), the majority remain here all yea round, although they spread more widely around the coast. Even in winter they are strongly territorial and remain in pairs, always thinly spread. Slightly shorter and rounder than the whinchat, the stonechat has a less streaked back and never shows the pale stripe over the eye of the whinchat. The distinctive male in breeding plumage has a black head with a contrasting white collar and very red breast. There is usually a clear area of white on the rump and white flash on the wing. Females and young birds are less well marked, but retain the round-headed appearance with a large dark eye and at least a trace of a dark chin.

The stonechat has a clear attachment to gorse, which the male will use as a song perch and from which he will launch into the characteristic song flight, when he appears to dance in the air.

▧ *Rather robin-like in general appearance, with a large rounded head, long legs, an upright stance and bright red breast in the male. Always perches in an open position on top of a bush or fence post and has a close affinity with gorse bushes.*
▧ *The distinctive pattern of the male is visible, in subdued coloration, on the female.*
▧ *In flight, the male shows prominent white patches on wings and rump.*

Whinchat
SAXICOLA RUBETRA

A summer visitor from wintering grounds in tropical Africa, the whinchat is rather patchy in its distribution through Britain. Most numerous in the open countryside of the north and west, it definitely favours the open hillsides and edges of moorland, where isolated bushes or fence posts provide suitable look-out points and song posts. It is extremely easy to locate within its territory.

For differences from the closely related stonechat see above, but the whinchat always shows a pale stripe above the eye and pale patches on either side at the base of the tail. The streaked upperparts contrast with the warmish flush of pink or buff on the underparts, and the male presents a contrasting white flash in the wing.

Rather resembling a rather short-tailed robin in shape, the whinchat sits very upright on long black legs. When perched on the ground it can be mistaken for a wheatear, but it differs in that it regularly bobs its body and flicks both wings and tail.

Ever alert, the whinchat lives on its nerves, perhaps aware of its dangerously exposed position.

▧ *The striking and contrasting plumage of the male is distinctive, particularly the black face mask.*
▧ *Less well marked than the male, the female still shows the streaked back and pale stripe above the eye.*

Adult male

Adult female

LENGTH: 13CM WEIGHT: 16.5–23.5G **WHERE TO LOOK:** OPEN COUNTRY WITH BUSHES **NEST:** ON GROUND, OF GRASS, LINED WITH HAIR **EGGS:** 5–6, BLUISH, FINELY SPECKLED BROWN **FOOD:** MAINLY INSECTS **VOICE:** A SWEET WARBLING SONG; MIMICS OTHER SPECIES. CALL NOTE A WHISTLE AND A *TAP-HWEET-TAK*

Redstart
PHOENICURUS PHOENICURUS

LENGTH: 11.5CM **WEIGHT:** 12–19.5G **WHERE TO LOOK:** OLD WOODS OR PARKLAND **NEST:** HOLE IN TREE, WILL USE NEST BOX. NEST OF GRASS LINED WITH FEATHERS. **EGGS:** 5–7, UNMARKED PALE BLUE **FOOD:** MAINLY INSECTS **VOICE:** BRIEF WARBLING SONG AND PLAINTIVE CALL NOTE *HWEET*

Adult female

Juvenile

Adult male

Although widely distributed throughout Britain, redstarts are very much birds of the western and northern oak woods. The older trees provide the holes and cavities that make ideal nesting sites, and the open spaces and leaf-litter give good feeding.

Among the earlier returning summer migrants, many redstarts are back from their African wintering grounds by the middle of April, when their arrival is announced by the distinctive song issuing from high on an exposed woodland perch. They are very active birds, constantly flitting and hovering through the branches. When perched, they bear some resemblance to robins, which are of a similar size.

In all plumages, redstarts differ from all but black redstarts in having contrasting dark central tail feathers in a chestnut-red tail that is continually moved up and down in a characteristic quivering motion. The adult males, with their strikingly patterned plumage of black, white, red and blue-grey, must be among the most distinctive and most beautiful of all British birds.

■ *Appearance is rounded or sleek. Male has brightly coloured and distinctive plumage.*
■ *Lacking the bright plumage pattern of the male, females retain the tail coloration.*

Black Redstart
PHOENICURUS OCHRUROS

Until the middle of the 20th century, the black redstart was considered a migrant species, occurring in both spring and autumn on the south and east coasts of England. It was rare in the north and west, and on the few occasions when a pair remained to nest it was usually at rocky coastal sites in Kent. Following World War II, a remarkable colonisation took place at the London bomb sites and the black redstart became an established British breeding species. Since that time the numbers increased, and although still very much of south-east distribution, the bird can now be encountered in towns and at such places as power stations far from central London. Railway yards and canal wharves are often appreciated!

The presence of breeding pairs is easily overlooked, for although the brief song is distinctive (the final phase has been likened to a handful of metal balls shaken together), the birds are inevitably in a noisy urban setting and only in the very early morning, before the town awakens, can the song be easily heard.

■ *The black body plumage of the adult male contrasts with the white wing panel and red tail.*
■ *The greyness of the female is good camouflage when on the nest.*
■ *Young males can closely resemble females – but they may sing, hold territories and breed.*

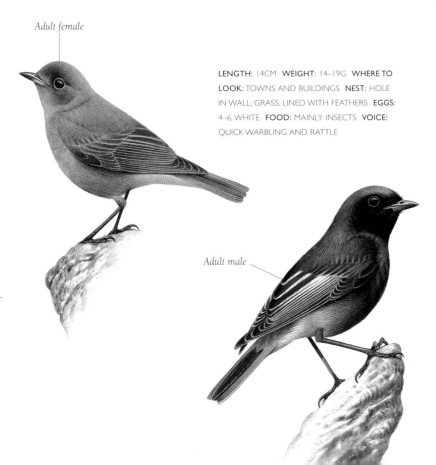

Adult female

Adult male

LENGTH: 14CM **WEIGHT:** 14–19G **WHERE TO LOOK:** TOWNS AND BUILDINGS **NEST:** HOLE IN WALL; GRASS, LINED WITH FEATHERS **EGGS:** 4–6, WHITE **FOOD:** MAINLY INSECTS **VOICE:** QUICK WARBLING AND RATTLE

Robin

ERITHACUS RUBECULA

LENGTH: 14CM **WEIGHT:** 16–22G **WHERE TO LOOK:** GARDENS, WOODS AND HEDGES **NEST:** IN BANK, LEDGE OR NEST BOX. LEAVES AND MOSS, DOMED, WITH HAIR LINING **EGGS:** 5–7, WHITE WITH RED SPOTS **FOOD:** INSECTS, WORMS AND BERRIES **VOICE:** FINE SONG; CALL *TIC-TIC-TIC*

Adult

Juvenile

As Britain's 'national' bird, the robin must be familiar to everyone. Its association with Christmas dates from the 1860s, when greeting cards became fashionable and postmen wore red tunics and were known as 'robins'. Britain's robins are resident, and are joined by paler northern European immigrants in the winter. These European birds are less confiding and more skulking than Britain's birds – perhaps due to the continuing massacre of migrant birds in southern Europe.

Robins may live to be as much as ten years old, but only a quarter of all robins manage to live beyond their first birthday. The greatest enemies of robins are domestic cats and traffic, which both take a heavy toll. When nesting, the male robin defends the territory and responds to almost any small patch of red – a red flag to a robin would be a better saying than a red rag to a bull. Fights between males can be extremely vicious and may even be to the death. The perky little chap that waits on the spade handle for worms is really quite a nasty piece of work!

Although robins generally build their nests in hedges and shrubs, they will choose some unlikely spots too, including old kettles, and garden sheds are a favourite site.

■ *Male and female robins look the same and will sing in autumn to mark out winter territories. The autumn song is quieter and less forceful than in spring.*

■ *Young robins are spotted and have no red breast. They moult into adult plumage in autumn.*

■ *They stand very upright, bobbing their heads and flicking their wings and tail when they are excited.*

■ *They are highly territorial and will display their red breasts vigorously to any intruders.*

■ *Though mainly insectivorous, they will eat fruit and seeds. They are particularly fond of mealworms and can become hand tame if fed with them.*

■ *Robins pair up from late December to early March. The female chases the male until she is accepted and, once paired, the male feeds her as part of courtship.*

■ *During severe winters robins relax their territorial nature and several birds can be seen feeding at a bird table together.*

Nightingale
LUSCINIA MEGARHYNCHOS

Adult

LENGTH: 16CM **WEIGHT:** 18–26.5G **WHERE TO LOOK:** SCRUB AND DENSE THICKETS SUCH AS OVERGROWN COPPICE WOODLAND **NEST:** AMONG VEGETATION CLOSE TO GROUND, MADE OF LEAVES, LINED WITH GRASS AND HAIR **EGGS:** 4–5, HEAVILY SPECKLED ON BLUISH-GREEN BACKGROUND **FOOD:** INSECTS, FOUND ON GROUND, PLUS SOME FRUIT AND BERRIES IN AUTUMN **VOICE:** SONG RICH, VARIED AND VIGOROUS, DELIVERED DAY AND NIGHT. ALARM A HARSH, HARD *TACK, TACK*; GRATING CROAK; LOUD *HWEET*

Juvenile

Nightingales have acquired a place in British folklore, not for their looks or familiarity, but for their voice alone. One of the earliest outdoor radio broadcasts included a nightingale from a Surrey wood. In fact, they can be extremely difficult to see as they are generally skulking birds whose brownish plumage hides them well in the dense vegetation that they prefer. Very much a species of south-east England, nightingales are scarce in the west and north even as migrants.

Returning as a summer migrant from wintering grounds south of the Sahara, the nightingale's far-carrying, rich and varied song fills some English woods from mid-April onwards, peaking during the first half of May. Contrary to popular belief, the nightingale does not only sing at night. Indeed, as a songster it is equally vocal in daylight, and can often appear to survive without sleep, as the singing will continue day and night during warm spring periods. By early June it is more sporadic and the brief song period comes to an end.

Although the plumage lacks distinctive features, when the bird is seen clearly the contrasting rusty-red tail, often held in a cocked position, is characteristic and gives the general impression of a rather outsized robin. The similar red tail of the redstart differs in having dark central feathers. Plainness in looks can be easily forgiven, though, when the bird has such a wonderful voice!

■ *An extremely difficult bird to see, the uniform plumage blends with the shadows when well hidden in foliage. Watch for movement and look for the distinctive large black eye.*

Ring Ouzel
TURDUS TORQUATUS

The ring ouzel spends the winter in the Mediterranean region, with some British breeding birds reaching North Africa. It is the only thrush that is a summer visitor to Britain. An early arrival, the first individuals reach southern England in early March and quickly return to the hills, where they occupy wild, open country.

Its upland breeding areas have earned the species the alternative name of 'mountain blackbird', and the differences between ring ouzel and blackbird are not always striking. The white breast crescent is only obvious in the adult males, but in all plumages the ring ouzel has a greyer look, caused by the pale fringes to the feathers. Paleness on the wing feathers results in a distinctive pale area visible on the upperwing as the bird flies.

Ring ouzel flight shows a somewhat similar quality to that of the blackbird, but it appears stronger on the wing and is rather erratic. The flight is accompanied by a deep, throaty, chattering call. The rign ouzel's song is a simple, loud piping, audible over very long distances.

■ *The largely black plumage gives the male a sooty appearance. The white breast crescent and yellow bill are obvious on the adult male, as are the pale grey fringes to the wing feathers.*

■ *The female is a brown, less strikingly plumaged bird.*

Adult female

Adult male

LENGTH: 24CM **WEIGHT:** 95–130G **WHERE TO LOOK:** MOUNTAINS AND MOORLAND **NEST:** OF GRASSES AND TWIGS AMONG ROCKS AND CREVICES **EGGS:** 5–6, BLUISH-GREEN, BLOTCHED BROWN **FOOD:** INSECTS, BERRIES AND FRUIT **VOICE:** HARSH RATTLE, PIPING SONG

Blackbird
TURDUS MERULA

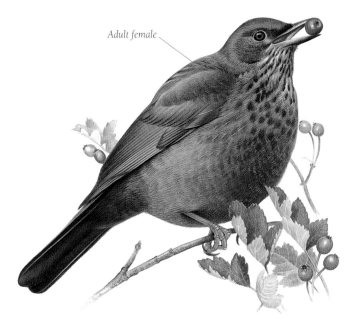

LENGTH: 25CM **WEIGHT:** 80–110G
WHERE TO LOOK: DENSE WOODLAND TO
OPEN MOORLAND, COMMON IN GARDENS
NEST: A LITTLE WAY UP, IN TREES AND HEDGES,
SOMETIMES IN BUILDINGS. CONSTRUCTED OF
MUD AND MOSS LINED WITH GRASS
EGGS: 3–5, BLUISH-GREEN, SPECKLED BROWN
FOOD: INSECTS SUMMER, BERRIES WINTER
VOICE: RICH FLUTY SONG, RATTLING ALARM

Adult female

There can be few places in Britain where it is not possible to find the blackbird throughout the year. The British breeding individuals are resident, but each autumn large numbers of migrants from northern Europe arrive on their way south to milder wintering grounds. Spectacular arrivals on the east coast can be seen in late October and November when, at times, hundreds of blackbirds, accompanied by other thrushes, may drop from the sky.

Many of these migrants remain in Britain throughout the winter, joining the resident birds at communal feeding grounds (orchards with waste apples being a particular favourite), and at traditional roosting sites that may be used year after year.

Blackbirds are very susceptible to albinism and individuals often have substantial numbers of white feathers. On such dark birds these feathers are particularly obvious and at times may resemble the crescent shape on the ring ouzel. A few birds are occasionally seen that are pure white, especially in urban areas where they may not be receiving a proper diet. Such individuals are obvious not only to our eyes, but also to those of predators, and so seldom last for many seasons.

▨ *Males live up to their name. Females are sooty brown, much darker than song thrush, but throat can be very pale, with dark streaks. Legs are dark, unlike thrushes'.*

▨ *Berries and fruit form a major portion of the winter diet. If the ground remains soft, worms predominate.*

▨ *A blackbird searching the lawn for worms is a familiar sight. Mainly ground-feeders, they move about in a series of short hopping runs, pausing to cock their head as if listening (in fact looking) for food. The struggle between blackbird and worm as the prey is slowly but steadily drawn from the ground is a familiar garden sight.*

▨ *The song, delivered from a very prominent song post, consists of loud clear notes combined to make phrases which last for some six seconds with a pause between of similar length.*

▨ *Blackbirds sing between March and June, whereas the mistle thrush starts in late December and has short phrases repeated over and over again.*

Sunbathing posture

Adult male

Song Thrush
TURDUS PHILOMELOS

LENGTH: 23CM **WEIGHT:** 70–90G **WHERE TO LOOK:** HEDGEROWS, GARDENS AND WOODLAND **NEST:** MADE OF LEAVES AND TWIGS, LINED WITH MUD **EGGS:** 4–5, BLUE, SPOTTED WITH BLACK **FOOD:** WORMS, SNAILS, FRUIT AND BERRIES **VOICE:** ALARM RATTLE, THIN *SIP* IN FLIGHT

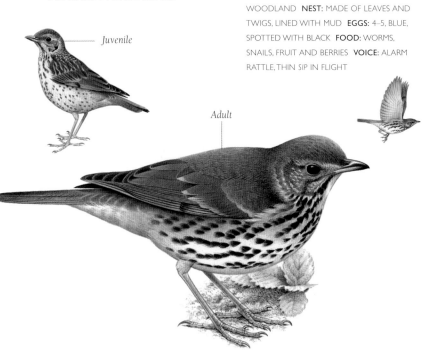

Juvenile

Adult

Although this is principally a resident species, found in towns and gardens throughout the year, some British song thrushes move south for the winter, to be temporarily replaced by arrivals from Scandinavia and northern Europe. Many of these birds, which are seeking the milder maritime winter climate, will pass on through Britain to spend much of the winter in western France or Spain. Most of the arrivals take place in October and are usually slightly in advance of the true 'winter thrushes' – the redwing and the fieldfare.

The presence of a song thrush in an area is often indicated by the discovery of a thrush's 'anvil', the site where snail shells are broken against a prominent stone or the concrete of a garden path to gain access to the soft, nutritious body inside. This behaviour is unique to the song thrush, although other species, notably the blackbird, have developed the habit of robbing the thrush as soon as the work of opening the snail has been completed, and flycatchers have occasionally been known to break a snail open.

■ *The long-legged, upright stance is typical of all ground-feeding thrushes. The birds are usually solitary, but will roost communally in cold weather.*
■ *Song thrushes are regular visitors to bird tables and garden 'feeding stations', preferring to collect items dropped beneath the table rather than using the table itself.*
■ *The superb song is delivered from a lower perch than that of the mistle thrush, a low bush or building being typical.*

Redwing
TURDUS ILIACUS

LENGTH: 21CM **WEIGHT:** 55–75G **WHERE TO LOOK:** OPEN COUNTRY AND GARDENS **NEST:** GRASSES AND TWIGS IN TREES OR BUSHES **EGGS:** 5–6, GREENISH, WITH RED-BROWN MARKINGS **FOOD:** WORMS, INSECTS, BUT ALSO BERRIES IN WINTER **VOICE:** SIMPLY FLUTY SONG. CALL DISTINCTIVE *SEEIP*

The British breeding population of redwings is usually confined to northern Scotland, where nesting was first recorded in 1925. The population increased slowly, and now numbers some 100 pairs in most years. There is little evidence of a westward spread in range and it is speculated that Britain's breeding birds are migrants which have simply failed to return to Scandinavia, rather than being the vanguard of an extensive colonisation. Isolated breeding has been recorded as far south as Kent.

Two distinct populations reach Britain each winter, one from Scandinavia, the other from Iceland. The Icelandic birds spend winter in the west, around the Irish Sea, the Scandinavia birds in the east. Although at first glance the two populations are very similar, the Icelandic birds are in fact distinctly darker and larger. The greater size gives longer wings, necessary to carry them on the lengthy, over-sea migration. The Icelandic birds have recently colonised the Faeroes and may also be responsible for some of the British breeding birds.

■ *Slightly smaller and darker than the song thrush, the distinctive shade of olive on the upperparts is a good feature once noted.*
■ *A standing bird will show distinctive lines or streaks on an almost white breast. Dull red flanks are usually visible. Note paler stripes on face.*
■ *In flight, the smallness of this species can at times make it appear rather lark-like, particularly in a migrating flock. The tawny-red underwing can be very obvious and quite unlike the yellow-buff of the song thrush.*

Mistle Thrush
TURDUS VISCIVORUS

LENGTH: 27CM **WEIGHT:** 110–140G **WHERE TO LOOK:**
GARDENS AND WOODLAND **NEST:** IN FORK OF TREE, BUILT OF
ROOTS AND GRASS **EGGS:** 3–5, VARIABLE IN COLOUR, BUT WELL
SPOTTED WITH BROWN **FOOD:** FRUIT, BERRIES AND INSECTS
VOICE: LOUD, FAR-CARRYING BLACKBIRD-LIKE SONG. HARSH,
CHURRING FLIGHT CALL

The largest of the common thrushes, the mistle thrush is the earliest to start nesting. The song, often delivered from the top of a tall tree in very windy conditions (the bird's alternative name is 'storm cock'), can be heard from December onwards, and this is one of the few birds in full song at the beginning of the year. Eggs may be laid as early as February, and young may have left the nest by the end of March.

When breeding, the mistle thrush can be very aggressive, showing a complete lack of fear in driving cats and dogs away from its nesting area. Some individuals will even attack people, to the extent of regularly striking at the head and preventing people from entering their own gardens!

This is the greyest of the speckled thrushes, most readily identified by the large size, large round spots on the underparts, very upright stance and pure white underwing that is easily visible in flight.

On the ground, the stance is very upright and birds move about with strong hopping, almost bounding, leaps. In winter the birds can often appear larger and rounder in contrast to the sleeker summer appearance.

Two identification features visible when the bird is in flight are the gleaming white underwing (obvious) and the whitish tips to the outermost tail feathers (less so).

The song is always delivered from a very exposed position and consists of up to six blackbird-like phrases repeated again and again in regular sequence.

Fieldfare
TURDUS PILARIS

LENGTH: 26CM **WEIGHT:** 80–130G **WHERE TO LOOK:**
PARKLAND, OPEN COUNTRY **NEST:** IN FORK OF TREE, MADE OF
GRASSES AND TWIGS **EGGS:** 5–6, SPECKLED GREENISH-BLUE.
RARE AND ERRATIC NESTING SPECIES IN BRITAIN **FOOD:** MAINLY
WORMS, INSECTS, BUT FRUIT AND BERRIES IN HARD WEATHER
VOICE: NASAL *EE-EEP*; HARSH *CHA-CHA-CHA-CHACK* FLIGHT CALL.
SONG RATHER WEAK, BLACKBIRD-LIKE

Fieldfares first nested in Britain in 1967, when a nest with fledged young was discovered in the Orkneys, but the subsequent colonisation has not been particularly dramatic. It is rare for more than ten pairs to have been recorded nesting in any one year, and these have almost always been in Scotland. The species has been steadily extending its breeding range westward through Europe, but this expansion may now have ceased.

Traditionally looked upon as a winter visitor to Britain, fieldfares may begin to arrive as early as August, but peak numbers are not reached on the east and south coast until late October or November. In suitable weather conditions, flocks of several hundred at a time will cross the southern North Sea, often arriving exhausted. Of all the winter visitors, the fieldfare is one of the latest to depart, with small parties regularly seen well into May.

Mixed thrush flocks in winter tend to be dominated by fieldfares and redwings, which behave in a noisy, nomadic fashion. Although fieldfares are usually found in the open countryside feeding on farmland and playing fields, cold weather will rapidly drive them into gardens where fruit and any remaining berries will be readily eaten and where they will join other birds at tables and feeding stations.

The yellow base to the bill and contrasting plumage pattern, with smooth grey head and rump, makes the fieldfare the most elegant of all the thrushes. Note red-brown back.

Behaviour is typical of all thrushes, with an upright stance and hopping run.

Flocks will suddenly arrive on berry bushes and remain until the supply is exhausted.

Welneys' Birds

Stroll along the Summer Walk at Welney Washes
to a great bird reserve.

Distance: 4.25 miles (6.8km)

Time: 1hr 30min (allow time for
 birdwatching)

Paths: Boardwalks and grass paths
 with benches

Landscape: Reedy wetlands, lagoons
 and fen

Map: OS Explorer 228 March & Ely

Grid reference: TL 545944

Parking: WWT Welney car park,
 signposted off A1101

Public Toilets: At visitor centre near car
 park

Note: Summer Walk open in summer
 only; contact WWT Welney (01353
 860711) to check path is open. Dogs
 not permitted

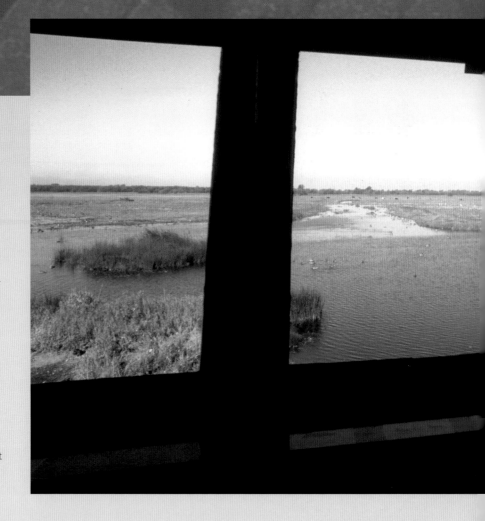

The Wildfowl and Wetlands Trust (WWT) reserve at Welney Washes is tucked away in the southeast corner of Norfolk, on the border with Cambridgeshire. It covers 850 acres (344ha) of freshwater grazing marshland that floods regularly – the largest such area remaining in Britain. This unique habitat was formed when two massive drainage channels were created, leaving a strip of land between them about 0.5 mile (800m) wide. This area is known as the Ouse Washes.

The Ouse Washes were not created with the intention of providing breeding areas for birds. Instead, they were designed to act as a reservoir to hold excess water when the main drainage system is unable to cope. Several attempts were made to drain the Fens – by the Romans and by medieval engineers – but it was not until the 17th century that this wilderness of sedge, reed and bog was finally vanquished. The wealthy Duke of Bedford owned a large expanse of fenland, and wanted to do more with it than graze sheep in the summer and watch it flood all winter. He employed a talented Dutch engineer called Cornelius Vermuyden to design a new river system that would allow flood water to be channelled more directly out to sea, rather than flowing into the meandering River Great Ouse.

The cut between Earith in Cambridgeshire and Denver in Norfolk, was named the Old Bedford River and was completed in 1637. Although it vastly improved the duke's summer grazing grounds, his land still flooded in winter. A second cut was made, running parallel to the first, and called the New Bedford River. The banks on both rivers were raised, so that the area between them could take surplus water during times of flood – the Ouse Washes. When you

visit you will see information boards telling you how each river bank has been built up to allow controlled flooding, but to prevent overflowing into the surrounding low-lying land.

Today, the area between the two channels is much as it always was: grazed or cut for hay during the summer and flooded during the winter. Because of this, and because parts are closed during the bird breeding season, this walk is only open for part of the summer – usually July and August – but it's well worth the wait.

Walk Directions

This walk takes you through some of the most spectacular birdwatching territories in the country. As visitors are asked not to make a noise or sudden movements that might startle the birds, many species seem totally unaware that they are under scrutiny. A visit to Welney is magical at any time of year, even when the footpath is closed and walkers are restricted to the Screenbank Walk that takes you between hides. Try coming in November, when thousands of swans crowd into the flooded washes to rest for the night. The noise is spellbinding and white necks poke up like periscopes as far as the eye can see.

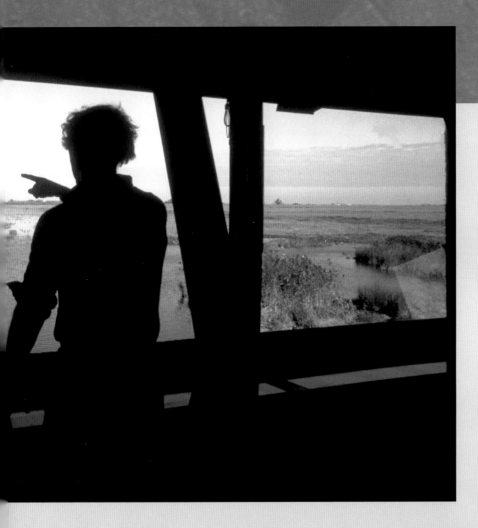

Begin at the car park and walk up the ramp to cross the bridge. Go down the steps and turn left. This is called the Screenbank Walk and wooden boards shield the Washes to the north from any sudden movements, although there are gaps that allow you to view the wildlife. Soon signs will direct you to the right to the Reedbed Boardwalk. This is a taste of what comes later.

When you finish the boardwalk, turn right along the Screenbank Walk until you see a sign to your right for the Summer Walk. Follow the waymarkers in a figure-of-eight configuration through reeds and marsh. The route is clearly marked, and easy to follow. Information boards at regular intervals tell you exactly what birds to look for. After completing its loops, the Summer Walk leads back to the Screenbank Walk. Turn left, and retrace your steps to the footbridge.

At the footbridge, continue straight ahead, along the northern part of the Screenbank Walk. Eventually you reach Buxton Hide, Lyle Hide, Allport Hide and Friends' Hide, all on your left. This part of the walk is linear, but you will see so many different birds that it won't feel like it. At Friends' Hide, retrace your steps back to the footbridge, cross it, and return to the car park.

LOOKING OUT OVER THE OUSE
WASHES FROM A WILDLIFE AND
WETLAND TRUST OBSERVATORY.

WHILE YOU'RE THERE For those who are interested in still more birdwatching, the RSPB has a large reserve at Ouse Washes, to the south of Manea at Welches Dam. Facilities include a car park, a visitor centre and several free hides.

WHERE TO EAT AND DRINK There is a little tearoom in the visitor centre at Welney, where you can sit and read the information about the site. It sells cakes, snacks, teas and coffee.

WHAT TO LOOK FOR Don't miss a spell in the WWT's observatory looking over the Bewick's swan lagoon. Twenty wildfowl species have been recorded here, but most impressive are the sheer numbers of birds that arrive in winter. Counts have included 3,000 Bewick's swans, 1,000 whooper swans and 30,000 wigeon.

Marsh Tit
PARUS PALUSTRIS

LENGTH: 11.5CM **WEIGHT:** 11G **WHERE TO LOOK:** DECIDUOUS WOODLAND, GARDENS. **NEST:** IN A HOLE, USUALLY IN A TREE **EGGS:** 6-10, WHITE, SPOTTED RED **FOOD:** INSECTS, SEEDS AND FRUITS **VOICE:** AN EXPLOSIVE *PITCHU; CHIKA-DEE-DEE-DEE*, ETC. SONG A REPEATED *CHIP-CHIP-CHIP*

Marsh and willow tits are about as common as each other and although not rare, are much less frequently seen than blue or great tits. They usually occur in ones and twos, and both marsh and willow tits join nomadic tit flocks in the winter. They pose one of the classic identification challenges and even experts cannot always tell them apart.

The two species live subtly different lives. Marsh tits prefer deciduous woodland, rarely occurring in conifer woods or scrub. They regularly drop to the ground, for instance to pick up beech-mast, and they hammer open this and other seeds, such as those of yew, honeysuckle and spindle. Marsh tits usually nest in ready-made holes in trees, walls and banks – perhaps doing a little enlarging work: for some reason they rarely use nest boxes. They come regularly to gardens and bird tables, and can often be seen carrying food away to hide, usually in crevices under bark, but sometimes in the ground. Such food is regularly recovered, but whether by searching likely places or by precise memory is not yet known.

▧ *In adults the cap is glossy black, the neck is 'slim', the bib neat, and there is little or no pale panel in the wing. The flanks and belly are a similar grey-white.*
▧ *Adult male and female marsh tits are alike in colour and pattern. The young bird has a browner cap and bib and is whiter below; it is very like the young willow tit.*
▧ *Marsh tits have strong bills and will hammer at tough seeds, such as beech-mast, while holding them under one foot.*

Willow Tit
PARUS MONTANUS

LENGTH: 11.5CM **WEIGHT:** 10G **WHERE TO LOOK:** WOODS, SCRUB, GARDENS **NEST:** SELF-EXCAVATED, LOW IN A STUMP **EGGS:** 6-10, WHITE, SPOTTED RED **FOOD:** INSECTS, SEEDS AND FRUITS **VOICE:** A NASAL *AIR-AIR-AIR*, HIGH, THIN CALLS, ETC. SONG IS A CLEAR *PIU, PIU*

The willow tit has the distinction of being the most recent British breeding species to be recognised. It was only separated from the marsh tit at the end of the last century, and the differences between the two species can still be very difficult to spot in practice. Plumage differences are slight, especially in summer when adults have worn feathers: juveniles can be inseparable even in the hand. However, the calls and song are fortunately very distinctive.

There are other differences, too. Although they occur more patchily across the country, willow tits live in a wider variety of woods than marsh tits, including conifer plantations. This may explain their slightly finer bills, which could be useful for feeding among bunches of conifer needles. They feed low down, but only very rarely on the ground, nor do they appear to 'hammer' food. Yet they excavate a new nest hole each year, typically in soft, rotten wood, and ignoring older apparently suitable holes, even in the same stump. This may be to avoid a build-up of parasites, which live in old nests. Willow tits will use nestboxes, especially if these are filled with wood chips or polystyrene for the bird to excavate.

▧ *Compared with the marsh tit, adults have a duller black cap, a bull neck and a more diffuse bib; in fresh plumage, pale wing panel and bright buff flanks.*
▧ *The marsh tit's distinctive sharp, sneezing* pitchu *sounds annoyed. The willow tit's deliberate, very nasal, air-air-air is unique. Both calls are frequent.*
▧ *Both species sometimes occur in the same wood, and both join in roving tit flocks.*
▧ *The female excavates a new hole each year, low in a rotten stump.*

Blue Tit
PARUS CAERULUS

Juvenile

Adult

Blue tits literally put all their eggs in one basket, producing a single brood of chicks each year to coincide with the general abundance of juicy, nutritious caterpillars. If that brood fails, there is no second chance. This contrasts with the strategy of the blackbird, whose dependable supply of worms allows three broods of four at a time, spread through the summer.

The blue tit is one of the most popular and familiar garden birds in Britain. Despite its eagerness to profit from people – quickly discovering a bag of peanuts or sunflower seeds, searching the window frames of houses for spiders, using an artificial box for nesting – the blue tit is essentially a woodland bird, especially where there is oak or birch.

In winter the blue tit population spreads out, even feeding in reed beds and much more open places – almost anywhere, in fact, where food might be available. In a mixed feeding flock in a wood it is interesting to watch the great tits going to the ground using the bigger branches, while the blue tits tend to feed out on the slimmer twigs, using the extra agility to the full.

▧ *Pale yellow underside, with thin dark streak. Young birds have greener wing coverts.*

▧ *Extremely acrobatic and active, blue tits are so light that they can seek food at the tips of the thinnest twigs, unlike great tits.*

▧ *Fledglings have greener caps and yellower faces than their parents, but the basic pattern still helps to identify them.*

▧ *A fresh-plumaged, bright blue tit has a vivid blue cap, blue wings and tail and clean yellow breast. In dull light it tends to look rather drab, paler beneath, and the white face with black lines is then the best feature.*

▧ *Blue tits may not easily be forgiven for stealing cream from milk bottles, pecking putty or even tearing wallpaper if they get the chance.*

▧ *The great tit is bigger with a blacker head; the coal tit has no blue, green or yellow. Blue tits feeding in tree tops with thin, high calls may easily be confused with other tits and goldcrests.*

LENGTH: 11.5CM **WEIGHT:** 9–10G **WHERE TO LOOK:** BROADLEAVED WOODS, ESPECIALLY OAK AND BIRCH, LESS IN CONIFERS; GARDENS, WIDESPREAD IN WINTER **NEST:** HOLE IN TREE, NEST BOX, ALMOST ANY KIND OF CAVITY. NEST OF MOSS WITH GRASS AND BARK STRIPS, LINED WITH FEATHERS **EGGS:** 7–13 (SMALLER CLUTCHES IN GARDENS), TINY **VOICE:** WHITE NOTES, CHURRS AND TRILLS – *TSEE, TSEE-SEE-CHUCHUCHUCH*

Great Tit
PARUS MAJOR

Adult male

Great tits are the 'tough guys' of the tit family, as anyone who has watched them at a bird table can testify. They usually stop short of serious violence, but that stout beak, which can hack open a hazelnut, is a formidable weapon, and there is evidence that they occasionally kill other birds and may eat portions of them. There is even a remarkable record of one killing a goldcrest and carrying it away in its feet, like a miniature hawk.

Despite these unendearing habits, the great tit is a fascinating species. It has been well studied, partly because it nests very readily in boxes, and also because it is reasonably easy to distinguish the male from the female – the black band on his belly is thick and unbroken, especially as it passes between the legs.

Males take little or no part in building the nest, but feed the hen when she is laying and incubating the eggs. If disturbed at the nest, she will hiss like a snake and this may frighten predators away, or startle them enough for her to escape.

The young are fed, as in other tit species, mainly on caterpillars, and the birds time their families to coincide with peak numbers of these. This peak varies in timing from year to year. But how do the birds know – some weeks in advance – when the peak will be?

In Autumn and winter, great tits roam the woods in flocks, often with other species. They regularly drop to the ground, where they toss leaves aside and tear up moss and fungi in search of food.

■ *Their large size, plus their striking combination of white cheeks, yellow breast, black crown and bib, make great tits unmistakable.*

■ *The tail is blue-grey with obvious white outer feathers.*

■ *Females have less glossy caps, and less black on the belly.*

■ *Juvenile birds have washed-out, duller colours and their cheeks are yellowish, not white.*

■ *Scores of different calls have been described for this species.*

■ *Most of these calls have a distinctive metallic or ringing quality which helps to identify them; in a wood, 'if you don't know the call, it's probably a great tit!'*

■ *Great tits are adaptable, taking advantage of unusual nest sites, such as pipes, letter-boxes, etc. Like blue tits, they have learned to open milk bottles and, in experiments, to perform very complex tasks to obtain food.*

Juvenile

LENGTH: 14CM **WEIGHT:** 19G **WHERE TO LOOK:** WOODS, HEDGES, GARDENS **NEST:** IN A NATURAL OR ARTIFICIAL HOLE **EGGS:** 5–12, WHITE WITH RED SPOTS **FOOD:** MAINLY INSECTS, SEEDS, FRUITS **VOICE:** VERY VARIED; CALLS ARE MOSTLY METALLIC AND RINGING, SUCH AS *CHINK*. SONG, A LOUD *TEACHER-TEACHER-TEACHER*, VERY STRIDENT

Coal Tit
PARUS ATER

LENGTH: 11CM **WEIGHT:** 9G **WHERE TO LOOK:** WOODS,
ESPECIALLY CONIFEROUS; GARDENS **NEST:** IN A HOLE LOW IN A
TREE, OR IN THE GROUND **EGGS:** 7–11, WHITE, SPOTTED RED
FOOD: CHIEFLY INSECTS AND SEEDS **VOICE:** BRIGHT, *PEET*; SONG,
GREAT TIT-LIKE, BUT FASTER, SOFTER

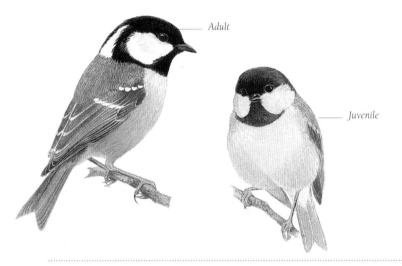

Adult

Juvenile

The coal tit occurs regularly in deciduous woodland, but it is with conifers that most birdwatchers associate it. In a mixed woodland, it will often be found flitting around in the top of a pine. It is even common in conifer plantations, where few other birds may be present. It overcomes the shortage of natural cavities in plantation trees by nesting in a hollow among the roots, or even in a mouse-hole. It often uses nest boxes and, given the choice, prefers one on a conifer to one on a deciduous tree.

In the winter, the coal tit often visits gardens, where it tends to be dominated by the larger blue and great tits. It manages quite well, however, by taking small prices of food discarded by the other birds, and also by carrying food away and storing it.

▓ *The large, white patch on the nape is unique and distinctive.*
▓ *The distinctive double wing bar is often easier to see than the nape-patch: at close range the bars show as separate white spots.*
▓ *Another distinguishing feature is the obvious olive-grey hue of the back.*
▓ *The black bib is more extensive than on other small tits.*
▓ *Males and females look alike, while juveniles have yellower cheeks, nape and wingbars. Fresh plumage, clean and bright.*
▓ *The smallest of the tits, it often looks dumpy and short-tailed.*

Crested Tit
PARUS CRISTATUS

Although a very few crested tits have occurred in England (probably all vagrants from the Continent), the only place in Britain where there is a realistic chance of seeing them is in the old pine woods of Highland Scotland, particularly in the valley of the River Spey. Even here, there are only a few hundred pairs, and the bird can be very difficult to find. The best approach is to choose a stretch of this ancient Caledonian forest (with plenty of dead wood, which the birds and their insect food love) and to listen for the soft, purring call. The first view may well be of an apparently drab, grey-brown and buff like bird, neck-achingly high in a pine. However, with patience, the 'bridled' face pattern and the upstanding black and white crest may be seen, especially if the bird drops low to inspect some cracked or rotten stumps as a possible nest site. If, as our modern pine plantations age, more sites become available, or if crested tits learn to use nestboxes more regularly, they may well be able to expand their range.

▓ *This is the only small British bird with a crest, but this feature can be surprisingly difficult to see, especially on a bird overhead. Nor is the distinctive face pattern always obvious in brief views.*
▓ *Males and females look alike: juveniles are a littler duller with shorter crests.*
▓ *Crested tits often feed by clinging to the trunk of a tree.*

LENGTH: 11.5CM **WEIGHT:** 11G **WHERE TO
LOOK:** OLD PINE FORESTS **NEST:** SELF-
EXCAVATED IN A STUMP, ETC **EGGS:** 5-7, WHITE,
BLOTCHED RED **FOOD:** INSECTS, SEEDS AND
FRUIT **VOICE:** THIN CALLS LIKE OTHER TITS
AND DISTINCTIVE, PURRING *CHOORRR*,
REPEATED AS SONG

Bearded Tit
PANURUS BIARMICUS

The fascinating 'beardie' is not a tit at all, but belongs to an Asian family, the parrotbills. It lives in reed beds, climbing with agility among the stems and often perching with each foot on a different reed. In windy weather it keeps low, but a chorus of unmistakable ringing calls will give away a flock, or the birds may fly, like tiny pheasants, just above the reed tops. Sometimes, with tails cocked up, they will feed on the ground, but always near reeds.

The bearded tit suffers badly in severe winters, but breeds prodigiously (a pair may raise four broods in a season!) and soon builds up its numbers again. After particularly good seasons, flocks 'erupt' from their breeding grounds, and appear in reed beds where they have not been seen for years, if ever.

Regular migrations also take place between summer and winter sites, often hundreds of miles apart. Birds may be very faithful to two such sites or ring the changes; it seems likely that they are influenced by others that they encounter – or perhaps by a new mate.

■ *Adult males have 'moustaches', grey heads and black undertail coverts. Females plainer; shape and behaviour distinctive.*
■ *Young birds are more golden, with black backs and tail sides.*

Adult female
Adult male

LENGTH: 16.5CM WEIGHT: 15–16G WHERE TO LOOK: REED BEDS NEST: LOW IN REEDS EGGS: 5–7, WHITE SPECKLED WITH BLACK FOOD: MAINLY INSECTS IN SUMMER AND SMALL SEEDS IN WINTER VOICE: UNIQUE AND MEMORABLE: A METALLIC *CHING* AND A HARD *TIK*, REPEATED

Long-tailed Tit
AEGITHALOS CAUDATUS

LENGTH: 14CM WEIGHT: 8G WHERE TO LOOK: HEDGES, BUSHES, WOODS IN WINTER NEST: IN A BUSH OR IN A TREE FORK EGGS: 8–12, WHITE, SPOTTED WITH RED FOOD: MAINLY INSECTS VOICE: A THIN *ZI-ZI-ZI*; *TUP*; A ROLLING *TRRR*: ALL DISTINCTIVE. SONG RARE

Adult
Juvenile

Despite appearances, this bird is not really a tit, and may be related to the exotic babbler family: like them it has fluffy plumage and sociable habits. A flock in winter will defend its territory against other flocks and roost communally, the birds huddling together for warmth. In fact this bird seems to like tight places – both adults will roost in the nest with the brood of up to a dozen young! The nest is a wonderful, elastic construction of moss and spiders' webs, disguised with lichen (or even pieces of polystyrene!) and lined with hundreds, perhaps thousands, of feathers. It may be low in a thorn bush or high in a tree, and the adults sometimes take 20 days to build it. After the breeding season, family parties and larger flocks wander through woods and along hedges, often joined by tits and other small birds. Long-tailed tits take mostly insects, but they also peck lichen and green algae from trunks and branches. They are wonderfully acrobatic and will hang upside-down by one foot, holding large food items in the other to eat them. They visit birdtables only rarely, but when they do decide to do so, they may come regularly, sometimes for more than one winter.

■ *Adults are black, white and pale pink.*
■ *Juveniles have dark cheeks, no pink and shorter tails.*
■ *An unmistakable 'ball and stick' shape, both perched and in flight.*
■ *Roving bands of these birds move with agility through trees and bushes, crossing gaps in single file and calling ceaselessly as they go.*
■ *Unique nest is an oval purse of moss, webs and lichen, feather-lined.*

Nuthatch
SITTA EUROPAEA

LENGTH: 14CM **WEIGHT:** 20–22G **WHERE TO LOOK:** WOODS, PARKS **NEST:** IN A TREE HOLE **EGGS:** 6–11, WHITE, SPOTTED WITH RED **FOOD:** INSECTS, NUTS, SEEDS **VOICE:** A VARIETY OF CLEAR, RINGING WHISTLES

Nuthatches behave like sparrow-sized woodpeckers, but have the unique ability to climb down trunks and branches as well as up. They do this by moving obliquely, hanging from the upper foot and propped by the lower one. Unlike woodpeckers, they are no carpenters (they nest in ready-made holes), but they are plasterers, and exclude starlings and predators such as weasels with a hard, mud rim to the nest-hole. They even do this to a nest-box hole – and fill in any cracks in the top and sides as well! The young are fed mainly on insects, taken from both bark and leaves. In autumn, nuthatches pick up beech-mast, acorns and hazelnuts, carrying them to a favoured branch, wedging them in the bark and hacking them open with energetic and noisy whacks of the bill. They sometimes visit bird tables, and access to this easy food supply may now be helping the bird to extend its range further north and west in England and Wales, though not as yet into Scotland or Ireland.

■ *A big-headed, short-tailed and perky little bird, rather like a miniature woodpecker in shape and actions, always on the move.*
■ *The most striking feature is the broad, black eye-stripe.*
■ *Blue-grey above, with white cheeks and corners to the tail; buff below. Chestnut flanks are brighter in the male.*
■ *The birds often plaster the nest-hole entrance with hard-drying mud, to keep out predators and larger competitors.*
■ *In a tree, the bird climbs just as readily down a trunk as up it, using its tail as a prop.*

Treecreeper
CERTHIA FAMILIARIS

LENGTH: 12.5CM **WEIGHT:** 9G **WHERE TO LOOK:** WOODLAND AND PARKS **NEST:** IN A CRACK IN A TREE, OR BEHIND LOOSE BARK **EGGS:** 4–8, WHITE, SPOTTED RED **FOOD:** INSECTS **VOICE:** A THIN, HIGH *TSIT* OR *TSU*. SONG IS A PENETRATING *TSIP-TSEE-TSEE-TSEE*, ENDING IN A FLOURISH

The treecreeper is usually seen flitting across a clearing, landing low on a tree trunk and then jerkily working its way up, propped on the stiff and pointed feathers of its tail. The down-curved, fine-tipped bill is ideal for probing in crevices in the bark. The bird spirals as it goes (quite why is not clear) appearing and disappearing from view, and it climbs along under branches as readily as on top. At any point it may abandon the tree and fly down to the base of another: unlike the nuthatch, it rarely climbs downwards. In winter, treecreepers often join tit flocks; they do not visit bird tables, but they will sometimes feed on fat if it is smeared into tree bark.

Some birds hollow out winter nests in the soft wood of certain tree trunks (Wellingtonias are a favourite). The birds make several hollows and choose one on the lee side of a tree, according to the weather. Just occasionally treecreepers can be persuaded to breed in a wedge-shaped nest box with a hole in the side. But beware if you are standing nearby when the young emerge – there is a record of a fledgling mistaking a man for a tree… and climbing him!

■ *A delicate looking bird with a fine, down-curved bill. Adults are warm brown above and silvery white below, streaked with buff; juveniles are greyer and more spotted.*
■ *Treecreepers, nuthatches and woodpeckers all cling to trees. The lesser spotted woodpecker is small enough to confuse, but is obviously black and white. The nuthatch is blue-grey with black eye-stripe. The treecreeper is brown, and thin-billed.*
■ *Treecreepers usually fly between one tree and the next. Longer flights are unusual.*

House Sparrow
PASSER DOMESTICUS

LENGTH: 14.5CM **WEIGHT:** 22–31G **WHERE TO LOOK:**
ASSOCIATED WITH HUMAN HABITATION, RURAL AND
URBAN **NEST:** UNTIDY GRASS AND STRAW, IN BUILDINGS
OR HEDGES **EGGS:** 3–7, GREYISH, FINELY SPECKLED
FOOD: VARIED, MAINLY SEEDS AND BUDS **VOICE:** NOISY,
TWITTERING AND CHEEPING NOTES

There is no species more closely associated with mankind than the house sparrow. From the centre of large cities to farm buildings in the most rural settings, this cheerful exploiter of human rubbish and wastefulness is found in abundance. They are inventive opportunists and have managed to colonise much of the world – especially those areas explored by Europeans. They followed the army camps across the North African desert in World War II, and they take rides on the London Underground and on cross-Channel ferries where discarded food is available. They appear in all kinds of isolated places where people settle – but how do they find them?

The normal breeding cycle is from May to July, often with three broods, but there has been an increasing trend towards year-round nesting, a sign of a very successful species. Any month with a spell of fine weather may trigger breeding activity and nest building, and although many of these out of season attempts are doomed to failure, an unusually long mild spell can result in fledged young being seen in mid-winter.

■ *Male has rather striking and distinctive plumage which is duller in winter than spring.*
■ *The rather drab female and the young show distinctive broad pale band over eye and plain underparts.*
■ *In flight, the males exhibit a striking contrast between the clear grey rump, brown back and wings with white wing-bar and chestnut side of neck.*
■ *Food provided in gardens will always attract large numbers of house sparrows, which have learnt to feed from peanut feeders.*
■ *On the ground, progress is by a series of hops or shuffles.*

Adult male

Adult female

Tree Sparrow
PASSER MONTANUS

LENGTH: 14CM WEIGHT: 19–25G WHERE TO LOOK: AREAS OF
OPEN WOODLAND, FARMS AND BUILDINGS IN WINTER NEST: IN
HOLES OF STRAW AND GRASS EGGS: 4–6, STIPPLED BROWN
FOOD: MAINLY SEEDS, BUT SOME INSECTS VOICE: *CHEEP* CALL
HIGHER PITCHED AND MORE METALLIC THAN HOUSE SPARROW,
FLIGHT NOTE A DOUBLE *TCHUR TCHUR* OR *TEK TEK*

Adult male

Less widespread than the more familiar house sparrow, the tree sparrow differs in several distinctive ways. It is a smaller, plumper bird than the house sparrow, lively and bold, but less inclined to exploit gardens and human waste, and more characteristic of open woods, parks and farmland with scattered trees. To look at, there is no difference between the sexes and even the recently fledged young resemble the adults.

A hole-nesting species that will frequently take over tit nest boxes in a woodland, it is dominant over any tits using the chosen box. Tree sparrows have even built on top of a brood of young blue tits, which the parents continued to struggle to feed until they were eventually stifled by the accumulating nest material gathered by the sparrows. Another favoured nesting site is within the base material of a larger nest, such as that of a crow, magpie or heron. The owner of the main nest apparently tolerates the squatters quite happily.

▨ *Smaller than the house sparrow, but more active and jerky with tail almost permanently cocked and hopping movements on the ground.*

▨ *Ground-feeding birds can appear to have a dark head and white collar, as in reed buntings.*

▨ *Plumage lacks variation between sexes, age and season; these are distinguished only by behaviour.*

▨ *Male and female tree sparrows share incubation, unlike house sparrows, where the job is the female's. The female is always at the nest during the night, brooding the young until seven days old.*

▨ *A regular migrant, there is an annual late-autumn immigration into Britain from continental Europe often associated with other finches.*

▨ *White cheeks with contrasting black spot is very distinctive. Chocolate-covered crown and double white wingbars are good features.*

▨ *In flight the shorter tail and rather more bouncy action separates the tree sparrow from the house sparrow.*

▨ *The distinctive double flight call is somewhat reminiscent of the redpoll.*

Chaffinch
FRINGILLA COELEBS

The chaffinch, among the most popular spring songsters, is one of Britain's commonest and most widespread breeding species, with 7 million pairs distributed throughout Britain and Ireland. Largely resident, British chaffinches rarely move more than 5km from home. The numbers are swollen each winter by a marked immigration from northern and eastern Europe. In these cases movements in excess of 2,000km are not unusual. Spectacular migrations can be watched on the east and south coasts during October and November and it is calculated that 10–20 million chaffinches arrive each autumn.

Producing only one brood per year, chaffinches build a beautifully camouflaged nest in the fork of a tree or dense bush. The outside of the nest is covered with lichen stripped from the surrounding bark. They are extremely long lived for small birds, ringing recoveries indicating that individuals may survive for up to 12 years. Where cause of death is known, the majority have been killed by traffic or by cats.

LENGTH: 15CM **WEIGHT:** 19–23G **WHERE TO LOOK:** HEDGEROWS, GARDENS AND FARMLAND **NEST:** IN BUSH OR LOW TREE, OF GRASSES DECORATED WITH LICHEN **EGGS:** 4–5, DARK SPOTTED, GREENISH **FOOD:** VARIED **VOICE:** *SPINK* CALL, RATTLING SONG ENDS WITH FLOURISH; *CHOOP* IN FLIGHT

Adult female

Adult male

- *Females show white in the wing; unstreaked; ground feeders.*
- *The male's contrasting plumage is highlighted by the pink breast.*
- *Winter flocks use a distinctive* choop *flight call; no twittering.*
- *In flight, the distinctive white outer tail feathers and wingbars are equally apparent.*

Brambling
FRINGILLA MONTIFRINGILLA

Adult male, spring

LENGTH: 14.5CM **WEIGHT:** 22–30G **WHERE TO LOOK:** BEECH WOODS OR FARMLAND **NEST:** ODD PAIRS MAY BREED IN SCOTLAND **FOOD:** INSECTS IN SUMMER, BEECH-MAST AND OTHER SEEDS IN WINTER **VOICE:** TWANGING *SWEEK*; NASAL GREENFINCH-LIKE *DWEEEE*; HARD *CHUP* IN FLIGHT

Adult male, winter

Adult female

In shape and behaviour the brambling is very similar to the chaffinch, and the two frequently mix in winter flocks. The conspicuous white rump is the most striking field characteristic of bramblings when the birds are in flight and is the best way of spotting them in a finch flock. A more prolonged view will show the orange breastband of both male and female and the pale orange shoulder patch and, in spring, the black head of the male. The black is obscured by pale grey in winter.

In recent years small numbers have been recorded nesting in Scotland and northern England, but there has been little evidence of major colonisation. The species is still principally a winter visitor from northern Europe, arriving each autumn in October and early November in variable numbers. In peak seasons as many as 2 million may be involved, but this is quite exceptional. A roost site one winter in northern England was estimated to hold over 150,000 individuals. The wintering flocks, however, are very nomadic, wandering erratically, but remaining in each site long enough to exhaust the available food supply. They can be elusive, but a good flock is worth seeking out.

- *The male is highly distinctive, with a striking black head.*
- *Both sexes show orange breast and white belly, characteristics that distinguish them from the chaffinch.*
- *In flight, the prominent white rump is a key feature.*
- *Mainly a ground feeder, the preferred food is beech-mast, but many small seeds are eaten.*

Hawfinch
COCCOTHRAUSTES COCCOTHRAUSTES

LENGTH: 18CM WEIGHT: 48–62G WHERE TO LOOK: MIXED WOODS AND ORCHARDS NEST: ROOSTS ON FOUNDATION OF TWIGS, USUALLY IN FRUIT TREES EGGS: 4–6, BLUISH GREEN, SPOTTED FOOD: LARGE SEEDS AND FRUIT STONES VOICE: QUIET WHISTLING SONG, ROBIN-LIKE *TICK* CALL

The massive bill and rather short tail gives the hawfinch a most distinctive silhouette, both in flight and when perched. At times it will appear to be so 'top heavy' that it seems in danger of tipping forwards. The thick neck and large head add to a most striking flight appearance which is quite unlike any other British finch, but clear views are unusual.

Generally considered a shy and secretive species, often difficult to locate, it will frequently perch on the very top-most branches, but obtaining good views is not an easy task for the birdwatcher. The broad white patch on the wing coverts and border to the tail contrasts with the warm-brown back and provides a striking pattern as the bird flies away, but other details demand closer study, which in turn requires patience and care.

The exceptional structure of the bill, together with massive jaw muscles, enables the hawfinch to tackle food ignored by other finches. Cherry stones are a regular feature of the diet, but softer seeds are taken and dealt with in a delicate manner.

■ *A bird of tree tops, but will feed on ground when soft fruit is available in orchards.*
■ *Secretive when breeding, they are a little more obvious in winter when flocks form to roost communally.*
■ *Mixed woods and orchards are preferred, but beech, hornbeam and wild cherry are most favoured.*
■ *Scattered populations throughout England, but mainly a south-eastern species.*

Bullfinch
PYRRHULA PYRRHULA

Adult male

Adult female

LENGTH: 15CM WEIGHT: 21–27G WHERE TO LOOK: UNDERGROWTH NEAR WOODS AND GARDENS NEST: FINE TWIGS, BUILT IN THICK COVER EGGS: 4–5, CLEAR GREEN-BLUE FOOD: BUDS, BERRIES AND SEEDS VOICE: A DISTINCTIVE LOW, PIPING *TEU*, WHICH CARRIES WELL

Throughout orchards and gardens in south-east England bullfinches have a justified reputation for damage to buds on fruit trees, often seriously affecting far more than they eat and reducing the crop. Many birds are trapped and destroyed. Two factors may affect the amount of damage. The number of suitable nest sites near the orchard will determine the population level in the area, and the available 'natural' food supply in late winter controls the change of diet to buds. When the ash-key crop is good, bullfinches remain in the woodland and fruit farmers sleep more easily.

Although males have a remarkably bright plumage, bullfinches can be very secretive. Their presence in an area – and they are far more numerous in south-east England than the rest of the country – is revealed by the distinctive, far-carrying piping call and the prominent white rump which stands out as they fly away.

Never far from dense cover, keeping to bushes and trees, they rarely settle on the ground. When they do, movement is by a series of ungainly hops. Pairs remain together throughout the year, with family parties in autumn and occasionally small flocks in winter.

■ *Males with contrasting plumage of grey back, jet-black cap and striking pink-red underparts. Inner flight feathers with red.*
■ *Unlike the male, the female has pinkish-grey underparts, but retains black cap and white rump. Young birds resemble female, but have no black cap.*
■ *White rump striking in flight.*
■ *In spring, rarely welcomed by gardeners concerned for the buds.*

Greenfinch
CARDUELIS CHLORIS

LENGTH: 14.5CM **WEIGHT:** 25–31G **WHERE TO LOOK:** OPEN WOODLAND, GARDENS AND FARMLAND **NEST:** OF TWIGS AND MOSS IN HEDGES AND BUSHES **EGGS:** 4–6, SPOTTED, OFF-WHITE **FOOD:** MAINLY SEEDS AND BERRIES **VOICE:** TWITTERING SONG; DRAWN OUT NASAL *TSWEEE*

Increasingly familiar garden birds, greenfinches have been attracted more and more to birdtables with sunflower seeds and other goodies. Together with house sparrows these confident, distinctive birds have quickly learnt how to feed from peanut feeders in winter and, being rather aggressive when competing for food, will drive away other more timid birds, including tits.

The stout bill on this rather heavily built finch enables it to deal with some of the larger seeds that become available, such as sea-buckthorn in the winter. In gardens they like mezereon, yew and cotoneaster berries. In spring they like tall hedges and are happy in big shrubberies and parks, their tinkling trills and wheezy notes livening up a sunny morning.

Flight, in common with all finches, is distinctly undulating, but in the breeding season the very characteristic song-flight of the male consists of a circling pattern on strangely erratic, slow, bat-like wing-beats, during which the bell-like calls are given non-stop. In winter, flocks burst up from the ground with a loud rush, swirling over a field or into the nearest hedge.

■ *The olive-green plumage of the male is off-set by varying degrees of yellow, brighter on older birds.*

■ *Juvenile streaked brown above, with faint yellow underneath; pale yellow flashes on wing and tail.*

■ *The duller female is browner with subtle streaking on the underparts. The yellow flashes in wing and tail are more subdued.*

■ *Note the very stout bill and short, well forked tail.*

■ *The yellow in wings and tail is clearly visible on flying birds.*

■ *Winter numbers are boosted by migrants from continental Europe.*

■ *Although solitary when breeding, flocks form in winter, often mixed with other species in woods and open farmland. In competition will become aggressive.*

Siskin
CARDUELIS SPINUS

LENGTH: 12CM **WEIGHT:** 12–18G **WHERE
TO LOOK:** MAINLY CONIFERS WHEN
NESTING, ALDERS BY STREAMS IN WINTER
NEST: TWIGS AND MASS, HIGH IN CONIFERS
EGGS: 4–5, DEEP BLUE, WITH PALE SPOTS
VOICE: VARIED TWITTERING SONG AND
SHRILL *TSEWI* FLIGHT CALL

As a breeding species the siskin is closely associated with conifers, and recent expansion of the population within Britain has almost certainly been the result of increased afforestation and the development of mixed ornamental woodland. At one time confined to Scotland, the species now nests in small numbers in scattered places throughout the British Isles, including several locations on the south coast.

On the breeding grounds the very musical twittering song, delivered in flight as the males circle the tree tops, is a sure sign of the presence of nesting birds. Indeed the song-flight will continue well after the female has settled to incubate the eggs, and consists of very exaggerated wing-beats, the wings appearing to meet above the back. At the same time, the tail is usually spread, flashing vivid yellow patches.

Like the greenfinch, this is predominantly a yellow-green bird, but it is smaller and slimmer, and the male has a black chin and throat and yellow rump. The female is very much greyer, lacks yellow and has paler, striped underparts. The neat, complex wing pattern can usually be seen on this tiny bird.

▓ *The bill shape is ideal for extracting seeds of birch, alder and larch.*
▓ *Often mixed with redpolls.*
▓ *In early spring, siskins will discover the red string bags containing peanuts.*
▓ *Feeds on twigs like a party of tits.*
▓ *Very active. Shows a distinct notch in tail in bounding flight.*

Redpoll
CARDUELIS FLAMMEA

Juvenile

Adult

LENGTH: 13–14CM **WEIGHT:** 10–13G **WHERE
TO LOOK:** BIRCH AND ALDER WOODLAND
NEST: GRASSES ON A TWIG FOUNDATION,
USUALLY HIGH IN TREE **EGGS:** 4–5, BLUE,
SPOTTED AND STREAKED **FOOD:** MAINLY
SEEDS **VOICE:** TRILLING UNMUSICAL SONG IN
FLIGHT; CALL FAST *CHUCHUCHUH-UH*

In winter, redpolls often join siskins in mixed flocks. They feed together in the tops of alder and birch trees, extracting the tiny seeds. Their behaviour is very tit-like, birds often hanging upside down at the very end of the branches. Such flocks are often associated with areas of running water, cress beds or riverside banks. Migrant flocks can be found in open areas of scrub or waste ground, feeding on low clumps of vegetation such as seeding willow-herb. In spring they feed on the ground on fallen birch seeds, bursting up into the trees if disturbed.

The presence of redpolls is frequently first indicated by the distinctive metallic twittering flight call; a close view will reveal the crimson on the forehead and small black chin patch. Some males have a noticeable pink flush to the underparts, but this may be absent from other individuals. Some are very colourful in spring.

Still rather sparsely distributed in south-west England, redpolls have increased and spread quite dramatically since the 1950s and are now widespread throughout the rest of Britain, although numbers fluctuate greatly from year to year.

▓ *Variable in size and colour, larger and paler individuals from northern localities are occasional winter visitors.*
▓ *Females lack the pinkish flush; some males vivid in spring; Juvenile lacks red.*
▓ *Breeding birds fly over a large area during display.*
▓ *The bouncy, undulating flight is accompanied by the distinctive three- or four-note flight call.*
▓ *Feeding in tree tops, their behaviour is very tit-like and agile.*

Goldfinch
CARDUELIS CARDUELIS

Adult

One of the most colourful and distinctive of all the British finches, the goldfinch is the 'thistle-finch', with a decided preference for eating the seeds of thistles. It is particularly appropriate that the collective noun for such an attractive bird is 'charm'. A slim, delicate-looking finch, it is usually seen like manner among the seed heads of low-growing vegetation. Although flight action retains the usual undulations of all finches, the goldfinch has a peculiar bouncing quality in its movements.

Where some finches are ground-feeders and others tree-top feeders, the goldfinch is very much a bird of the lower vegetation, favouring plants of open waste ground such as teasels and hawkweeds. It can hop on the ground but is more likely to be seen hanging from the seed-heads in a tit-like manner; flocks also feed in trees.

The striking plumage consists of a mixture of black, white, brown, yellow and red – goldfinches have white rumps, but this is often overlooked among the wealth of other bright colours. Sexes are similar in appearance, although the red extends behind the eye only in the male. Young birds are 'grey pates' without the colourful head pattern, and slightly streaked beneath.

At one time this was a very popular cage bird, and one form of trap for small birds is known as a 'chardonneret' – the French name for the goldfinch.

■ *Unforgettable and unmistakable. Identification is easy.*

■ *In all plumages the black feathering of the wings is contrasted with the bright yellow flash that gives the bird its name.*

■ *In addition to the band of brilliant yellow, the black wing feathers each have a prominent pale tip. Black tail feathers have pale tips and oval patches.*

■ *The striking pattern on the head of all adults is unique. In spring there are patches of brown each side of the breast.*

■ *On leaving the nest, young birds lack the adult face patterns, but acquire these within two months.*

■ *Outside the breeding season flocks rarely mix with others, but may be with siskins in alders.*

Juvenile

LENGTH: 12CM **WEIGHT:** 14–17G **WHERE TO LOOK:** GARDENS AND ORCHARDS, ROUGH AND OPEN GROUND **NEST:** BUILT OF WOOL AND MOSS AT END OF BRANCH **EGGS:** 5–6, SPOTTED AND STREAKED, BLUISH **FOOD:** SEEDS, MAINLY THISTLES, AND INSECTS **VOICE:** LIQUID TWITTERING CALLS AND SONG

Linnet
CARDUELIS CANNABINA

LENGTH: 13.5CM WEIGHT: 15–21G **WHERE TO LOOK:** AREAS OF GORSE IN SUMMER, FARMLAND AND SHORE IN WINTER **NEST:** GRASSES NEAR GROUND **EGGS:** 4–6, SPOTTED, BLUISH **FOOD:** SMALL SEEDS AND INSECTS **VOICE:** VARIED, MUSICAL TWITTERING SONG, RAPID FLIGHT CALL

Male summer plumage

Female

Male winter plumage

Widespread throughout Britain, the linnet is often thought of as a bird associated with heaths, commons and gorse bushes. In fact it is also found in open country and farmland far from gorse. A semi-colonial species, small groups of ten or more pairs can often be located, and then the bird will appear absent for some distance until the next group is found. Large numbers form lively flocks in winter, but can be difficult to locate. Quite extensive areas can seem empty of linnets, but rather than there being a genuine reduction in numbers, it is just that all the birds tend to assemble in one place where there is plentiful food.

Although quite large numbers and concentrations may be encountered on southern and eastern coasts in late autumn, the amount of migration undertaken by linnets is still something of a mystery. It appears that a small number of British birds move south for the winter, travelling as far as Iberia; a somewhat larger number from Scandinavia probably arrives to spend the winter in Britain, spreading southwards from eastern Scotland.

■ *The male's strongly contrasting plumage of grey head and crimson breast and crown is lost in winter and absent in females.*

■ *Open farmland or coastal salt marshes are very much favoured during the winter months. Small seeds are taken all year round.*

■ *Feeds on bushes in summer, but a ground-feeder in winter.*

Twite
CARDUELIS FLAVIROSTRIS

LENGTH: 13.5CM WEIGHT: 13–17G **WHERE TO LOOK:** MOORS AND MOUNTAINS IN SUMMER, COASTS IN WINTER **NEST:** BUILT OF GRASS NEAR GROUND **EGGS:** 5–6, BLUE WITH BOLD MARKINGS **FOOD:** SEEDS **VOICE:** SONG A LINNET-LIKE TWITTERING, CALL A VERY NASAL *TSOOEE, DWEYE*

Very linnet-like in appearance, the twite is often known as the 'mountain linnet'. Although very much a bird of the higher ground, mountains and moorland, in summer it is also found nesting at sea level in northern and western Scotland and parts of Ireland. The breeding areas are largely deserted in winter and there is a general movement to coastal localities where it feeds on the seeds of salt marsh plants, often in company with linnets and skylarks.

Flight, behaviour and shape are all reminiscent of the linnet, but this is a slightly smaller bird with a relatively longer tail. Generally much darker, it lacks the chestnut back and red crown of the male linnet. In mixed flocks twites can be distinguished by having pinkish rumps (males) and yellow bills in winter.

Lacking clear-cut identification features, the twite is probably frequently overlooked, but it is estimated that the British breeding population numbers some 20,000 pairs, with perhaps 100,000 individuals present in winter.

■ *Overall appearance of dark tawny brown with bright orange-buff colouring around face and breasts; neat tawny wingbar.*

■ *The bill is rather greyish in summer, pale yellow in winter.*

■ *In flight shows pink rump and very little white in wing.*

■ *Colonial as a breeding species; small numbers grouping together. Flocks form during the winter months.*

■ *Favours open country all year; breeds in Pennines, northern Scotland and western Ireland. Winters on coast.*

Crossbill and Scottish Crossbill
LOXIA CURVIROSTRA AND LOXIA SCOTICA

LENGTH: 16-17CM **WEIGHT:** 34-48G **WHERE TO LOOK:** CONIFER WOODS AND PLANTATIONS **NEST:** GRASSES ON TWIG FOUNDATION, BREEDING BETWEEN JANUARY AND JULY **EGGS:** 4, OFF-WHITE WITH BOLD SPOTS **FOOD:** ALMOST EXCLUSIVELY SEEDS FROM CONES OF PINE, LARCH AND SPRUCE **VOICE:** LOUD, PERSISTENT *CHIP CHIP* FLIGHT CALL. SONG OF TRILLING NOTES FOLLOWED BY GREENFINCH-LIKE CALLS

Adult male

Adult female

Crossbills are the most specialised of all the finches. Most obvious are the crossed mandibles, which enable the birds to extract seeds from pine cones. Other adaptations include particularly strong asymmetrical jaw muscles which assist the twisting movement necessary to extract the seed. In normal circumstances the feeding activity follows a regular routine. The cone is broken from the tree, usually requiring a considerable effort, with the bird apparently making use of every muscle. It is then carried to a convenient branch where it is held firmly by the feet while each seed is extracted in a systematic manner.

The numbers and distribution of crossbills in Britain vary greatly from year to year, for this is an 'invasion species'. Factors as varied as food supply and prevailing weather conditions will control the number of migrants reaching Britain in the autumn, and in many cases the subsequent size of the breeding population early the following year. The Scottish crossbill is a different but very similar species, found only in Scottish pine woods.

■ *Adult males are often a bright brick-red; females and young are usually a yellowish-green, with a yellower rump.*
■ *In flight, the short, deeply forked tail together with the heavy neck and bill, and disctinctive call, readliy identify the crossbills.*
■ *Scottish crossbill is a separate species with a larger, blunter bill and larger body; it is Britain's only unique species.*

Yellowhammer
EMBERIZA CITRINELLA

Adult male

Adult female

LENGTH: 16.5CM **WEIGHT:** 27G **WHERE TO LOOK:** FARMLAND, HEATHS, SCRUB, HILLSIDES **NEST:** BULKY, OF GRASS OR STRAW, WITH CHARACTERISTIC PLATFORM, LOW DOWN OR ON GROUND IN GRASS CLUMP OR BUSH **EGGS:** 3–5, PALE WITH DARK 'SCRIBBLING' AND SPOTS **FOOD:** CEREALS, GRASS SEEDS; INSECTS IN SUMMER **VOICE:** FAMILIAR 'LITTLE-BIT-OF-BREAD-AND-NO-CHEESE' **FLIGHT CALL:** *TWICK* OR *TWITICK*

The derivation of the curious English name becomes clear upon learning that the German word for bunting is 'Ammer'. The two languages have a distant common origin. The dark, irregular lines on the eggs have given rise to the yellowhammer's country name of 'scribbling lark'.

The phrase 'bread-and-cheese' recalls the song of this familiar bunting only in rhythm: in fact the song is rather variable and sometimes lacks the final (higher or lower) 'cheese'. On drowsy high-summer days it is often the only bird sound accompanying the hum of insects.

Aggressive when setting up territory, the male pursues his prospective mate in a rapid, twisting courtship flight. Once paired, both birds often feed together, and indeed gather food for the young, away from their nesting territory. The young are fed almost entirely on green caterpillars and insects.

In winter yellowhammers are social. They may roost in large numbers in rank vegetation, sometimes in reed beds with reed and corn buntings, and even on occasion in snow burrows. Ringing reveals that up to 70 per cent of adults spend the winter within 5km of the nest site.

■ *Long, notched tail shows white on sides when spread, but is less obvious than on reed bunting.*
■ *Juveniles are darker, well-streaked, and may show very little yellow, but plumage extremely variable.*
■ *Feeds almost exclusively on the ground. When disturbed, flocks fly up into bushes.*

Corn Bunting
MILIARIA CALANDRA

LENGTH: 18CM **WEIGHT:** 44–54G **WHERE TO LOOK:** OPEN FARMING COUNTRY **NEST:** LARGE, LOOSE, OF COARSE GRASSES, OFTEN IN SCRAPE ON GROUND **EGGS:** 3–5, USUALLY PALE WITH BOLD, DARK SCRIBBLES AND BLOTCHES **FOOD:** SEEDS, INSECTS **VOICE:** UNIQUE, DISCORDANT JANGLING

Britain's largest bunting, this nondescript bird makes up for its drab appearance with a fascinating sex life! It is one of a very few truly promiscuous passerines, both male and female mating with several partners. The males return to the breeding sites in midwinter, the largest birds securing the best territories. The females do not leave the winter flock until April, and they alone deal with all the domestic duties, leaving males free to court other hens. Males sing, head thrown back, from a prominent low perch, or from overhead wires, in almost every month of the year, and at any time of day.

Although one of the few species at home in modern agricultural 'prairies', the corn bunting has, for reasons unknown, decreased this century to the point of extinction in much of the west and north. The British population is sedentary, flocking outside the breeding season to feed on stubble and in farmyards. Winter roosts in reed beds or scrub may contain 100 or more birds. The distinctive flight call is a low-pitched dry but loud *kwit* or *quilp kwit-it*.

■ *A bulky, clumsy-looking, sparrow-like bird; rather neckless appearance. Large, dark eye in rather pale face. No white in shortish tail. Sexes alike in plumages.*
■ *May fly short distances with legs dangling, on fluttering wings.*
■ *Pursues rivals or prospective mates low over cornfields.*
■ *Paler, less buff in summer. Streaking most dense in centre of breast, forming diffuse dark spot.*

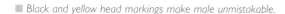

Cirl Bunting
EMBERIZA CIRLUS

Not discovered as a British bird until 1800, in Devon, the cirl bunting expanded during the 19th century to become widespread, if local, north to the midlands and Wales. A decline was first noticed in the 1930s, accelerating since the late 1950s to the present precarious position of perhaps 150 pairs, almost all in Devon. The recent colder, wetter springs and summers are probably responsible, for the cirl bunting is essentially a Mediterranean species at the edge of its range in Britain.

The bird is easily overlooked until the song is learnt. Like the other farmland buntings, the song period is long: it may be heard regularly from late February to early September, and occasionally at other times, though bursts may be irregular, even during the main song period. It may recall a distant lesser white-throat but with an unmistakable, sharper, bunting quality. The breeding territory is unusually large, and given the bird's relative secrecy, and tendency to fly quite long distances, it can be very elusive. Nevertheless, a recent survey revealed that three out of five territories contained a house or farm building.

■ *Black and yellow head markings make male unmistakable.*
■ *Female distinguished by olive-grey rump, buffy rather than yellowish breast, with neat, dark streaks.*
■ *Call a soft, penetrating ssi.*

LENGTH: 16.5CM **WEIGHT:** 22G **WHERE TO LOOK:** FARMLAND WITH HEDGES AND TALL TREES, BUSHY SLOPES, CLIFFS. **NEST:** NEAT, WELL-CONCEALED, OF MOSS AND GRASS. **EGGS:** 3–4, BLUISH-WHITE, BOLDLY MARKED. **FOOD:** SEEDS, INSECTS. **VOICE:** METALLIC RATTLE ON ONE NOTE.

Snow Bunting
PLECTROPHENAX NIVALIS

LENGTH: 16CM WEIGHT: 30–40G **WHERE TO
LOOK:** RARE BREEDER, HIGH, MOUNTAIN TOPS.
COMMONER IN WINTER IN NORTHERN HILLS,
EAST COAST **NEST:** IN CREVICE **EGGS:** 4–6,
OFF-WHITE, BLOTCHED BROWN **FOOD:** SEEDS,
INSECTS **VOICE:** RIPPLING TRILL; *TEW*

Adult female, summer

Adult male, summer

Winter plumage

Breeding right around the Arctic Circle in Eurasia and North America, the snow bunting reaches further north than any other small bird, right up to the summer limit of ice in Greenland. The first British nest was found in 1886. These lovely buntings remain a prize summer find on the barren, hostile tops of the highest mountains, the sweet musical song being uttered in a short display flight. The nest often has a warm lining of ptarmigan feathers.

In winter, they are often delightfully confiding. Sometimes called 'snowflakes', a flock in flight does indeed fancifully recall a flurry of snow as each bird flies in deep undulations, seeming to dance along, then swooping low and fast before landing, flashing white in wings and tail. A feeding flock moves in rolling fashion, each bird running rapidly, pecking and leap-frogging over its companion in short flights, frequently calling.

Inland lowland sightings are unusual, and reports in gardens can usually be related to partially albino sparrows.

▧ *Yellow bill with dark tip in winter. Some white always visible in the wing in flight.*
▧ *Breeding male black and white, female cold grey-brown and white.*
▧ *Winter birds usually show lovely warm rusty-buff wash over crown and breast, reddest on females.*
▧ *Numbers wintering in Britain very greatly. Highly sociable, flocks of a thousand or more on record, usually under 50.*

Reed Bunting
EMBERIZA SCHOENICLUS

The brief, unmusical song is delivered *ad nauseam* from a prominent song-post such as a tall reed or dock. A widespread bird, with breeding recorded from every county in Britain and Ireland, it is mainly sedentary, though deserting upland areas in winter when it moves into all types of open country. Most reed buntings move only a little way, yet, curiously, studies at roosts in central and southern England have revealed two males for every female: perhaps the females simply do not all come to the communal roost. Prolonged heavy snow cover may make it difficult for this ground feeder to find enough seeds to eat, and heavy mortality may result. They are increasingly visiting gardens for free handouts in winter.

Although primarily birds of wet and damp areas, there has been a trend this century for breeding to spread into the drier habitats normally occupied by yellowhammers or corn buntings, with little evidence of competition between these species where they coexist. More recently this spread seems to have halted. Farmland reed buntings do not require the taller trees favoured by yellowhammers, being content with low song-posts, more like their usual marshy homes.

▧ *The male's handsome black and white head and breast in breeding plumage are unmistakable. Note the long, deeply notched tail, typical of British buntings.*
▧ *Usually perches upright on plant stem, with tail at rakish angle or twisted to one side.*

Adult female

Adult male

LENGTH: 15.5CM WEIGHT: 19G **WHERE TO LOOK:** ALL TYPES OF
WET AREAS, FARMLAND, SCRUB, PLANTATIONS, ALSO GARDENS
IN WINTER **NEST:** SUBSTANTIAL, OF GRASSES, ON GROUND OR
LOW IN TUSSOCKS, HEDGEROW BUSHES **EGGS:** 4–5, BUFF, OR
OLIVE-BROWN, BOLDLY MARKED WITH DARK STREAKS, SMUDGES
FOOD: SEEDS, INSECTS AND INVERTEBRATES IN SUMMER **VOICE:**
MONOTONOUS SHORT SONG. CALL SHRILL *TSEEU*; HIGH *SEE*

Index

The following organisations can help you further your interest in birdwatching:

The Royal Society for the Protection of Birds (RSPB)
The Lodge, Sandy, Bedfordshire SG19 2DL
Tel: 01767 680551

Wildfowl & Wetlands Trust
Slimbridge, Gloucestershire GL2 7BT
Tel: 01453 890333

British Trust for Ornithology (BTO)
The Nunnery, Nunnery Place, Thetford, Norfolk IP24 2PU
Tel: 01842 750050